ISBN: 9781313539364

Published by:
HardPress Publishing
8345 NW 66TH ST #2561
MIAMI FL 33166-2626

Email: info@hardpress.net
Web: http://www.hardpress.net

BX
4720
P36M
1828

CORNELL
UNIVERSITY
LIBRARY

BOUGHT WITH THE INCOME
OF THE SAGE ENDOWMENT
FUND GIVEN IN 1891 BY
HENRY WILLIAMS SAGE

Date Due

APR 1 2 1948 H		
NOV 2 0 1948 J		
DEC 1 3 1949		
NOV 14 1952 K U		
NOV 3 0 1953 H S		
DEC 1 1954		
OCT 1 9 1955 H X		
NOV 2 6 1957 H X		
JAN 1 7 1958 K U		
APR 1 3 1960 B R		
fine pd		
NOV 2 9 1993		

Cornell University Library
BX4720 .P36 1828

Provincial letters, containing an exposu

3 1924 029 444 381

olin

PROVINCIAL LETTERS,

CONTAINING

AN EXPOSURE

OF THE

REASONING AND MORALS OF THE JESUITS,

BY

BLAISE PASCAL.

ORIGINALLY PUBLISHED UNDER THE NAME OF

LOUIS DE MONTALTE.

TRANSLATED FROM THE FRENCH

TO WHICH IS ADDED,

A View of the History of the Jesuits,

AND

THE LATE BULL FOR THE REVIVAL OF THE ORDER IN EUROPE.

The bishop of Lueon, son of the celebrated Bussy, told me, that asking one day the bishop of Meaux what work he would covet most to be the author of, supposing his own performances set aside, Bossuet replied, *The Provincial Letters.* Examples of all the species of eloquence abound in them.—*Voltaire.*

NEW YORK:
PUBLISHED BY J. LEAVITT, 182 BROADWAY.

BOSTON:
CROCKER & BREWSTER, 47 WASHINGTON-STREET.

1828.

A. 139171

1158 A 71

Vanderpool & Cole, Printers.

TRANSLATOR'S PREFACE.

"THE name of PASCAL (that prodigy of parts, as Locke calls him,") says Mr. Dugald STEWART,* " is more familiar to modern ears than that of any of the other learned and polished anchorites who have rendered the sanctuary of *Port-Royal* so illustrious. Abstracting from his great merit in mathematics and in physics, his reputation rests chiefly on the ' *Provincial Letters ;*' a work from which Voltaire, notwithstanding his strong prejudices against the Author, dates the *fixation* of the French language ; and of which the same excellent judge has said, ' MOLIERE'S BEST COMEDIES DO NOT EXCEL THEM IN WIT, NOR THE COMPOSITIONS OF BOSSUET IN SUBLIMITY." The author was originally induced to compose and publish them by a very casual circumstance. Accustomed frequently to visit a sister, who had taken the veil in the monastery of Port-Royal, he was introduced to the society of some celebrated Jansenists, particularly M. Arnauld, who had recently been engaged in a dispute with the doctors of the Sorbonne. The subjects of difference related chiefly to those points of faith which have continually divided Arminians and Calvinists in the Protestant community ; the Jesuits being allied in sentiment to the former, and the

* Supplement to Encyc. Brit. vol. i. p. 1.

Jansenists to the latter. The Jesuits had selected five propositions from a posthumous work of Jansen or Jansenius, bishop of Ypres, which his adherents believed to contain the doctrine of the Scriptures and the Fathers on the litigated articles of faith, and procured their condemnation by the Faculty of Theology at Paris and by Pope Innocent X. Arnauld published a letter in 1655, in which he declared that the condemned propositions were not to be found in the book of Jansenius, and then proceeded to controvert the Jesuitical notion of efficacious grace. Being at this time a member of the Sorbonne, violent altercations arose; and as his adversaries were in power, they procured his expulsion from the Faculty of Theology, by a decree in January 1656. The defence which he made was not in itself very satisfactorily written, and some of his friends intimated their wish to M. Pascal, with whom they had become recently acquainted, and of whose talents they had formed a very just idea, that he would write something upon the subject. This occasioned his first letter, which being much admired, was soon succeeded by others, under the fictitious name of Louis de Montalte; the consequence was, the Jesuits became the objects of ridicule and contempt to all Europe.

It is quite needless to accumulate testimonies in favour of the extraordinary merit of this work; otherwise the encomiums of numerous French writers might be introduced; and our elegant GIBBON is said to have possessed so enthusiastic an admiration for the book, that he was accustomed to read it through once every year. Amongst those, however, who are always entitled to marked attention, must be ranked d'Alembert, whose words are as follow: " This master-piece of pleasantry and eloquence diverted and moved the indignation of all Europe at their (the Jesuits') expense. <u>In vain they replied that the greatest part of the Theologists and Monks had taught, as well as them, the scandalous doctrine with which they were reproached.</u> Their answers, ill written and full of gall, were not read, while every body knew the 'Provincial Letters' by heart. This work is so much the more admirable, as Pascal, in composing it, appears to have theologized two things which seemed not made for the theology of that time—language and pleasantry. The (French) language was very far from being formed, as we may judge by the greater part of the works published at that time, and of which it is impossible to endure the reading. In the 'Provincial Letters,' there is not a single word that is grown obsolete; and that book, though written above a hundred years ago, seems as if it had been written but yesterday.

" Another attempt, no less difficult, was, to make people of wit, and good people, laugh at the questions of *sufficient grace* and *next power*, and the decisions of the casuists—subjects very little favourable to pleasantry, or, which is worse still, susceptible of pleasantries that are cold and uniform, and capable, at most, of amusing only priests and monks. It was necessary, to avoid this rock, to have a delicacy of taste so much the greater, as Pascal lived very retired, and far removed from the commerce of the world. He could never have distinguished, but by the superiority and delicacy of his understanding, the kind of pleasantry which could alone be relished by good judges in this dry and insipid matter. He succeeded in it beyond all expression; several of his *bon-mots* have even become proverbial in our language, and the 'Provincial Letters' will be ever regarded as a model of taste and style."

A considerable portion of the merit of this performance, consists in the ingenious manner in which Pascal has brought together the extravagant maxims of the principal Jesuitical writers, so as to make them appear truly ridiculous. He does not, as Voltaire, (who, otherwise, bestows upon him great praise,) insinuates, collect his citations from a few individuals, whose sentiments are unwarrantably adduced as a fair specimen of the principles of the whole society, for he uniformly appeals to the very best of their writers, and particularly to the *twenty-four* elders, who were so designated on account of the entire confidence which the whole body of the Jesuits reposed in their statements. In fact, Pascal adopted no other than the usual and authorized method of obtaining the real opinions of any extensive society. If their own publications—the publications of their most eminent men; be not the proper standard of appeal, by what other means can their opinions be obtained? Besides, none of their writings were issued without the sanction of the superiors of their order.

One peculiarity of these 'Letters,' it is impossible to perceive through the medium of a translation. The *words*, selected by the writer, are uniformly the purest which the language furnished; and, according to the testimony of Voltaire, "not a single word occurs, savouring of that vicissitude to which living languages are so subject. Here, then, we may fix the epocha, when our language may be said to have assumed a settled form." The conversational form in which the subject is treated, precludes that oratorical elegance and Ciceronian flow which delights the ear. A certain sprightliness and humour constitute their chief characteristics, interspersed with passages of grave instruction, which prove that Pascal wrote for a higher purpose than to furnish a comedy, or to gratify a malignant feeling. After all, a severe critic might detect in this work some minor faults of composition, as redundancies and repetitions, unless, as is most probable, even *he* should be too much occupied with its numerous beauties.

CONTENTS.

LETTER I.

Remarks on the Disputes of the Sorbonne, and on the Invention of the Term NEXT POWER, employed by the Molinists to draw a Censure upon M. Arnauld 25

LETTER II.

On the Subject of sufficient Grace 35
Reply of the Provincial to the two former Letters of his Friend 45

LETTER III.

The Injustice, Absurdity, and Nullity of the Censure upon M. Arnauld 47

LETTER IV.

Of actual Grace, and of Sins of Ignorance . . . 55

LETTER V.

The Design of the Jesuits in establishing a new Morality. Two kinds of Casuists amongst them: the great Remissness of the one, and the equal Rigidity of the other. Reason of this Difference. Explanation of the Doctrine of Probability. A

Crowd of modern and obscure Authors substituted for the Holy Fathers 68

LETTER VI.

The different Artifices of the Jesuits to evade the Authority of the Gospel, the Councils, and the Popes. Consequences which follow from their Doctrine of Probability. Their Abatements in favour of the Clergy, Monks, and Servants. History of John d'Alba 82

LETTER VII

On the Method of directing the Attention. The Permission to kill in defence of Honour and of Property, which is extended to Priests and Friars. A curious Question proposed by Caramuel, namely, whether the Jesuits may kill the Jansenists? . . 95

LETTER VIII.

Corrupt Maxims of the Casuists respecting Judges, Usurers, the Contract *Mohatra*, Bankrupts, Restitutions, &c.—Various other extravagant Notions . 111

LETTER IX.

The false Worship of the Virgin Mary which the Jesuits have introduced. The various Facilities they have invented to procure Salvation without any Trouble and amidst the Indulgences of Life. Their maxims respecting Ambition, Envy, Gluttony, Equivocation, mental Reservations, the Liberty which young Females enjoy, the Habits of Women, Gaming, and the Manner of hearing Mass . 127

LETTER X.

Mitigating Expedients of the Jesuists with regard to the Sacrament of Penitence. Their Maxims respecting Confession, Satisfaction, Absolution, Occasions of Sin, Contrition, and the Love of God . . . 142

LETTER XI.

Ridiculous Errors may be refuted by Raillery. The Precautions it is necessary to use, which the Author has observed, but which have not been regarded by the Jesuits. The impious Buffooneries of Fathers le Moine and Garasse 159

LETTER XII.

Refutation of the Quirks and Turns of the Jesuits on the Subjects of Almsgiving and Simony . . . 174

Refutation of the Reply of the Jesuits to the last Letter 190

LETTER XIII.

The Doctrine of Lessius respecting Murder the same with that of Victoria. The Ease with which we pass from Speculation to Practice. Reason why the Jesuits make use of this vain Distinction, and how unavailing it is to their Justification . . 205

LETTER XIV.

Jesuitical Maxims on the Subject of Homicide refuted by the holy Fathers. Reply, in passing, to some of their Calumnies, and a Comparison of their Doctrines with the Form observed in pronouncing Judgment in Criminal Cases . . . 221

LETTER XV.

The Jesuits omit Calumny in their Catalogue of Crimes, and make no Scruple of using it against their Enemies 237

LETTER XVI.

The horrible Calumnies of the Jesuits against pious Ecclesiastics and holy Monks 254

LETTER XVII.

By the unanimous Consent of all the Divines, and particularly of the Jesuits, the Authority of the Popes and of Œcumenical Councils is not infallible in questions of Fact 276

LETTER XVIII.

Evidence still more incontestable adduced even from Father Annat's Reply, that no Heresy exists in the Church. Every body condemns the Doctrine which the Jesuits impute to Jansenius; and thus all Christians agree on the Subject of the Five Propositions. Difference respecting the Questions of Right and Fact pointed out. With regard to the latter, one ought to rely more upon our own Senses than upon any human Authority . . 297

A VIEW

OF THE

HISTORY OF THE JESUITS.

A SOCIETY, which at one period extended its influence to the very ends of the earth, and proved the main pillar of the papal hierarchy, which not only wormed itself into almost absolute power, occupying the high places, and leading captive the ecclesiastical dictator of the world, must be an object of some curiosity to the inquisitive mind, especially as it has been recently restored by the present pope, from that ruin to which Clement XIV. had reduced it.

IGNATIUS LOYOLA, a native of Biscay, is well known to have been the founder of this, *nominally*, religious order. He was born in 1491, and became the first page to Ferdinand V. king of Spain, then an officer in his army. In 1521, he was wounded in both legs at the siege of Pampeluna, when having had leisure to study a 'Life of the Saints,' he devoted himself to the service of the Virgin; and his military ardour becoming metamorphosed into superstitious zeal, he went on a pilgrimage into the Holy Land. Upon his return to Europe, he studied in the universities of Spain, whence he removed into France, and formed a plan for the institution of this new order, which he presented to the pope. But, notwithstanding the high pretensions of Loyola to inspiration, Paul III. refused his request, till his scruples were removed by an irresistible argument addressed to his self-interest : it was proposed that every member should make a vow of unconditional obedience to the pope, without requiring any support from the Holy See The order was therefore instituted in 1540, and Loyola appointed to be the first General.

The plan of the Society was completed by the two immediate successors of the founder, Lainez and Aquaviva, both of whom excelled their master in ability and the science of government ; and, in a few years, the Society established itself in every Catholic country, acquiring prodigious wealth and exciting the apprehensions of all the enemies of the Romish faith.

To Lainez are ascribed the *Secreta Monita,* or secret instructions of the order, which were first discovered on Christian, duke of Brunswick, seizing the Jesuits' college at Paderborn, in Westphalia, when he gave their books and manuscripts to the capuchins, who found these secret instructions among the archives of their rector. After this, another copy was detected at Prague, in the college of the Jesuits.

The Jesuits are taught to consider themselves as formed for action, in opposition to the monastic orders, who retire from the concerns of the world ; and engaging in all civil and commercial transactions, insinuating themselves into the friendship of persons of rank, studying the disposition of all classes, with a view of obtaining an influence over them, and undertaking missions to distant nations ; it is an essential principle of their policy, by every means to extend the Catholic faith. No labour is spared, no intrigue omitted that may prove conducive to this purpose.

The constitution of this Society is monarchical. A General is chosen for life by deputies from the several provinces, whose power is supreme and universal. Every member is at his entire disposal, who is required to submit his will and sentiments to his dictation, and to listen to his injunctions, as if uttered by Christ himself. The fortune, person, and conscience of the whole Society are at his disposal; and he can dispense his order not only from the vows of poverty, chastity, and monastic obedience, but even from submission to the pope, whenever he pleases. He nominates and removes provincials, rectors, professors, and all officers of the order, superintends the universities, houses, and missions, decides controversies, and forms or dissolves contracts. No member can have any opinion of his own; and the Society has its prisons, independent of the secular authority.

There are four classes of members,—the noviciates or probationers, the approved disciples the coadjutors, and the professors of the four vows. The education of youth was always considered by them as their peculiar province, aware of the influence which such a measure would infallibly secure over another generation: and before the conclusion of the sixteenth century, the Jesuits had obtained the chief direction of the youthful mind in every Catholic country in Europe. They had become the confessors of almost all its monarchs, and the spiritual guides of nearly every person distinguished for rank or influence. At different periods, they obtained the direction of the most considerable courts, and took part in every intrigue and revolution.

Notwithstanding their vow of poverty they accumulated, upon various pretences, immense wealth. They claimed exemption from tithes under a bull of Gregory XIII. who was devoted to their interests; and, by obtaining a special licence from the court of Rome to *trade* with the nations whom they professed to convert, they carried on a lucrative commerce in the East and West Indies, formed settlements in different countries, and acquired possession of a large province in South America, where they reigned as sovereigns over some hundred thousand subjects.

Their policy is uniformly to inculcate *attachment to the order*, and by a pliant morality, to soothe and gratify the passions of mankind, for the purpose of securing their patronage. They proclaim the duty of opposing princes who are inimical to the Catholic faith, and have employed every weapon, every artful and every intolerant measure, to resist the progress of Protestantism.

In *Portugal*, where the Jesuits were first received, they obtained the direction of the court. which for many years delivered to them the consciences of its princes, and the education of the people. Portugal opened the door to their missions, and gave them establishments in Asia, Africa, and America. They usurped the sovereignty of Paraguay, and resisted the forces of Portugal and Spain, who claimed it. The court of Lisbon, and even Rome herself, protested in vain against their excesses. The league in France was, in reality, a conspiracy of the Jesuits, under the sanction of Sixtus V to disturb the succession to the throne of France. The Jesuits' college at Paris was the grand focus of the seditions and treasons which then agitated the state and the ruler of the Jesuits was president of the Council of Sixteen, which gave the impulse to the leagues formed there and throughout France. Matthieu, a Jesuit and confessor of Henry III. was called 'The Courier of the League,' on account of his frequent journies to and from Rome, at that disastrous period.

In *Germany* the Society appropriated the richest benefices, particularly those of the monasteries of St. Benedict and St. Bernard. Catharine of Austria confided in them, and was supplanted; and loud outcries were uttered against them by the sufferers in Vienna, in the states of Styria, Carinthia, Carniola, and elsewhere. Their cruelties in Poland will never be forgotten. They were expelled from Abyssinia, Japan Malta, Cochin, Moscow, Venice, and other places, for their gross misconduct; and in America and Asia, they carried devastation and blood wherever they went. The great object of the persecution of the Protestants in *Savoy* was the confiscation of their property. in order to endow the colleges of the Jesuits. They had, no doubt a share in the atrocities of the duke of Alva. in the Low Countries. They boasted of the friendship of Catherine de Medicis, who espoused their cause, and under whose influence the massacre of St. Bartholomew was executed. Louis XIV. had three Jesuit confessors, which may explain the revocation of the edict of Nantz.

The Jesuits have been notorious for attempting the lives of princes. The reign of Queen Elizabeth presents a succession of plots. In her proclamation, dated Nov. 15, 1602. she says, that ' the Jesuits had fomented the plots against her person, excited her subjects to revolt, provoked foreign princes to compass her death, engaged in all affairs of state, and by their language and writings, had undertaken to dispose of her crown."

Lucius enumerates five conspiracies of the Jesuits against James I. before he had reigned a year. They contrived the gunpowder plot. So late as the time of George I. both houses of parliament reported, that the evidence examined by them on the conspiracy of Plunket and Layer, had satisfactorily shown that it had for its object the destruction of the king, the subversion of the laws, and the crowning of the popish Pretender; and they state, that " Plunket was born at Dublin, and bred up at the Jesuits' college at Vienna." Henry III. of France was assassinated by Clement, a Jesuit, in 1589. The Jesuits murdered William Prince of Orange, in 1584. They attempted the life of Louis XV. for imposing silence on the polemics of their order, besides innumerable other atrocities.

The pernicious spirit and constitution of this order, rendered it early detested by the principal powers of Europe; and while Pascal, by his ' Provincial Letters,' exposed the morality of the Society, and thus overthrew their influence over the multitude, different potentates concurred, from time to time, to destroy or prevent its establishments. Charles V. opposed the order in his dominions : it was expelled in England, by the proclamation of James I. in 1604 ; in Venice, in 1606 ; in Portugal, in 1759 ; in France, in 1764 ; in Spain and Sicily, in 1767, and suppressed and abolished by pope Clement XIV. in 1775. Recently, however, the pope has dared to re-establish it, though Clement had acted on the entreaties of even Catholic sovereigns, who deemed it incompatible with the existence of civil society. It must be acknowledged, indeed, to be a fit instrument for ecclesiastical despotism, and may therefore be regarded with indifference by all who are unconcerned to secure the liberties of their fellowmen; but those who feel as men and think like Christians, will read the following BULL for the revival of the order of the Jesuits, with no ordinary sensations.

Pius, Bishop, Servant of the Servants of God.

"(Ad perpetuam rei memoriam.)

"The care of all the churches confided to our humility by the Divine will, notwithstanding the lowness of our deserts and abilities, makes it our duty to employ all the aids in our power, and which are furnished to us by the mercy of Divine Providence, in order that we may be able, as far as the changes of times and places will allow, to relieve the spiritual wants of the Catholic world, without any distinction of people and nations.

" Wishing to fulfil this duty of our apostolic ministry, as soon as Francis Kareu, (then living,) and other secular priests, resident for many years in the vast empire of Russia, and who had been members of the company of Jesus, suppressed by Clement XIV. of happy memory, had supplicated our permission to unite in a body, for the purpose of being able to apply themselves more easily, in conformity with their institution, to the instruction of youth in religion and good morals to devote themselves to preaching, to confession, and the administration of the other sacraments, we felt it our duty the more willingly to comply with their prayer, inasmuch as the then reigning Emperor Paul I. had recommended the said priests in his gracious despatch, dated August 11, 1800, in which, after setting forth his special regard for them, he declared to us that it would be agreeable to him to see the company of Jesus established in his empire, under our authority; and we, on our side, considered attentively the great advantages which these vast regions might thence derive; considering how useful those ecclesiastics, whose morals and learning were equally tried, would be to the Catholic religion, thought fit to second the wish of so great and beneficent a prince.

"In consequence, by our brief, dated March 7, 1801, we granted to the said Francis Kareu, and his colleagues residing in Russia, or who should repair thither from other countries power to form themselves into a body or congregation of the company of Jesus; they are at liberty to unite in one or more houses, to be pointed out by their superior, provided these houses are situated within the Russian empire. We named the said Francis Kareu, general of the said congregation; we authorized them to resume and follow the rule of St. Ignatius of Loyola, approved and confirmed by the constitutions of Paul III. our predecessor, of happy memory, in order that the companions in a religious union, might freely engage in the instruction of youth in religion and good letters, direct seminaries and colleges, and with the consent of the ordinary, confess, preach the word of God, and administer the sacraments. By the same brief we received the congregation of the company of Jesus under our immediate protection and dependence, reserving to ourselves and our successors the prescription of every thing that might appear to us proper to consolidate, to defend it, and to purge it from the abuses and corruptions that might be therein introduced; and for this purpose we expressly abrogated such apostolical constitutions, statutes, privileges, and indulgences granted in contradiction to these concessions, especially the apostolic letters of Clement XIV. our predecessor, which begin with the words, *Dominus ac Redemptor noster*, only in so far as they are contrary to our brief, beginning *Catholicæ*, and which was given only for the Russian empire.

"A short time after we had ordained the restoration of the order of Jesuits in Russia, we thought it our duty to grant the same favour to the kingdom of Sicily, on the warm request of our dear son in Jesus Christ, King Ferdinand, who begged that the company of Jesus might be re-established in his dominions and states, as it was in Russia, from a conviction that, in these deporable times, the Jesuits were instructors most capable of forming youth to Christian piety and the fear of God, which is the beginning of wisdom, and to instruct them in science and letters The duty of our pastoral charge leading us to second the pious wishes of these illustrious monarchs, and having only in view the glory of God and the salvation of souls, we by our brief, beginning *Per alias*, and dated the 30th July, 1804, extended to the kingdom of the Two Sicilies the same concessions which we had made to the Russian empire.

" *The Catholic world* demands with *unanimous* voice the re-establishment of the company of Jesus. We daily receive to this effect the most pressing petitions from our venerable brethren, the archbishops and bishops, and the most distinguished persons, especially since the abundant fruits which this company has produced in the above countries have been generally known. The dispersion even of the stones of the sanctuary in those recent calamities, (which it is better now to deplore than to repeat;) the annihilation of the discipline of the regular orders, (the glory and support of religion and the Catholic church, to the restoration of which, all our thoughts and cares are at present directed,) require that we should accede to a wish so just and general.

" <u>We should deem ourselves guilty of a great crime towards God, if, amidst these dangers of the Christian republic, we neglected the aids which the special providence of God has put at our disposal</u>; and if, placed in the bark of Peter, tossed and assailed by continual storms, we refused to employ the vigorous and experienced rowers who volunteer their services, in order to break the waves of a sea which threatens every moment shipwreck and death. Decided by motives so numerous and powerful, we have resolved to do now what we could have wished to have done at the commencement of our pontificate. After having by fervent prayers implored the divine asistance, after having taken the advice and counsel of a great number of our venerable brothers the cardinals of the holy Roman church, we have decreed. with full knowledge, in virtue of the plenitude of apostolic power, and with perpetual validity, that all the concessions and powers granted by us solely to the Russian empire and the kingdom of the Two Sicilies, shall henceforth extend to all our ecclesiastical states, and also to *all other states*. We therefore concede and grant to our well-beloved son, Taddeo Barzorowski, at this time general of the company of Jesus, and to the other members of that company, lawfully delegated by him, all suitable and necessary powers, in order that the said states may freely and lawfully receive all those who shall wish to be admitted into the regular order of the company of Jesus, who, under the authority of the General *ad interim*, shall be admitted and distributed, according to opportunity, in one or more houses one or more colleges, and one or more provinces, where they shall conform their mode of life to the rules prescribed by St. Ignatius of Loyola, approved and confirmed by the constitutions of Paul III. We declare besides, and GRANT POWER that they may freely and lawfully apply to the education of youth *in the principles of the Catholic faith*, to form them to good morals, and to direct colleges and seminaries; we authorize them to hear confessions, to preach the word of God, and to administer the sacraments in the places of their residence with the consent and approbation of the ordinary. We take under our tutelage, under our immediate obedience, and that of the Holy See, all the colleges, houses, provinces and members of this order, and all those who shall join it ; always reserving to ourselves, and the Roman pontiffs our successors, to prescribe and direct all that we may deem it our duty to prescribe and direct to consolidate the said company more and more, to render it stronger and to purge it of abuses, should they ever creep in which God avert. It now remains for us to exhort with all our heart, and in the name of the Lord, all superiors, provincials, rectors companions, and pupils of this re-established Society, to show themselves at all times and in all places, faithful imitators of their father ; that they exactly observe the rule prescribed by their great founder ; that they obey with an always increasing zeal the useful advices and salutary counsels which he has left to his children,

"In fine, we recommend strongly, in the Lord, the company and all its members to our dear sons in Jesus Christ, the illustrious and noble princes and lords temporal, as well as to our venerable brothers the archbishops and bishops, and to all those who are placed in authority ; we exhort, we conjure them not only not to suffer that these religious be in any way molested, but to watch that they be treated with all due kindness and charity.

"<u>We ordain that the present letters</u> be inviolably observed, according to their form and tenor, in all time coming, that they enjoy their full and entire effect ; that <u>they shall never be submitted to the judgment or revision of any judge, with whatever power he may be clothed,</u> declaring null and of no effect any <u>encroachment on the present regulations,</u> either knowingly or from ignorance ; and this <u>notwithstanding any apostolical constitutions and ordinances, especially the brief of CLEMENT XIV.</u> of happy memory, beginning with the words *Dominus ac Redemptor noster,* issued under the seal of the Fisherman, on the 22d of July, 1773, which we expressly abrogate as far as contrary to the present order.

" It is also our will that the same credit be paid to copies, whether in manuscript or printed, of our present brief, as to the original itself, provided they have the signature of some notary public, and the seal of some ecclesiastical dignitary ; that no one be permitted to infringe, or by an audacious temerity, to oppose any part of this ordinance; and that should any one take upon him to attempt, let him know that he will thereby incur the INDIGNATION OF ALMIGHTY GOD, and of the HOLY APOSTLES PETER AND PAUL.

" Given at Rome, at Sancta Maria Major, on the 7th of August, in the year of our Lord, 1814, and the 15th of our pontificate.

  (Signed)   " Cardinal PRODATAIRE.
          " Cardinal BRASCHI."

PROVINCIAL LETTERS.

LETTER I.

Remarks on the Disputes of the Sorbonne, and on the Invention of the Term NEXT POWER, *employed by the Molinists to draw a Censure upon Mr. Arnauld.*

SIR,   *Paris, Jan.* 23, 1656.

WE have been greatly mistaken. It was only yesterday that I was undeceived; for, till then, I had imagined that the disputes of the Sorbonne were really of the utmost consequence to the interests of religion. The frequent meetings of a society so celebrated as the faculty of theology at Paris, in which have transpired so many extraordinary and unexampled things, have so raised universal expectation, that every one believes some great subject has been agitated. You will be much surprised, however, to learn by this communication, the issue of this splendid affair, which, as I have made myself thoroughly acquainted with it, I shall state in a few words.

The two subjects under examination relate—the one to a question of *fact*—the other to a question of *right*.

The former is to ascertain whether Mr. Arnauld be guilty of rashness, for saying, in his second letter, that he has carefully read the book of Jansenius, but has not been able to find the propositions condemned by the late Pope (Innocent X); nevertheless, as he condemns these propositions wherever they exist, he condemns them in Jansenius *if they should be there.*

The question, therefore, is, whether it be not extremely rash to intimate a doubt respecting these propositions actually occurring in Jansenius, after the bishops have affirmed that they do?

This affair being proposed in the Sorbonne, seventy-one doctors undertook the defence of Mr Arnauld, maintaining that he could give no other reply to the numerous inquirers into his opinion of the existence of these propositions in the said book than this, that he had not seen them there, nevertheless he condemned them if they were.

Some went further, and declared that after a diligent search they had not been able to discover them, but that they had even found some quite of a contrary nature. They then proceeded with some warmth, to require that if any doctor had seen them, he would be good enough to point them out. This they pleaded was so easily done, that no person could refuse the request, and it was an infallible way of convincing every one, even Mr. Arnauld himself. This, however, has never been conceded.

Such have been the proceedings on one side; on the other, eighty secular doctors and about forty mendicant friars have condemned Mr. Arnauld's statement without any examination into its truth or falsehood; and have even affirmed that the question did not respect the truth of his assertion, but merely his rashness in advancing it.

Moreover, fifteen were indisposed to concur in the censure; and they are called *the indifferent*.

In this manner the question of *fact* terminated, about which I confess I feel very little concern; for whether Mr. Arnauld be or be not guilty of rashness, does not at all affect my conscience. If I had any curiosity to ascertain whether the propositions occur in Jansenius, his book is neither so scarce nor so voluminous, as to prevent my reading it for my own satisfaction, without consulting the Sorbonne.

But were I not apprehensive of being rash myself, I believe I should agree with almost every body I meet, who having hitherto adopted the general belief that these propositions were in Jansenius, really begin to mistrust it, on account of this strange refusal to point them out. I positively have not found a single individual who could say he had seen them. This censure then, I fear, will do more harm than good, and give those who may be acquainted with the circumstances, quite a different impression from what is intended. In fact, people are now becoming so mistrustful, they will believe nothing but what they see. This point however, as I observed before, is of little importance, since it does not touch our faith.

The question of *right* seems at first sight more momentous; I have therefore taken the utmost pains to inform myself upon the subject; but you will be gratified to find that this is as insignificant as the former.

The investigation respected Mr. Arnauld's words in the same letter, "that the grace without which we can do nothing, was deficient in St. Peter when he fell." You and I expected that the great principles of grace would have been examined, as, whether grace be bestowed on all men, and whether it be certainly efficacious. Alas! how were we deceived! For my part I am become a great divine in a very little time, of which you shall have some signal proofs!

To ascertain the real truth, I went to my near neighbour, Mr. N., a doctor of the college of Navarre, who is, as you know, one of the bitterest opponents of the Jansenists; and as my curiosity rendered me almost as zealous as himself, I inquired if, to prevent all future doubts, they would not come to a formal decision, "that grace is given to all men." But he repelled me with great rudeness, saying, that was not the point, although some of his party maintained 'that grace is not given to all," and that even the examiners had declared in full assembly, that this opinion was *problematical*. This, indeed, was his own sentiment, which he confirmed by a celebrated passage of St Augustin: "We know that grace is not given to all men."

I apologized for mistaking his meaning, and requested to know whether they would not, at least, condemn that other opinion of the Jansenists, which had excited so much clamour, "that grace is efficacious, and determines the will in the choice of good." But I was again unlucky; " You know nothing about it," said he; "that is no heresy; it is perfectly orthodox; all the Thomists maintain it, and I have done the same myself in my Sorbonnic disputations."

I dared not proceed—still, I could not discover where the difficulty lay; but to gain some kind of information, I begged him to state wherein consisted the heresy of Mr. Arnauld's proposition. "It is in this," said he, "that he does not admit that the righteous possess the power of fulfilling the commands of God, in the manner in which WE understand it."

After this information I withdrew, elated with having found out the difficult point of the question. I hastened to Mr. N., who was sufficiently improved in his health to accompany me to his brother-in-law, a most thorough Jansenist, but *nevertheless a very good man!* In order to secure a better reception, I pretended to be of his party, and asked if it were possible that the Sorbonne should introduce such an error as this into the church, "that the just always possess a power of fulfilling the commands of God?" "What," replied he, "are you saying?" Do you call such a Catholic sentiment as that an error, a doctrine which none but Lutherans and Calvinists ever oppose?" "And is not this *your* opinion then?" returned I "Certainly not: we condemn it as heretical and impious." All astonishment, I perceived that I had now over-acted the Jansenist, as I had before, the Molinist. But not being fully satisfied with this reply, I entreated him to tell me ingenuously if he really maintained, "that the just always had a real power to keep the divine precepts" My gentleman grew a little angry at this—but it was all a holy zeal of course—and said he would never disguise his sentiments for any consideration in the world! that this was his firm belief, that both he and all his party would defend it to the last moment of life, as the genuine doctrine of St. Thomas and St. Augustin their master.

He was so serious that I could not disbelieve him: and

I instantly returned to my first doctor, to assure him, with the utmost satisfaction, that I was confident peace would soon be restored in the Sorbonne ; that the Jansenists were agreed upon the just possessing power to perform the commandments ; that I would answer for it, and would make them all sign it with their blood. "Hold," said he, "a man must be an excellent divine to discriminate these niceties ; so fine and subtle is the difference between us, that we can scarcely discern it ourselves ;—you therefore cannot be supposed to comprehend it ; but rest satisfied that the Jansenists will tell you, that the just always possess a power of fulfilling the divine commandments, which we do not dispute, but they will not inform you that this is *next power*. This is the point.

This term was to me quite new and unintelligible. I understood the matter till this moment ; but now all was obscurity, and I could imagine no otherwise than that this kind of phraseology was invented solely to confuse the subject. I therefore requested some explanation, but he made a great mystery of it, and dismissed me without any further satisfaction, to inquire of the Jansenists whether they admitted this *next power*. My *memory*, you will observe, retained the expression ; but, as to my *understanding*, verily it had no concern with it. Fearful of forgetting it, I hastened off to my Jansenist, and after the first compliments. "Pray," said I, "do you admit of a *next power ?*" He fell a laughing, and coldly replied, "Tell me yourself, in what sense you understand it, and I am then prepared to say what I believe." But as I was not wise enough for this, I could find no answer ; but unwilling to lose my visit, I answered at random, "I understand it in the sense of the Molinists." "O," returned my gentleman, without the least emotion, "and to which of the Molinists would you refer me ?" "All of them," said I, "as they constitute but one body and are animated by one spirit."

"You know little," said he, "of the subject. They are so much disunited in opinion, that they are quite opposite to each other. In one thing, however, they are all agreed, *to ruin Mr. Arnauld ;* and accordingly have determined, by mutual consent, to use the term *next*, though they understand it in very different senses, that by a similarity of language and an external conformity, they may seem to constitute a more considerable body, and be able to seek his ruin with the greater confidence of success."

This answer filled me with astonishment: still, I was unwilling to receive an impression of the base designs of the Molinists upon the word of an individual, and my only concern being to ascertain the different senses in which they employ the term *next power*. He assured me of his perfect readiness to explain it, but remarked, "You will see such gross contrariety and contradiction, as will almost surpass your belief, and make you suspicious of my veracity. But you will be better satisfied to have it immediately from themselves; and if you allow me to direct you, I should recommend a separate visit to a Mr. le Moine and father Nicolai." "I have no acquaintance," said I, "with either of these gentlemen." "But possibly you may know some others I may name, who entertain the same opinions." This was, in fact, the case. "Do you not know," continued he, "some of the Dominicans, who are called the new Thomists, and all agree with father Nicolai?" I was acquainted with some of them, and being resolved to avail myself of his advice and pursue my object, I immediately left him, and went to one of the disciples of M. le Moine.

I entreated him to inform me what it was to *have the next power to do any thing*. "O," said he, "this is sufficiently obvious; it is to have whatever power is requisite to accomplish it, in such a manner that nothing is wanting to complete the action." "So then," answered I, "to have the *next power* to cross a river, is to have a boat, watermen, oars, and other requisites, so that nothing be wanting." "Quite right." "And to have the *next power* to *see*, is to have good eyes and a good light. For, in your estimation, if a person possessed good eyes in the dark, he would not have the *next power* to see, because light would be needed, without which it is impossible to see at all." "Very logical indeed." "Consequently," continued I, "when you say that all the just, at all times possess the next power of observing the commandments, you mean that they always have all the grace which is necessary for their performance; at least that nothing is wanting on the part of God." "Gently," said he, "the just always possess whatever is requisite for their obedience, or at least what is requisite to ask it of God." "I understand, very well, said I, "they have all that is necessary to seek divine assistance by prayer, but need no other grace to enable them to pray." "Perfectly correct." "But is not an efficacious grace requisite to excite us to pray?" "No," returned he, following the opinion of M. le Moine.

To lose no time, I hastened to the Jacobins, inquiring for those whom I knew to be Thomists of the new school; and I begged them to give me information respecting this *next power*: first asking if it were not that in which nothing was deficient in point of active energy. The answer was categorically, "No." I asked, "Pray, Fathers, do you call it *next power* when any such deficiency exists; and will you affirm, for instance, of a person in the night, without any kind of light, that he has the *next power to see?*" "Most assuredly, if he be not blind." "I have no objection to this," said I, "but M. le Moine has quite a different view of the subject." "True, but I tell you how *we* understand it." To this I bowed. "For I will never," returned I, "dispute about a term, if I am only informed of the meaning attached to it. I perceive that when you state that the just always have the *next power to* pray to God, you intend that they require some other aid, without which they could never pray at all." "Excellent, excellent," replied one of the Fathers, embracing me,— "most excellent; for the just need an efficacious grace not bestowed upon all men, and which influences their will to pray; and whoever denies the necessity of this efficacious grace is a heretic."

"Excellent, indeed, very excellent," exclaimed I, in my turn: "but, according to your opinion, the Jansenists are orthodox, and M. le Moine a heretic; for they affirm that the just have power to pray, but efficacious grace is nevertheless essential, which you approve ; he says that the just can pray without efficacious grace which is the statement you condemn." " True," said they, ' but then M. le Moine calls that power by the distinguishing epithet of *next power*.

" But really good Father," continued I, " it is a mere play upon words to say that you agree respecting the same common term, but use it in a contrary sense." To this I had no reply ; but most fortunately, in came the disciple of M. le Moine I had before consulted. This struck me at the time as a marvellous coincidence ; but I have since learned that these fortunate *accidents* are not uncommon, as they are in the habit of perpetual intercourse.

Addressing myself instantly to M. le Moine's disciple, " I know a gentleman," said I, " who maintains that all the just have always, at all times, the power to pray, but that nevertheless they never will pray without an efficacious grace to impel them, which God does not always vouchsafe to all the just. Is this heretical ?" " Stop," said the doctor, " you take me by surprise—hold a little—*distinguo*—if he call that power *next power*, he is a Thomist, and therefore orthodox—if not, he is a Jansenist and consequently a heretic." " But he neither calls it next nor not next." " Then he is a heretic—I appeal to these good Fathers." However, I did not take the opinion of these judges, for they had already given consent by a significant nod, but proceeded.—" The gentleman refuses to adopt the term *next*, because he can obtain no explanation of it." One of the Fathers, upon this, was going to favour us with a definition, but the disciple of M. le Moine interrupted him, saying, " Why do you wish to renew our quarrelsome disputations ? Have not we agreed not to explain the term *next*, and to use it on both sides without defining what it signifies ?"—to this he instantly assented.

I was now let into the secret ; and, rising to take my leave, " Fathers," I exclaimed, " verily I feel extremely apprehensive that the whole of this affair is mere chicanery, and whatever may result from your meetings, I will venture to predict, that whatever censure may be inflicted. peace will not be established. For, if it should be agreed to pronounce the syllable *next*, who does not perceive that, as no explanation is given, each party will claim the victory? The Dominicans will say it is understood in their sense. M. le Moine will affirm it is in his; and there will arise more disputes respecting the signification of the word, than about its being introduced; for, after all, there would be no great hazard in receiving it without affixing any meaning, since it can only do mischief by its meaning. It would, however, be unworthy of the Sorbonne and the faculty of theology to make use of ambiguous terms without giving some explanation; but, Fathers, I beseech you, only this once, what must I believe in order to be an orthodox Catholic?" 'You must," said they, all speaking together, "you must say, that all the just possess the *next power*, without attaching any meaning to the words—*Abstrahendo à sensu Thomistarum, et à sensu aliorum Theologorum.*

"That is to say," returned I, taking my leave, "this word must be pronounced with the lips, through fear of being stigmatized with the name of heretic. Is it a scriptural term?" "No." "Is it used by the Fathers, the councils, or the Popes?" "No." "Is it patronised by St. Thomas?" "No." "Whence then arises the necessity of using it at all, since it is neither supported by any authority, nor has any peculiar signification of its own?" "You are prodigiously obstinate," they exclaimed, "but you *shall* pronounce it, or be accounted a heretic, and Mr. Arnauld also; for our party constitutes the majority, and, if it be necessary, we can compel as many of the Cordeliers to vote as will carry the point."

This last reason was so forcible, that I bowed, and withdrew to give you this statement, by which you will perceive that none of the following points have been examined, and consequently neither condemned nor approved. 1. That grace is not given to all men. 2. That all the just have power to keep the divine commandments. 3. That nevertheless they need efficacious grace to determine their will to obey them, and even to pray. 4. That this efficacious grace is not always given to all the just, and that it depends solely on the mercy of God. So that there is nothing but the poor word *next*, without any meaning, that runs any risk.

Happy the people who live entirely ignorant of it? Happy they who existed before the birth of this *next!!* I see no remedy, if the gentlemen of the academy do not, by some authoritative mandate, banish this barbarous term out of the Sorbonne—a term which has occasioned so many divisions. Unless this be done, the censure must be confirmed; but I can see no other evil consequence than that of rendering the Sorbonne contemptible, which however will annihilate the authority it ought to possess on other occasions.

Now I have you at liberty to vote for or against the term *next*, for I have too much affection for you to persecute you upon so frivolous a pretext.

If this account should afford you any gratification, I shall continue to give you every information of what passes.

I am, &c.

LETTER II.

On the Subject of sufficient Grace.

Sir,   *Paris, Jan. 29, 1656.*

At the very moment I was sealing up my last letter, our old friend Mr. N. came in, most fortunately for my curiosity, for he is thoroughly acquainted with the controversies of the day, and is perfectly in the secret of the Jesuits, being with them constantly, and intimate with their principal men. After mentioning the particular purpose of his visit, I requested him to state, in a few words, the points in debate between the two parties.

These, with the utmost readiness, he told me were chiefly two: the one respecting *next power*, the other *sufficient grace*. The first I have already explained; allow me to speak of the second.

The difference, then, on the subject of sufficient grace is chiefly this; the Jesuits maintain that there is a general grace bestowed upon all mankind, but in such a sense subordinated to free will, that this grace is rendered efficacious or inefficacious as the will chooses, without any additional assistance from God, and without needing any thing exterior to itself to make its operations effectual; on which account it is distinguished by the epithet *sufficient*. The Jansenists, on the contrary, affirm that no grace is actually sufficient, unless it be also efficacious, that is, that all those principles which do not determine the will to act effectively, are insufficient for action, because, they say, no one can act without efficacious grace.

Wishing afterwards to be informed respecting the doctrine of the new Thomists, " It is," exclaimed he, " quite ridiculous ; for they agree with the Jansenists, to admit of a *sufficient grace* given to all men, but insist that they can never act with this alone, and that it is still necessary that God should bestow an *efficacious grace* really to influence the will, and which is not bestowed upon all." " Then," said I, " this grace is at once sufficient and insufficient." " Very true," he answered ; for if it be sufficient, nothing more is requisite to produce the action ; and if not, it cannot be called *sufficient*."

" But," I inquired, " where is the difference between them and the Jansenists ?" " They differ," said he, " in this, that the Dominicans at least acknowledge that *all men have sufficient grace*." " I understand you ; but they *say* so without *thinking* so, because they proceed immediately to state, that in order to act, we must possess *efficacious grace, which is not given to all* ; and hence, although they agree with the Jesuits in using the same nonsensical terms, they contradict them in the substantial meaning, and agree with the Jansenist." " True." " How is it then," I asked, that the Jesuits and these men are so united, and why do not they oppose them as well as the Jansenists, for they will always find them powerful opponents ; who, while asserting the necessity of efficacious grace to determine the will, prevent the establishment of that which they deem to be of itself sufficient ?"

" The Dominicans," said he, " are a powerful body, and the Jesuits are too cunning openly to encounter them. They are content with having brought them to admit the term *sufficient grace*, though the sense in which they use it is widely different ; by which means they gain the advantage of easily making their opponents' sentiments appear indefensible whenever they please. For, supposing that all men have sufficient principles of grace it is quite natural to infer that efficacious grace is not necessary to action, because the sufficiency of the general principle will preclude the necessity of any thing additional. He who uses the term *sufficient*, includes whatever is essentially requisite, and it will be of no avail for the Dominicans to protest that they impute a different sense to the expression. The people accustomed to the general use of the word, will not listen to their explanation. Thus the society of Jesuits has profited abundantly by the expression adopted by the Dominicans, without urging them farther; and were you acquainted with what occurred during the popedoms of Clement VIII. and Paul V., and how the Dominicans opposed the efforts of the Jesuits to establish the doctrine of sufficient grace, you would no longer be surprised at the present cessation of hostilities, and the ready consent of the latter to their enjoying their own opinion, provided they have equal liberty, especially as the Dominicans have adopted and agreed publicly to their favourite term.

This complaisance is satisfactory, and the Dominicans are in consequence not required to deny the necessity of efficacious grace. This would be advancing a step too far: friends should not be tyrannized over; the Jesuits have gained enough; for the world is satisfied with words, little solicitous of penetrating into things; so that the name *sufficient grace* being equally received by both parties, though with a wonderful difference of meaning, there are no persons, except it be some of the most sharp-sighted theologians, but will think that Jacobins and Jesuits agree in sense as much as in expression." I acknowledged that I thought the Jesuits a shrewd set of people: and, availing myself of my friend's advice, I went straight to the former, at whose gate I found a good friend of mine, a staunch Jansenist (for you must know I have friends of all parties,) who was in search of one of the Fathers, though not the same. However, I persuaded him after much entreaty, to accompany me. Asking for one of the new Thomists, who was delighted to see me— "Oho!" said I, "my good Father, it is not enough for all men to have *a next power*, by which they can in fact do nothing; they must possess *sufficient grace*, by which they can do—as little. Is not this the doctrine of your schools?" "Yes, certainly," returned he, "and I firmly maintained it in the Sorbonne this very morning: I spoke out my half-hour; and, but for the *hour-glass*, I should have exterminated that abominable proverb which is so current in Paris—*he votes with his cap like a monk in the Sorbonne.*" "And pray, what may you mean by your half-hour and your hour-glass? Do they confine your speeches so exactly to a specified time?" "Yes," said he, "they have done so for some days past." "And are you obliged to occupy your half-hour?" "O no, you may speak as little, but not as much as you please." "A capital regulation for an ignoramus! A noble excuse for such as have nothing worth hearing to say! But to the point, Father. Is this grace, which is given to all men *sufficient?*" "Yes," said he, "and yet it is of no avail without efficacious grace!" "No." "And all men have *sufficient*, but all have not *efficacious* grace?" "Exactly so." "That is to say, all men have grace enough, and all have not grace enough—this grace is sufficient and it is not sufficient—that is, in fact, it is nominally sufficient and really insufficient. Upon my word, Father, this is a very fine doctrine! Have you forgot, since you quitted the world, what the term *sufficient* signifies? Do you recollect that it includes all that is necessary to an action? You cannot have forgotten this; for to take a very obvious illustration, if your table were only supplied with two ounces of bread and a glass of water per day, should you be satisfied with your Prior, upon his pleading that with one thing more, which however he would not furnish, you would have quite sufficient for your support? How then can you state that all men have sufficient grace for acting, while you confess something more, which all do not possess, is absolutely necessary? Is this so unimportant an article of faith, that every one is left at liberty to decide whether efficacious grace be or be not requisite? Or is it altogether a matter of indifference?" "What do you mean," replied the good Father, "by indifferent? This is *heresy*, rank *heresy*. To admit the necessity of efficacious grace to act effectually, is *faith;* but to deny it is downright *heresy.*"

"Where are we now," exclaimed I, "and which side am I to take here? If I deny sufficient grace, I am a *Jansenist;* if I admit it with the Jesuits in such a sense, that there is no necessity for efficacious grace, I am, say you, a *heretic;* and if I concur with you, I sin against common sense. I am a madman say the Jesuits. What then am I to do in this inevitable necessity of being deemed a madman, a heretic, or a Jansenist? [And to what a situation are we reduced, if the Jansenists alone avoid confounding faith and reason, and thus save themselves at once from absurdity and error."]

My good friend the Jansenist seemed pleased with my remarks, and thought he had already gained me. He said nothing to me, however; but turning to the Father— "Pray," said he, " in what respects do you agree with the Jesuits?" He replied, " In this, that we both acknowledge that sufficient grace is given to all men." "But," returned he, "there are two things in the term sufficient grace; the sound, which is mere air, and the sense, which is real and significant. So that when you avow an agreement with the Jesuits in the *word*, but oppose them in the *sense*, it is obvious that you disagree with them in the essential matter, though you accord in the term. Is this acting with openness and sincerity?" "But," said the good man, "what cause of complaint have you, since we deceive no one by this mode of speaking? for in our schools we publicly declare that we understand the expression in a sense quite opposite to the Jews." " I complain," said my friend, ' that you do not declare to all the world, that by *sufficient grace*, you mean a grace which is not *sufficient*. Having changed the signification of the usual terms in religion, you are obliged in conscience to declare, that when you admit of sufficient grace in all men, you really intend that they have *not* sufficient grace. Every one understands the word sufficient in the same sense, the new Thomists alone excepted. Women of all classes, who constitute one half of the world, the whole court, the army, the magistrates, lawyers, merchants, artificers, and in fact the mass of mankind, the Dominicans apart consider the word *sufficient* as denoting whatever is necessary. And no one is aware of your singular interpretation; every where it is said that they maintain the doctrine of sufficient grace. What then is the natural inference, but that their opinion is, that all men possess grace sufficient for action? Especially when they are seen to coalesce with the Jesuits, who receive it in this sense, for selfish and intriguing purposes? Is not the uniformity of your expressions connected with this union of party, an undeniable exposition and proof of the uniformity of your sentiments?"

"Christians inquire of divines, what is the real condition of human nature since the fall? St. Augustin and his disciples reply, that it does not possess sufficient grace, unless it pleases God to bestow it. The Jesuits come forward and assert that all do absolutely possess it. Consult the Dominicans upon this contradictory representation, and what is the consequence? They coalesce with the Jesuits. By this artifice their numbers appear so considerable. They divide from those who deny sufficient grace and declare that all men have it; and who would imagine otherwise than that they sanction the Jesuits? When, lo! they proceed to intimate that this *sufficient* grace is useless, without the *efficacious*, which is not bestowed upon all men!

"Shall I present you with a picture of the church amidst these different sentiments? I consider it like a man who, leaving his native country to travel abroad is met by robbers who wound him so severely that they leave him half dead. He sends for three physicians resident in the neighbourhood. The first after probing his wounds, pronounces them to be mortal, assuring him that God alone can restore him; the second, wishing to flatter him, declares he has sufficient strength to reach home, and insulting the first for opposing his opinion, threatens to be the ruin of him. The unfortunate patient, in this doubtful condition as soon as he perceives the approach of the third, stretches out his hands to welcome him who is to decide the dispute. This physician, upon examining his wounds, and ascertaining the opinions already given, coincides with the second, and these coalesce against the first to turn him out with contempt; and they now form the strongest party. The patient infers from this proceeding, that the third physician agrees with the second, and upon putting the question, he assures him most positively that his strength is sufficient for the proposed journey. The wounded man, however, expatiating upon his weakness, asks upon what he founds his opinion? 'Why, you have still got legs, and legs are the means which, according to the constitution of nature, are sufficient for the purpose of walking.' 'Very true,' replies the wounded traveller; 'but have I all the strength which is requisite for making use of them: for really they seem useless to me in my present languishing condition?' 'Certainly they are.' returns the physician, 'and you never will be able to walk unless God vouchsafes some extraordinary assistance to sustain and guide you.' 'What then,' says the infirm man, 'have not I sufficient strength in myself to be fully able to walk?' 'O no, far, very far from it.' 'Then you have a different opinion from your friend respecting my real condition.' 'I candidly admit, I have.'

"What do you suppose the wounded man would say to this? He complains of their strange proceeding, and of the ambiguous language of this third physician. He censures him for coalescing with the second, when he was in fact of a contrary opinion, though they agreed in appearance and for driving away the first, with whom he really coincided; and then, after trying his strength, and finding by experience the truth of his weakness, he dismisses them both; and recalling the first, puts himself under his care, follows his advice, and prays to God for the strength which he confesses he needs. His petitions are heard, and he ultimately returns home in peace."

The good Father was all astonishment at this parable, and made no reply. Anxious to encourage him, I said, in the softest manner, "But after all, what do you think, my good Father, of applying the term *sufficient* to a grace which, you say, it is a point of faith to believe is really *insufficient?*" "You," said he, "are at liberty to speak whatever you choose upon these subjects, being a private person; I am a monk and belong to a society. Cannot you perceive the wide difference; We are dependent on our superiors: they depend elsewhere, and have promised our votes. What do you suppose would become of me?"— Half a word was sufficient, and we recollected that one of his brethren was banished to Abbeville on a a similar occasion.

"But," inquired I, "how is it that your community pledges itself at all upon the subject of this grace?" "Oh, that is another question: all I can say is, our order has most strenuously maintained the doctrine of St. Thomas respecting efficacious grace. How zealously did it oppose that of Molina from the very moment of its introduction! How has it laboured to establish the necessity of the efficacious grace of Jesus Christ! You cannot be ignorant surely of what was done under Clement VIII. and Paul V., that the former being prevented by death, and the latter by some Italian affairs, from publishing his bull, our arms were retained in the Vatican. But the Jesuits, who, from the very commencement of the heresies of Luther and Calvin, took advantage of the peoples' incapacity to discern between the truth and falsehood of the doctrine of St. Thomas, circulated their sentiments with such rapidity, that they soon obtained a dominion over the popular faith, and we should have been decried as Calvinists, and treated as the Jansenists now are, if we had not qualified the truth of an efficacious grace by the acknowledgement, at least in *appearance*, of a sufficient one. In this dilemma what better expedient could be devised, at once to preserve the truth and save our credit, than that of admitting the *name* of sufficient grace, but denying the *reality?* This then is the state of the case."

He spoke in so melancholy a tone, that I really pitied him; but not so my friend, who continued, "Do not flatter yourself with having preserved the truth; if she had no other protectors, she would have perished in such feeble hands. You have received the name of her enemy into the church, which is as baneful as having received the enemy himself. Names are inseparable from things. If the term *sufficient* grace be once established, it will be vain to say that you understand a grace which is *insufficient*. It will never do; the explanation will be detested: the world uses more sincerity on the most unimportant occasions: the Jesuits will triumph; for this will in fact be establishing their sufficient grace, while yours will be only nominal, and thus you will propagate an article of faith which is contrary to your own belief."

"No," said the Father " we would all suffer martyrdom, rather than consent to the establishment of sufficient grace in the Jesuitical sense of the term. St. Thomas, whom we have sworn to follow, even to death, is diametrically opposed to it." My friend, more grave than I could be, replied, " Your fraternity, Father, has received an order which is miserably managed: it abandons the grace which was entrusted to it, and which was never before abandoned from the creation of the world. That victorious grace which the patriarchs anticipated which the prophets predicted, which was introduced by Jesus Christ, preached by St. Paul, explained by St. Augustin, the greatest of the Fathers, embraced by all his followers, confirmed by St. Bernard, the last in the succession of the Fathers, maintained by St. Thomas, the angel of the schools, transmitted from him to your society, maintained by so many of your Fathers, and so gloriously defended by your fraternity under the popes Clement and Paul; this efficacious grace which has been thus committed to you as a sacred deposit, in order to secure, by means of an indissoluble holy order, a succession of preachers, to proclaim it to the end of the world, is at length deserted for the most unworthy considerations. It is high time for others to arm in its defence. It is time for God to raise up some intrepid supporters of the doctrine of grace, who, happily unacquainted with the principles of the age, shall serve God from motives of genuine love. The Dominicans may no longer defend it; but it will not therefore be destitute of protectors, for it will raise and qualify others by its own almighty energy. Grace demands holy and sanctified hearts—hearts which she purifies herself, and detaches from those worldly interests which are so incompatible with the Gospel. Reflect, seriously, my Father, and take care lest God remove the candlestick from its place, and leave you in darkness and dishonour, as a punishment for your indifference to a cause of such vital importance to his church."

He would have said much more, for he kindled as he proceeded, but I thought proper to interrupt him, and getting up, said, " Verily, Father, had I any influence in France, I would have it proclaimed with the sound of a trumpet—' KNOW ALL MEN, that when the Jacobins state that sufficient grace is given to all, they mean that all have not the grace which is really sufficient.'—After which you might state the same, but no otherwise, as often as you pleased." Thus our visit terminated.

You will perceive from this communication, that there is a *political sufficiency* not dissimilar to a *next power;* and yet it seems to me, that any one who is not a Jacobin, may, without incurring any hazard, doubt of both *next power* and *sufficient grace.*

As I am folding up my letter, I hear that the censure is inflicted; but as I know nothing respecting the wording of it, and as it will not be made public till the 15th of February, I shall write no more till the next post.

I am, &c.

Reply of the Provincial to the two former Letters of his Friend.

SIR,   *Feb.* 2, 1656.

I HAVE not kept your former letters to myself; every body sees, understands, and believes them. They are not only in high estimation with divines, but prove very amusing to others, and even to the ladies.

A gentleman of the academy, one of the most illustrious of that illustrious body, who had only read your first letter, wrote me as follows: "I wish that the Sorbonne, which owes so much to the memory of the late Cardinal, (Richlieu,) would acknowledge the jurisdiction of his French academy. The author of the letter ought to have satisfaction; for, as an academician, I would authoritatively condemn, banish proscribe—I am ready to say I would exterminate, with all my might, this next power, which creates such an unmeaning clamour about nothing: the mischief is that our academic power is so remote and circumscribed. I am extremely concerned about it: the more so, that my feeble ability is inadequate to render you a suitable return for your favours.

                                       I am, &c."

The following was written by a person whom I cannot name, to a lady who had sent him your first letter:

"It is impossible for you to conceive the obligation you conferred in sending the letter you conveyed to me: it is remarkably witty and well written. Its details are without tediousness, its statements respecting the most perplexed affairs perfectly clear; its raillery is in a fine style; it is instructive to those who are ignorant of these disputes, and renews the pleasure of such as were previously acquainted with them. It is moreover, an excellent apology, or, if you will, a delicate piece of satire, and quite innocent. In a word, there is so much skill, spirit, and judgment in it, that I am anxious to know the writer.

I am, &c."

And you. Sir, are desirous of knowing the person who could give such an account; but be content to respect without knowing him, and when you know him you will honour him the more.

Continue your communications, and let the censure come whenever it will, we are prepared to receive it. The terms *next power* and *sufficient grace* with which we are menaced alarm us no more. We have learned too well from the Jesuits, the Jacobins, and Mr. le Moine, how strangely they have been distorted, and how little there is in these new phrases to give us any concern.

Ever yours, &c.

LETTER III.

WRITTEN IN REPLY TO THE PRECEDING.

The Injustice, Absurdity, and Nullity of the Censure upon Mr. Arnauld.

Sir,   *Paris, Feb.* 9, 1656.

I RECEIVED your letter, and at the same time, a manuscript copy of the censure. I find myself as well treated in the one as Mr. Arnauld is ill used in the other. I am apprehensive there may be extremes on both sides, and that neither of us is sufficiently known by our judges: if we were, I feel assured Mr. Arnauld would have merited the approbation of the Sorbonne, and I the censure of the academy. Such is the contrariety that has awaited us! To defend *his* innocence he has only to procure publicity; to preserve *my* reputation I must seek the shades. Unable therefore to make my appearance, I must trouble you to discharge my duty to those excellent persons with whose approbation I have been favoured, while I communicate some farther information respecting the censure.

I freely confess, Sir, my extreme astonishment at it: expecting, as I did, nothing less than a condemnation of the most horrible heresies; but you will participate my surprise when informed, that all these splendid preparations vanished into nothingness at the very moment when the mighty effect was to be produced.

This will be obvious, if you will be good enough to recollect the strange accounts which have so long been circulated respecting the Jansenists. Of what cabals, errors, schisms, and conspiracies have they been accused! How have they been decried and blackened in the pulpit and from the press! And how prodigiously has this violent torrent increased within these few years, in which they have been openly and publicly accused, not only of being heretics and schismatics, but apostates and infidels, as denying the mystery of transubstantiation, and renouncing Jesus Christ and the Gospel!

After so many accusations, a resolution was taken to examine their writings, as the means of forming a correct judgment. The second letter of Mr. Arnauld was selected, as containing the worst errors. The examiners were his most avowed enemies, who, devoting their utmost attention to the search of objectionable passages, eventually produce a single proposition relating to doctrine, which they exhibit for censure.

What is the natural inference, but that the proposition selected under such circumstances, must contain the very essence of the vilest imaginable heresies? And yet there is nothing in reality which is not so plainly and formally expressed in the passage Mr. Arnauld quotes from the Fathers, that I have never found any individual capable of pointing out the least difference. Still it is believed an essential difference must exist, because the citations from the Fathers being unquestionably *orthodox*, the proposition of Mr. Arnauld must be perfectly contrary to become *heretical*.

The Sorbonne. it was of course anticipated, would afford the requisite explanation. All Christendom opened its eyes to discover in the censure they inflicted, that point which to vulgar minds was imperceptible. Mr. Arnauld defends himself by furnishing his own proposition and the passages in the Fathers whence he took it, in parallel columns, which rendered their conformity obvious to the meanest understanding. He shows in a quotation from St. Augustin, "that Jesus Christ exhibits a just man in the person of St. Peter, who teaches us by his fall to avoid presumption," and again, "that God left St. Peter destitute of grace, to prove that man can do nothing without it." He cites St. Chrysostom, as saying, " that the fall of St. Peter was not occasioned by any lukewarmness towards Christ, but from a want of grace ; and that this did not arise so much from that apostle's negligence, as from his being forsaken of God, which was to teach all Christians that without God they can do nothing." He then states his own criminal proposition, namely, " The Fathers point out to us a just man in the person of St. Peter, in whom grace, without which we can do nothing, was wanting "

Vain must be the attempt here to make Mr. Arnauld's statement as perfectly different from that of the Fathers, as truth is from error, and faith from heresy : for wherein does the difference consist ? Is it in his saying that " the Fathers point out a just man in the person of St. Peter ?" But these are the identical words of St. Augustin. Is it in the phrase, " Grace was wanting ?" But the same St. Augustin who says that " Peter was a just man," says that " he wanted grace on that occasion." Is it in the expression, that, " without grace we can do nothing ?" But does not St. Augustin declare the same in the very same paragraph ?—a truth which St. Chrysostom had before advanced, in these much stronger terms—" His fall did not originate in his lukewarmness, nor in his negligence, but from a defect of grace and through his being forsaken of God."

These considerations produced an universal suspense, to ascertain wherein the alleged diversity consisted, till at length this celebrated and long expected censure, which had occasioned so many meetings, appeared. But alas! alas! what a disappointment! Whether the learned doctors did not choose to condescend to instruct our feeble capacity, or for any other undivulged reason, certain it is they have done nothing else but pronounce the following words,— " This proposition is RASH, IMPIOUS, BLASPHEMOUS, ACCURSED, and HERETICAL !!!"

Is it incredible, Sir, that most people, deceived in their expectations, are very much displeased, and censure the very censurers themselves, and that they deduce the most charming inferences in favour of Mr. Arnauld's innocence ?

5

"What!" say they, "is this all that so many infuriated doctors, after so long an examination of his works, have been able to discover? What! only three objectionable lines, and these composed of the very words of the greatest divines of the Greek and Latin churches? Is this author to be ruined when his writings afford no better a pretext for his condemnation? who can possibly produce a nobler evidence of the faith of this accused, but excellent individual? How is it that this censure comprises so many imprecations, dreadful as were ever invented against Arius and Antichrist himself? *poison, plague, horror, rashness impiety, blasphemy, abomination, execration, anathema, heresy*—and all to combat what is imperceptible and invisible? If this war be waged against the words of the Fathers what becomes of faith—what of tradition? If it be against Mr. Arnauld's proposition, let them explain this prodigious disagreement; for really we can at present perceive nothing but the most perfect coincidence. Whenever we discover the guilt, we are prepared to detest it; but so long as we can see nothing but what the holy Fathers themselves believed and expressed in the identical terms, how can we possibly withhold our reverence?"

Such then is the unhappy situation of people who penetrate too deeply into these affairs; you and I, methinks, being not so profound, may remain at ease. Why should we be wiser than our masters? O let us by no means attempt it: we should wander into a boundless labyrinth! One step more and this censure will itself be heretical! Truth is of so delicate a nature, that the least deviation betrays us into error; but this error of Mr. Arnauld is so minute, that the slightest conceivable departure from it restores us to truth. The difference between this proposition and the true faith dwindles into an imperceptible point; the distance is so small, that being incapable of perceiving it, I became really apprehensive of opposing the doctors of the church, while aiming at too precise a conformity to the doctors of the Sorbonne. In this perplexity I deemed it necessary to consult one of those who remained neutral on the first question, for the purpose of ascertaining the real truth. Meeting with a very sensible person of this description, I entreated him to point out the circumstances of this difference, frankly owning myself incapable of discerning any. He replied, smiling at my simplicity, "Are you really weak enough to believe there is any difference? In what can it consist? Do you imagine, if it had been discovered, it would not have been announced triumphantly, and exposed to the people with the same eager delight as is evinced in decrying Mr. Arnauld?"—I now perceived that they who were neutral upon the first question, did not however disregard the second. Still being anxious to hear his reasons, I inquired why this proposition had been attacked? "Can you then," returned he, "be ignorant of two things. which even the most superficial inquirer knows, namely, that Mr. Arnauld always avoided asserting any thing which was not entirely founded on the tradition of the church—and that his enemies resolved nevertheless to excommunicate him at any rate? And as the writings of the one furnished no pretext to the designs of the other, they have been necessitated in order to gratify their malignity to take the very first proposition they found, and condemn it without saying why or wherefore? Are you not aware that the Jansenists hold them in check, and urge them so vehemently that if the least syllable escape them contrary to the opinions of the Fathers, whole volumes are instantly accumulated, to which they are obliged to yield? so that after such numerous evidences of their own weakness their opponents have thought it more convenient and more easy to censure than to reply, to find condemning monks rather than substantial arguments."

"But," said I, "if this be the case, their censure is unavailing, for who will attach any credit to what is utterly unfounded, and capable of being at once refuted?" "Ah," replied the doctor, "you would adopt a different language, were you acquainted with the spirit of the people. Their censure, all censurable as it is, will for a time produce nearly its intended effect: for, however invalid it may be proved to be, it will be regarded by the generality of people with as much deference, as though it were the justest censure in the world. Let it only be cried about the streets,—' Here is the censure of Mr. Arnauld —here is the condemnation of the Jansenists,'—and the Jesuits will have effected their purpose. How many, do you suppose, of those who read it, will understand it? How many will perceive that it is objectionable? Who will deeply interest himself in the affair, or take the trouble of giving it a thorough examination? You see then it will be prodigiously serviceable to the enemies of the Jansenists. They are sure, by this artifice, of a triumph: and however vain, as usual, it may be, it will at least continue some months, after which they will invent some new mode of subsistence. They live, according to the proverb, from hand to mouth. This is their present plan; sometimes they have a catechism, in which a child is made to anathematize their adversaries; then a procession, in which sufficient grace leads efficacious grace in triumph; anon a comedy, where the devils fly off with Jansenius; one while an almanack; and now—this said censure."

" Once, Sir," said I, " I thought the method of the Molinists indefensible, but after what you have said, I admire their prudence and policy. I see they could do nothing more judicious or more sure." " You understand it," returned he; · the safest expedient has always been to be silent, which made a learned divine say, 'the wisest among them are those who intrigue much, speak little, and write nothing.'

" It was in this spirit that from the very commencement of their meetings, they prudently decreed, that if Mr. Arnauld should come into the Sorbonne he should only be allowed simply to explain what he believed, and not enter the lists of controversy with any one. The examiners being desirous of some little deviation from this rule, found themselves much mistaken, and were too vigorously refuted by his second apology.

" In the same spirit they discovered this rare and novel invention of the half-hour and hour-glass: by which they avoided the urgency of those troublesome doctors, who undertook to refute all their reasons, to produce books to demonstrate their falsehood, to challenge them to answer, and to reduce them to total silence.

"They foresaw, that the secession of so considerable a number of doctors from their assemblies, in consequence of an abridgement of the liberty of discussion, would discredit their censure, and that Mr. Arnauld's protesting its nullity from the very first would prove but a miserable preamble to procure it a favourable reception. They are satisfied that those who have no prepossessions will, at least, respect the judgment of the seventy doctors who had nothing to gain by defending Mr. Arnauld, quite as much as that of others, who had nothing to lose by condemning him. But after all, they consider it a very fine thing to procure a censure- though it be from only a part of the Sorbonne, and not from the whole body; though it passed in defiance of the liberty of discussion, and succeeded by mean, unwarrantable artifices; though it furnish no explanation of the point of dispute; though it determine not wherein the alleged heresy consists; though in fact it speaks but little through fear of mistake. This silence itself is, to the generality, very mysterious; and this remarkable advantage will ensue, that the most critical and penetrating divines will never be able to charge upon it one erroneous argument!

"Do not, then, disturb yourself; be assured there is nothing heretical in the condemned proposition: it is only offensive as being introduced into Mr. Arnauld's second letter. Are you incredulous? inquire of M. le Moine, the most zealous of the examiners, who, in speaking this very morning to a doctor, one of my friends, who happened to question him respecting the nature of this difference, and whether he might be allowed any longer to adopt the language of the Fathers, made this charming reply: "This proposition would be orthodox in any other mouth; it is only in Mr. Arnauld that the Sorbonne has condemned it." And now, do you not admire this Molinistical machinery, which produces such wonderful effects in the church, that what is orthodox in the Fathers, is heretical in Mr. Arnauld; that what is heretical in the semi-Pelagians, is orthodox in the writings of the Jesuits; that the ancient doctrine of St. Augustin is an untenable novelty, and that the novel inventions, which spring up every day, must pass for the ancient faith of the church?"

Here we parted; but to me the meeting was instructive, for I discovered a new species of heresy. The *sentiments of Mr. Arnauld are not heretical, but his person*. He is a heretic, not for any thing he has written or said, but solely because he is Mr. Arnauld. This is all that can be alleged against him. It is a *personal heresy*. Whatever he may do, never, never will he be a good Catholic till he ceases *to be*. The *grace* of St. Augustin will never be true, so long as *he* defends the doctrine. It will come to nothing, unless *he* oppose it: this would be the certain and almost the only method of establishing it, and of exterminating Molinism: such is his destructive influence upon the opinions he ventures to adopt!

Here then let us leave these differences: they belong to *divines, not to divinity*. We are no doctors, and have no right to intermeddle with their disputations. Let all our friends be informed of my account of the censure, and continue your affectionate confidence so long as

I remain, &c.

LETTER IV.

Of actual Grace, and of Sins of Ignorance.

Sir,   Paris, Feb. 25, 1656.

The Jesuits are an incomparable set of men. I have seen Jacobins, doctors, and all descriptions, but my knowledge was still incomplete. Others are mere copyists of them. The stream is purest at the spring-head; I therefore went to one of their most intelligent partizans, accompanied by my faithful Jansenist, who had been with me in my former visits.

Anxious to obtain full information respecting the dispute between them and the Jansenists, on the subject of what they call *actual grace*, I intimated to the good Father, the obligation he would confer in condescending to instruct me; and, as I did not even know the signification of the term, I entreated him to explain it. "Most readily," said he; "for I am pleased with people that are inquisitive. Our definition is as follows: <u>*actual grace* is an inspiration of God, by which he teaches us his will, and by which he excites within us a desire to fulfil it.</u>" "What then is the precise point of dispute," said I, "between you and the Jansenists?" "It is this," answered he; "<u>we maintain that God bestows actual grace upon all men in every temptation. Otherwise, if they did not possess actual grace to prevent the commission of sin, guilt could never be imputed to them; but the Jansenists affirm that sins committed without actual grace must be imputed</u>: but they are surely dreaming."

I perceived his drift; but, for the purpose of obtaining

clearer information, I said, "My good Father, this phrase, *actual grace*, perplexes me: I am really unaccustomed to it, and if you will have the goodness to state the meaning, without using the term, you will confer a great obligation." "Oh, that is to say, you wish me to substitute the definition for the thing defined. Very well, the sense will remain unaltered. We maintain then, as an incontrovertible principle, that an action cannot be deemed sinful, if, previous to the commission of it, God does not communicate the knowledge of what evil there is in it, and an inspiration which excites us to avoid it. Do you understand me now?"

Astonished at this doctrine, according to which all unpremeditated sins and those committed from forgetfulness of God, are not chargeable upon the criminal, I turned to my friend the Jansenist, and perceived from his manner, that he did not believe this statement; but, as he was silent, I remarked to the Father, that I should wish for some substantial proofs of the truth of his representations. "Do you require proofs?" said he. "I will furnish them, proofs the most irrefragable: trust me." Upon this, he withdrew to search after some books, and I in the meantime inquired of my friend if he thought any other being was of his opinion. "Is this, then," he replied, "such a novelty to you? Assuredly, neither the Fathers, the Popes, the Councils, the Scriptures, nor any book of devotion, ancient or modern, have delivered such sentiments; but as for Casuists and new Scholastics, he will produce them in prodigious numbers." "Oh, but I despise such writers as these, if they contradict tradition." "You are right," said he; and at that moment the good Father returned laden with volumes. "There, read that"—offering me the first of the load—"it is a summary of sins by Father Bauny, and as a proof of its excellence, this is the fifth edition." "This book," observed my Jansenist, in a whisper, "has been condemned at Rome, and by the bishops of France." "Turn to page 906," said the Father. I did so, and found these words —"To sin so as to be accounted guilty before God, it is necessary to know that what is going to be perpetrated is not good, or at least to be doubtful of it, to entertain apprehensions, or to suppose that God will be displeased with the premeditated action, and forbids it; notwithstanding which, it is done in defiance of every obstacle."

"This," I remarked, "is a fine beginning!" "And yet," said he, "mark the power of envy. Upon this very point, M. Hallier, previous to his uniting with us, ridiculed Father Bauny, by applying these words to him, *Ecce qui tollit peccata mundi,* 'See the man who takes away the sins of the world!'" "True," replied I, "this redemption of M. Bauny is rather of a novel description." He asked if I wished for a still higher authority? "Then read this performance by Father Annat, the last which he produced against Mr. Arnauld. Look at the thirty-fourth page which I have turned down and marked with a pencil: every syllable is gold." The words were as follow: "He who has no thought of God, or of his sins, nor any apprehension, that is, (as he explained it) any knowledge of his obligation to exercise acts of contrition or love to God, possesses no actual grace to exercise such acts; but it is true also that he does not sin in omitting them, and if he be finally condemned, it will not be as a punishment for this omission." A few lines lower it is added, "The same may be affirmed of committing sin."

"Do you observe," said the Father, "in what manner the author speaks respecting sins of omission and of commission? He forgets nothing. What say you?" "Oh, it is charming—the consequences deducible, how fine! I can already discern surprising mysteries! An incomparably greater number, I see, are justified by their ignorance and forgetfulness of God, than by grace and the sacraments of religion! But pray, Father, is this a well founded transport? Is there not some resemblance here to that *sufficiency* which does not *suffice?* I am tremendously apprehensive of the *distinguo*, having been already entrapped by it. Are you really in good earnest?" "How!" said the Father, with some warmth—"this is no jest: raillery, Sir, is inadmissible upon this subject." "Indeed

I am not in sport, but fear that what seems desirable may not prove to be true."

"For the purpose then," said he, "of further confirmation, study the writings of M le Moine, who has taught the same in full council. In fact, he learned it of us, but has had the merit to disentangle its intricacies: and how incontestable the evidence he has adduced! His doctrine is, that for an action to be sinful, all the following thoughts must pass in the mind—but read it yourself, and weigh every word." I then read the Latin original, of which I give you a translation. "1. On the one side God diffuses over the soul a certain love which disposes it to the thing commanded; and, on the other, a rebellious concupiscence allures it to disobedience. 2. God inspires it with the knowledge of its own infirmities. 3. God inspires it with the knowledge of the physician who must cure it. 4. God inspires it with the desire of being healed 5. God inspires it with the desire to pray and implore his aid."
"And," said the Jesuit, "if all these do not concur, the action is not properly sinful, and cannot be imputed, as M. le Moine states in this and the succeeding passage. Are you desirous of other authorities? Behold they are here" "Yes, yes," said my Jansenist, whispering; "but all *modern* authorities."—"I see them," replied I.—"But, my good Father, this would be a delightful thing for some of my acquaintance; really I must introduce them! Perhaps you scarcely ever saw such innocent people: they never think of God; vice has blinded their reason: they have never known any thing of their infirmities, or of the physician who can cure them: they have never cherished a wish for the health of their souls, much less have they besought God to bestow it; so that, to adopt M. le Moine's language, they are now as innocent as at their baptism: they have never entertained a thought of loving God, or of contrition for sin"—according to Father Annat, they never committed any sin through defect of charity or penitence: their life is one continual search after diversified pleasure, unattended with the least interruption from remorse. These excesses induced me to believe their

destruction inevitable ; but, my good Father, you have taught me, that these very excesses render their salvation the more infallible. O what a blessedness is yours to justify mankind in this manner! Others prescribe painful austerities to save the soul; but you demonstrate that such as were considered in the most desperate state, are perfectly well! O, what a glorious method to procure happiness both in this world and in another! I have always supposed that our criminality was enhanced in proportion to our forgetfulness of God ; but now I see, whenever one is able to arrive at this point, to be totally thoughtless, every thing henceforth becomes allowable and innocent. Away then with those who sin by halves, still retaining some attachment to virtue! These demi-transgressors will be all lost; but, as to open sinners, hardened offenders, sinners without restraint, whose iniquity is full and overflowing, there is no hell for *them;* they have cheated the devil by abandoning themselves entirely to his influence!"—

The good Father, who clearly perceived the connexion between his principles and my consequences, dexterously made his escape, and without exhibiting any symptoms of passion, either from a natural mildness of temper, or from motives of policy, merely said, "To explain our mode of avoiding these incongruities, you must understand that our statement respecting the transgressors of whom you speak is, that they would not incur guilt, if they had never thought of repentance or the dedication of themselves to God; but we maintain they have all cherished such thoughts, and that God never permits any man to commit sin without previously giving him a view of the evil he is about to perpetrate, and a desire to avoid it, or at least to implore his aid to enable him to shun it; none but Jansenists will contradict this statement."

"And," replied I, "does the heresy of the Jansenists consist in denying that every time sin is committed, the offender feels remorse of conscience, and that in defiance of it he overleaps every barrier, as Father Bauny observes? Really this is a curious kind of heresy enough! I have been accustomed to suppose that a man was condemned for being devoid of all good thoughts, but to be so for not believing that every one else possesses them—positively, I never imagined such a thing before! But Father, I feel myself bound in conscience to undeceive you, and to say, that there are thousands who cherish no such desires, who sin without any remorse, nay, who absolutely make a boast of their iniquities. Can any persons be better aware of this than yourselves? It is no surely that you do not *confess* any one of this description for they are usually found amongst people of the greates distinction: but beware, good Father, of the dangerou consequences of your doctrine. Are you unaware of the ef fect it may produce on libertines, who eagerly avail them selves of every means of discrediting religion? And witl what a pretext do you furnish them, by affirming as al indubitable article of faith, that they feel, on every fresl commission of sin, a secret restraint and a wish to abstain Is it not obvious that, being conscious from personal ex perience of the falsehood of your statement, they will ex tend the consequences beyond this single point? They wil maintain that your incorrectness on this subject, render you suspicious on others, and thus you will compel then to infer, either that religion is untrue or that you are to tally ignorant of it."

Here my friend interposed to second my remarks, b saying, "Father, you would promote your opinions bette by avoiding so lucid a statement as you have now give of the signification of the term *actual grace:* for how ca you expect persons to believe in so undisguised a senti ment as this, 'that no one can commit sin without bein previously acquainted with his infirmity, and his physician and cherishing a desire to be healed and to solicit a cur from God?' Is your mere affirmation sufficient to convinc the world that the avaricious, the impure, and those wh commit blasphemy, or indulge in murderous revenge, rob bery, and sacrilege, really wish to possess chastity, humi lity, and the other Christian virtues? Is it credible tha those philosophers who so highly celebrated the power c nature, knew its weakness and its remedy? Would you assert that such as confidently maintained this maxim—'that God does not bestow virtue, nor did any one ever solicit it of him'—really thought of asking it themselves? Who can imagine that the Epicureans, who denied the existence of a Divine Providence, felt any disposition to pray to God? They aver, 'that it is an affront to implore his interference in our necessities, as if he could descend to concern himself about *our* affairs!' Who can suppose that idolaters and atheists, amidst the incalculable diversity of their temptations to sin, entertain a desire to seek the true God, with whom they are utterly unacquainted, for the bestowment of real virtues, of which they are as ignorant?"

"Yes," said the good Father, in a firm and resolute tone—"yes, we *do*, and *will* say so; and rather than admit that it is possible to commit sin without clearly perceiving its vileness and cherishing an opposing wish, we will maintain that the whole world, including even the most impious and infidel of the human race, have these inward suggestions and desires in every moment of temptation. You can produce no evidence to the contrary at least from Scripture."

Here I interposed, and said, "What, Father, is it necessary to recur to Scripture to prove what is so obvious? This is no point of faith, nor of argumentation; it is a matter of fact: we see it, know it, and feel it."

My Jansenist, strictly adhering to the prescribed rules, replied, "If you really determine to be guided solely by the Scriptures, I readily consent, but at least do not resist that; and since it is written 'that God has not revealed his judgments to the heathen, but has left them to wander in their own ways,' do not say that God has enlightened those whom the sacred writings affirm to be left in darkness and in the shadow of death? Is not the error of your sentiment sufficiently exposed by St. Paul representing himself as the *chief of sinners*, for a sin which he declares he committed *through ignorance* and *unbelief?* Is it not obvious from the Gospel, that they who crucified Jesus

Christ needed that forgiveness which he solicited for them, though they know not the wickedness of their conduct, and which, according to St. Paul, they never would have perpetrated, had they been aware of it? Does not Jesus Christ forewarn us that persecutors will arise, imagining they do God service by aiming to destroy his church, showing that the sin which the apostle represents as the greatest of all others, may be committed by those who, so far from being conscious of its criminality, would really suppose they sinned in *omitting* to do it? Lastly, has not Jesus Christ himself taught us that there are two descriptions of sinners; the one sins knowingly, the other ignorantly; and both will suffer punishment, though in different proportions?"

Urged by so much Scriptural evidence, to which the good Father had appealed, he began to give way; and, allowing that the wicked were not under an immediate inspiration to sin, he claimed at least the admission that the righteous never sin, unless God gives them——"Oho," interrupting him, "you are for retracting your statement —you are abandoning your general principle; and, aware that it is unavailing with respect to sinners, you are desirous of a compromise, at least in behalf of the righteous. But even in this case it would be so circumscribed in its application, as scarcely to be of any service, and is not therefore worth an argument."

My friend, who seemed as profound in the subject as if he had been studying it that very morning, replied, "O Father, this is the last refuge to which your party repairs; but it is of little avail: the example of the righteous is by no means more advantageous to your cause. Who doubts that they are frequently surprised into sin? Do they not assure us that concupiscence often spreads its secret snares in their path, and that it is common for sober-minded persons to concede to pleasure what they only intended to yield to necessity? as St. Augustin admits with respect to himself in his confessions. How frequently do we see zealous people become exasperated in a discussion in defending their *own interests*, when at the moment they conscientiously believe themselves contending only for the *interests of truth*, and long retain the same conviction!

"But what shall we say of those who zealously do evil, imagining it to be really good, of which the history of the church furnishes many instances, and all of them admitted by the Fathers to be sinful? If not, how could any secret iniquities be imputed to the righteous? How would it be true that God only knows their extent and number? That no one knows whether he is deserving of love or hatred, and that the most holy persons ought to live in perpetual fear and trembling, although, in the language of St. Paul, 'they know nothing (criminal) by themselves?'

"These examples, then, of the righteous and the wicked, equally controvert the necessity which you imagine, of knowing the evil of an action and loving the opposite virtue, in order to constitute it sinful; since the passionate eagerness for their vices which the wicked manifest, is sufficiently demonstrative of their being destitute of all desire after virtue; and the attachment which the righteous have to virtue, strikingly evinces that they do not always know, as the Scriptures state, the sins which they are daily committing.

"It is thus evident that the righteous transgress through ignorance, and that the most eminent saints seldom sin otherwise; for how is it conceivable that such holy persons, who avoid, with so much care and diligence, the minutest thing which they believe to be displeasing to God, but who nevertheless commit many sins every day—how is it possible, that on every occasion, immediately previous to their fall, they should have a knowledge of their weakness, and of the physician, and possess a desire to be healed, and to solicit divine assistance; yet, in defiance of all these pious inspirations, these zealous souls should be left to overleap every opposing barrier, and rush into sin?"

"The inference, then, Father, is this, that neither the sinners, nor saints, are always in possession of this knowledge, these desires, and these inspirations; that is, to adopt your own phraseology, they have not always *actual grace* upon every such occasion. No longer, therefore, believe your new authors, who assert it is impossible to sin while in ignorance of what is right, but rather say, in concurrence with St. Augustin and the ancient Fathers, that it is impossible not to sin while continuing ignorant of what is right—*Necesse est ut peccet, à quo ignoratur justitia.*"

Though the good Father found that his sentiments, both with regard to the righteous and the wicked, were equally untenable, he was not totally discouraged; but, after a little pause—"I will now convince you," said he; and, again taking up Father Bauny, at the very page before cited, "Look, look at the reason on which his opinion is founded. I assure you he is not deficient in demonstration. Read his quotation from Aristotle, and after such express authority, you must either coincide with our opinion, or burn the writings of this prince of philosophers. Hearken to Father Bauny's principles. He first states 'that an action cannot be deemed criminal when it is involuntary.'" "True," said my friend. I remarked, "This is the first time I have ever seen you agree: this, then, is the very point at which you should stop: take my advice." "That would be doing nothing," returned he; "for you must be informed of the circumstances which are essential to a voluntary action." "I am very much afraid," said I, "you will disagree again." "O don't be alarmed, it is all right—Aristotle is on my side. Pray attend to Father Bauny; in order that an action be voluntary, it must be the action of a man who sees, knows, and well understands what degree of good and evil attaches to it—*Voluntarium est,* as we commonly say with the philosopher—(*Aristotle,* you know," said he, with great self-complacency, squeezing my hand) "*quod fit à principio cognoscente singula in quibus est actio;* so that when the will chooses or rejects inconsiderately and without investigation, before the understanding has been able to discover the evil of complying or refusing, doing or neglecting an action, it is neither good nor bad, inasmuch as, previous to this examination, this observance and reflection of the mind on the good or bad qualities of the object in view, the action is not voluntary.—Are you satisfied now?"

"Why, really," replied I, "Aristotle is of the same opinion with Father Bauny, but this does not lessen my surprise. What! <u>is it not acting voluntarily when one knows what he does, and does it with a fixed determination of mind? Is it requisite further, that he should 'see, understand, and fully investigate the degree of evil in that action?'</u> If this be the case, it is scarcely possible that *any* conduct should be strictly voluntary, for few persons have all these considerations in view. How many oaths in gaming, how many excesses in debauchery, how many irregularities in the Carnival must be involuntary, and by consequence neither good nor bad, because unaccompanied with these reflections on the good or evil qualities of the deed! But can Aristotle be really chargeable with such a sentiment? for I have understood he was a man of sense."

"I will soon explain this," said my Jansenist; and requesting to look into Aristotle's Ethics, he opened the volume at the commencement of the third book, whence Father Bauny had taken the very words already cited, saying, "I can forgive you, my good Father, for believing upon the testimony of Father Bauny, that this was the sentiment of Aristotle; but you would have thought otherwise, had you read him yourself. He states, indeed, that 'for an action to be voluntary, it is necessary to know its peculiarities: SINGULA *in quibus est actio:* but nothing else is meant by this than the particular circumstances of the action, as appears most obviously from the examples he adduces in justification of his position, such as those which refer to an ignorance of the circumstances, as, 'if a person, when exhibiting a machine, inadvertently shoots a dart at another,' and the instance of Merope slaying her son when intending to kill her enemy, with others of a similar nature.

"Hence it is apparent what description of ignorance that is which renders actions involuntary,—an ignorance of the particular circumstances, called, as you know, by the divines, *the ignorance of fact:* but, in the regard to the *ignorance of right*, that is, of the good and evil in an action, which is the present subject of our consideration, let us inquire whether Aristotle and Father Bauny agree. 'All the wicked,' says the philosopher, are ignorant of what they ought to do, and what they ought to avoid; and it is this which renders them wicked and vicious. On this account, it cannot be said, that because a man is ignorant of what is proper to be done to discharge his duty, his conduct is therefore involuntary. for this ignorance in the choice of good and evil does not constitute an action involuntary, but vicious. The same may be said of him who is unacquainted with the rules of duty, as this ignorance is blameworthy and not excusable: so that the ignorance which constitutes actions involuntary and pardonable, is that only which regards the fact in particular, with all its individual circumstances; we excuse and forgive the person whom we consider as having acted contrary to his will.'

"Will you now say, Father, that Aristotle is of your opinion? What must be the universal astonishment to perceive that a pagan philosopher was more enlightened than your doctors upon a point so important to morality and the conduct of souls, or the knowledge of those conditions which render actions voluntary or involuntary, and consequently which excuse or condemn them? Do not expect any support, then, from this prince of philosophers, and no longer oppose the prince of divines who decides the point in the following words (B. I. of his Retr. ch. 15:) 'They who sin through ignorance commit the action with the consent of the will, though they have not the intention of committing sin; so that a sin of this description cannot be perpetrated without the will, but the will induces the action only, not the sin, which, however, does not prevent the action being sinful, its contrariety to the interdicting precepts being a sufficient crimination.'"

The Jesuit seemed surprised still more at the quotation from Aristotle than that from St. Augustin: but, as he was revolving in his mind what reply to offer, a servant

came in to say, that Madam the Marechale of ———,
and Madam the Marquise of ———, requested an interview : and thus leaving us abruptly, " I will speak," said
he, " to some of our Fathers upon this subject : they will
be able to suggest a reply. We have some very subtle
divines amongst us, who are profoundly acquainted with
the controversy."

We understood him; and being alone with my friend,
I expressed my astonishment at the total subversion of
morals which this doctrine tended to produce. " How !"
said he, " I am absolutely astonished at *your* astonishment ! And do you not know, then, that they are much
greater delinquents in morality than even in other subjects ?"

He instantly furnished me with some monstrous examples, deferring more ample illustrations to another opportunity. The first time I enjoy the pleasure of an interview, these will supply matter for conversation.

I am, &c.

LETTER V.

The Design of the Jesuits in establishing a new Morality. Two kinds of Casuists amongst them: the great Remissness of the one, and the equal Rigidity of the other. Reason of this Difference Explanation of the Doctrine of Probability. A Crowd of Modern and obscure Authors substituted for the Holy Fathers.

Sir,   Paris, Mar. 20, 1656.

In fulfilment of my promise, I here transmit you the first outlines of Jesuitical morality, the views of those men who are so " eminent in learning and wisdom, who are all under the guidance of a divine wisdom, which is so much more certain than all the light of philosophy!"

You imagine, perhaps, I am jesting; indeed I am serious, this is their own language in their publication, entitled, *Imago primi seculi.* I have copied their words, which I shall continue to do in the following eulogium: " It is a society of men, or rather of angels, of whom Isaiah prophesied, 'Go, ye angels, prompt and swift.' Is not this prediction obvious? 'They have the spirit of eagles: it is a troop of phœnixes, so numerous are they. as a late author has shown: they have changed the face of Christianity." Their *ipse dixit* is doubtless sufficient, as you will see by their maxims which I am going to introduce to your notice.

Anxious to be fully informed, I was unwilling to confide implicitly in my friend's representations, but felt determined to converse with them personally. I found every syllable he had said correct: he had indeed never deceived me: you shall have an account of these conferences.

My friend had given such extravagant statements that I could scarcely credit them; but he pointed out his authority in their own publications, and no defence could be made, but that the opinions of individuals ought not to be imputed to the whole body, and I assured him that I knew some who were as rigid as those whom he quoted were lax. This gave him occasion to exhibit the true spirit of the society, which is by no means generally known, and which perhaps to you may be a desirable piece of information. He thus began:

"You suppose that it tells considerably in their favour to show that some of their fathers coincide as much with the maxims of the Gospel, as others oppose them; and hence you infer, that these lax opinions are not attributable to the whole society. I am well aware of this, for if it were the case, they would not tolerate such contradictions: but since they have those who maintain so libertine a sentiment, you must conclude that the spirit of the society is not that of pure Christianity: if it were, they would not endure those who so diametrically opposed it."
"What then," said I "what can be the design of the whole body? Doubtless they have no fixed principles, and every one is at liberty to say what he pleases." "No, this cannot be: so large a society could not subsist, were it so rash as to leave itself without a soul to govern and regulate its concerns. There is, besides, an express order that nothing shall be printed without the approbation of their superiors." "But how can the superiors themselves permit such opposing sentiments?" "I will explain it," said he.

"Their object is not to *corrupt* morals: this certainly is not their *design*: but neither is it their sole purpose to *reform* them: this would be bad policy. Their intention is this—Having the best opinion of themselves, they think it both beneficial and necessary to the interests of religion, that their reputation should be extended through the world, and that they should obtain the direction of every one's conscience; and as the strict maxims of the Gospel are adapted to govern some people, they make use of them whenever the occasion favours it: but inasmuch as these maxims do not accord with the views of the generality of mankind, they dispense with them in regard to such predilections, for the sake of affording universal satisfaction. On this account, as they are connected with persons of every condition in life, and of every country and clime, it becomes necessary to employ casuists whose varieties of sentiment should suit every existing diversity of circumstance. Hence you will easily perceive, that if they had none but casuists of lax notions, they would defeat their principal purpose, which is to please every body, because the truly religious are solicitous of a more rigorous leader. But as there are not many of this description they do not require many guides of the stricter class to direct them: a few of the one will suffice for a few of the other; while the multitude of lax casuists offer their services to the numerous classes that wish to be allowed an undisciplined remissness.

"It is by this *obliging* and *accommodating* conduct, as Father Petau calls it, that they open their arms to all the world. For, if a person should apply to them who was resolved upon the restoration of any thing he had obtained by fraudulent means, do not imagine they would attempt to dissuade him from his purpose; on the contrary they would applaud and confirm his determination. But if another should present himself soliciting absolution without restitution, it would be strange indeed if they did not furnish him with expedients, and guarantee his success.

"By this means they preserve all their friends, and defend themselves against all their enemies. If they should be reproached for their extreme laxity, they instantly exhibit to the public their austere directors with some volumes which they have composed on the strictness of the Christian law; and with these proofs they satisfy the superficial, who cannot fathom their depths.

"Thus they accomodate all descriptions of people, and are so well prepared with an answer to every question, that in countries where a crucified Jesus passes for foolishness, they suppress the scandel of the cross and preach only Jesus Christ in his glory, and not in a state of suffering; as in India and China, where they allow their Christians to practise idolatry itself, by the ingenious devise of making them conceal an image of Christ under their cloaks, to which they are instructed to address *mentally*, the adorations rendered publicly to the idols Cachin-choam and Keum-fucum. This is charged upon them by Gravina, a Dominican, and the same policy is described in a Spanish memorial presented to Philip IV., king of Spain, by the friars of the Philippine islands, as reported by Thomas Hurtado, in his book of Martyrology, p. 427. The cardinals of the society *de propaganda fide*, were obliged expressly to forbid the Jesuits, upon pain of excommunication, to allow the worship of idols under any pretext whatever, and to conceal the mystery of the cross from those whom they instructed in the faith, positively commanding them to admit no one to baptism till after such instruction, and enjoining them to exhibit a crucifix in their churches; as is amply detailed in a decree of the congregation on the ninth of July, 1646, signed by Cardinal Capponi.

"In this manner they have spread over the whole world by their doctrine of *propable opinions*, which is the spring and foundation of all this disorder. You must learn what it is from their own testimony,—for they take no more pains to conceal it than they do the facts I am stating, with this difference only, that they veil their *human and political* prudence under the pretext of *divine* and *christian* prudence, as if faith, supported by tradition, were not invariable in all times and places, as if the rule were to bend to the accommodation of the person who was to submit to it, and as if there were no other means for sinners to purify their stains of guilt, than corrupting the law of God; whereas 'the law of the Lord is perfect, *converting* the soul,' to conform to its salutary directions!

"Let me beg you to go and visit these worthy Fathers, and I assure you that you will at once perceive the reason of their doctrine respecting grace, in the laxity of their morals: you will see the Christian virtues so disguised and so completely divested of that charity which is their life and soul, you will witness so many crimes palliated, and so many disorders permitted, that it will no longer appear strange that they should maintain, 'that all men have at all times sufficient grace to lead, in their sense of the phrase, a religious life.' As their morality is entirely pagan, nature is sufficient to guide them. When we affirm the necessity of efficacious grace, the object presented to view embraces other virtues. It is not simply to cure vices by other vices, it is not to induce men to conform to the external duties of religion, but to practise a nobler virtue than that of the Pharisees or the sages of the pagan world. Law and reason are sufficient for these effects. But to detach the soul from the love of the world, to withdraw it from what is an object of the fondest affection, to make a man die to himself, and to love God with supreme and unalterable attachment, can be accomplished only by an omnipotent power. It is as irrational to pretend that we possess a perfect command over these graces, as it is to deny that those virtues which do not include the love of God, and which the Jesuits confound with Christian virtues, are not practicable by our own power."

Hitherto my friend spoke with much concern, for he is seriously afflicted at these disorders. For my own part I applauded the excellence of Jesuitical policy, and went immediately to one of their best casuists, with whom I wished, at this moment, to renew a former acquaintance. Knowing how to proceed, I had no difficulty in introducing and conducting the subject. Retaining his attachment to me, I was welcomed by a thousand expressions of kindness, and after some desultory conversation, I took occasion from the season, to make an inquiry respecting fasting for the purpose of leading insensibly to the particular object of my solicitude. I stated how difficult I felt it. He exhorted me to resist my own disinclinations; but persisting in my complaints, he became compassionate, and began to frame some excuses for me. Many which he offered did not exactly accord with my taste, till at length he asked if I could not sleep without a supper? "No," said I, "in consequence of which I am obliged to breakfast at noon and to sup at night." "I am very happy," answered he, "that I have discovered an innocent method of relieving your anxiety; go, go, you are under no obligation to fast. However, do not depend on my word, come with me into the library."

I went—"Here, here," said he, taking up a book, "is your proof, and oh, what a noble one it is! furnished by Escobar." "Who is Escobar?" "What, are you ignorant of the name of Escobar, of our society, who has compiled this moral theology from twenty-four of our Fathers, who in his preface compares this book to 'that of the Revelation which was sealed with seven seals,' and says that Jesus delivered it thus sealed to the four living creatures, Suarez, Vasquez, Molina, and Valentia, in the presence of four-and-twenty Jesuits, who represent the four-and-twenty elders?" All this allegory he read, which of course he found to be very just, and by which he gave a vast idea of the excellence of this work! When he turned to the passage respecting fasting —"See, see," he exclaimed; "Tr. 1, Ex. 13, N. 67, Is he who cannot sleep without a supper obliged to fast? By no means." "Are you now satisfied?" "Not entirely so," replied I, "for I can fast pretty well by making a breakfast in the morning and a supper at night." "Oho, then, look at what follows; there is not a single consideration omitted. If a person can content himself with a breakfast in the morning and a supper at night," —"That is exactly my case"—"he is not obliged to fast; for no one is under any obligation to disarrange the order of his meals." "Noble reason!" "But," continued he, "do you accustom yourself to much wine?" "No, Father, I exceedingly dislike it." "I said this," added he, "simply to intimate that you might take it in the morning, or whenever you pleased without breaking your fast; and a glass of wine is always cheering. Pray observe N. 75." "May a person, without breaking his fast, drink wine at any hour he pleases, and in considerable quantities?" "He may, and a dram too. I did not recollect the dram," said he, "I must note it down in my memoranda." "Truly this Escobar," said I, "is a fine man." "O," rejoined he, "every body admires him: he puts such lovely questions. Look again, N. 38, If a man doubt whether he be of age, is he obliged to fast? No. But suppose I should come of age to-night, at an hour after midnight, and to-morrow is to be a fast, should I be obliged to fast to-morrow? No: for you may eat as much as you please from twelve to one, because you would not yet have completed twenty-one years; and so having a right to break your fast, you are not obliged to keep it.'" "O," said I, "what an agreeable publication!" "Indeed it is—one is never tired of it. I pass whole days and nights in reading it: absolutely I can do nothing else."

The good Father seeing my satisfaction, proceeded in a perfect ecstacy: "Look here, at a passage in Filiutius, one of the twenty-four Jesuits, vol. ii. tr. 27. p. 2. ch. 6. n. 143. 'Suppose a person is fatigued, *ad insequendam puellam*, is he obliged to fast? Certainly not. But suppose he has fatigued himself for the express purpose of being released from fasting, must he then observe it? No—though it should be his premeditated design, he is not obliged.' Would you ever have believed this?" appealing to me. "Why, really I cannot tell how to believe it yet. What, is it no sin to break a fast when I can keep it? And is it allowable to seek opportunities of sinning, or rather are we under no obligations to avoid them? This is accommodating indeed!" "Not always, that is according———" "According to what?" said I, "Oh," replied the Jesuit, "suppose one has sustained any inconvenience in avoiding such opportunities, do you think there is still an indispensable obligation? If so, it is more than Father Bauny concedes, p. 1084: 'We must not refuse absolution to those who live on the confines of sin, if they should be so situated that they cannot quit them without becoming the subjects of public observation, or without bringing themselves into difficulties.'" "I am rejoiced at this, Father, and since we are allowed not to avoid opportunities of sin, it only remains that we be permitted deliberately to seek them." "Sometimes," he remarked, "even this may be granted; so says the celebrated casuist Basil Pontius, whose opinion is quoted and approved by Father Bauny, in his Treatise on Penitence, q. 4. p. 94: 'A person may seek an occasion to sin directly and by itself, *primo et per se;* when either our own temporal or spiritual good, or that of our neighbour, demands it."

"Verily," said I, "this must be a dream! Do I really hear religious people talk in this manner? Tell me, Father, are you absolutely and conscientiously of this opinion?" "No, certainly." "Why, then, speak against your conscience?" "Not at all: I did not speak according to *my* conscience, but in conformity to Pontius and Father Bauny; and you may follow them with safety, for they are skilful polemics." "What! because they have inserted these three lines in their writings, am I allowed to search out occasions and pretences to commit sin? I imagined that the Scriptures and the tradition of the church constituted the only rule of conduct, not your casuists!" "Why," said he, all astonishment, "you absolutely remind me of the Jansenists! Is it not in the power of Father Bauny and Basil Pontius to make their opinions *probable?*" "But I am not satisfied with *probability,* I am anxious to obtain certainty." "Oh," said he, "you know nothing respecting the doctrine of *probable opinions:* if you did, you would speak in a very different manner: you must really come under my instructions: your time is by no means thrown away. by coming here to-day, I can assure you: for without being acquainted with this doctrine, you can know nothing; it is the very foundation, the *a b c* of all our morality."

I was enchanted to find him at the very point I wished, and entreated him to state what was meant by a *probable opinion.* 'Our author," said he, " will furnish you with the best explanation. All of them, including the twenty-four elders, agree in the following representation *in princ.* ex. 3. n 8. ' An opinion is called *probable* when it is founded upon reasons of some importance. Hence it sometimes happens that only one very grave doctor can render an opinion probable ;' and observe the reason ; ' for a man who is particularly devoted to study, would not adopt an opinion unless he were induced by a good and sufficient reason.' " " And thus," I remarked, " a single doctor may turn and overturn, settle and unsettle the consciences of men at his own pleasure, and be always safe." " Sir," said he, " you must not ridicule or think of opposing this doctrine. Whenever the Jansenists have attempted it they have completely failed. No, no, it is too firmly established. Attend to Sanchez one of our most celebrated casuists, *Som.* l. 1. c. 9. n. 7 : 'You may perhaps doubt whether the authority of a single good and learned doctor be sufficient to render an opinion probable. I answer, it is ; and Angelus, Sylvius, Navarre Emanuel Sa, &c. assert the same, furnishing this proof ;—a probable opinion is that which has a considerable foundation, but the authority of a wise and pious man is not of small but of great importance ;—for— and pray listen to this reason—if the testimony of such a man possess sufficient weight to convince us that any occurrence took place, for example, at Rome ; why should it not be equally satisfactory in deciding a doubtful point of morality ?"

"This is a curious comparison indeed," said I, " between the ordinary events of the world and the scruples of conscience !" " Have patience, and Sanchez suggests the answer in the next paragraph—'and I disapprove of the limitation prescribed by certain writers, that the authority of such a doctor is sufficient in questions relating to human affairs, but not in those which refer to religious concerns ; for it is of the greatest importance in both.' "

"Father," speaking frankly, " I can place no dependence

upon this rule. Who can assure me, while your doctors assume such a liberty of examining every thing by mere reason, that what appears certain to one shall appear the same to all? The diversity of opinions is so considerable———" "You do not understand," interrupting me, "their views are indeed frequently different, but this is nothing to the purpose; every one may render his own probable and certain. We are well aware their opinions are not all coincident: so much the better; in fact, they scarcely ever agree; for a very few questions can arise in which you will not find one say *yes* and another *no*; but each of these contrary opinions is *probable*, as Diana states on a certain subject, part 3. tom. 4. v. 244: 'Pontius and Sanchez are of an opposite opinion, but inasmuch as they are both learned men, each one makes his own sentiment probable."'

"But, Father, in such cases it must be very embarrassing to know which to prefer." "O no, not at all; it is only to follow the one which is most agreeable to yourself." "But what if the other opinion should be the most *probable?*" "It does not signify." "But what if it should be the most *sure?*" "Still it does not signify; only observe the explanation of Father Emanuel Sa, of our society, in his Aphorisms *de Dubio*, p. 183:—'A person may do what he conceives to be permitted by one probable opinion, although the contrary be more sure; but the opinion of one grave doctor is sufficient." "But suppose an opinion is both *less probable* and *less sure*, is it permissible to follow it, rejecting that which is believed to be *more probable* and *more sure?*" "Yes," once more: hear that great Jesuit Filiutius, *Mor. Quæst.* tr. 21. c. 4. n. 128. 'It is allowable to follow the opinion which is less probable, though it be also less sure. This is the concurrent sentiment of modern authors.' Is not this explicit?" "Most certainly," said I, "we are left at the most perfect liberty, reverend Father, thanks to your probable opinions! Our consciences are entirely free and unconstrained! Pray, as to your other casuists, do you enjoy the same license in your answers?" "O yes: we give what answers we please, or rather whatever they please who consult us. Our rules are deduced from our Fathers Laiman, *Theol. Mor.* l. 1. tr. 1. c. 2, § 2. n 7; Vasquez, *Disp.* 62. c. 9. n. 47; Sanchez, in *Sum.* l. 1. c. 9. n. 23; and from our twenty-four *in prin.* ex. 3. n 24 The words of Laiman, which the twenty-four elders have followed, are, ' When a doctor is consulted, he may give his advice not only as *probable*, according to his opinion, but contrary to his opinion, if it should be deemed *probable* by others when the advice which is opposed to our own is more favourable and agreeable to the person who consults him; *si forte et illi favorabilior seu exoptatior sit:* but I say farther, that he will not act without reason, if he should give those who consult him an opinion, held probable by some learned individual, though he felt confident at the same time it was absolutely false."

"Charming, charming my good Father; your doctrine is admirably accommodating indeed!" To have a reply always at hand, yes or no, just as you please—what an inestimable privilege, and how can it be sufficiently valued! Now I perceive the use which you doctors make of their contrary opinions on all subjects; one is always for you, and the other is never against you; if you do not find your account in one way, you are sure to do so in another; and thus you are always safe." "True, true; and we can say with Diana, who found Father Bauny on his side when Father Lugo was in direct opposition,— *Sape premente Deo fert Deus alter opum,* i. e. ' if one God distress us, another will defend us.' " "I understand this very well: but another difficulty strikes me. After having consulted one of your doctors, and taking his opinion, which left me at entire liberty, suppose one should be entrapped by a confessor who refuses absolution without a total change of sentiment: have you provided for such a case, Father?" "To be sure; they are obliged to absolve their penitents who hold some *probable opinions,* upon pain of committing a mortal offence; so that they can never be at a loss. This is luminously stated by our Fathers: amongst others, by Father Bauny, tr. 4. *De Pœnit.* q. 13. p. 93. ' When the penitent,' says he, ' follows a probable opinion, the confessor must *absolve* him, although his opinion be contrary to that of the penitent." "But, Father, he does not affirm that it would be a mortal sin not to absolve him." "How hasty you are! Hear, hear! he proceeds with this express conclusion: 'To refuse to absolve a penitent who acts conformably to a *probable* opinion, is a sin in its own nature mortal;' and he quotes, in confirmation of this sentiment, three of our most distinguished divines, Suarez, tom. 4. dist. 32. sect. 5; Vasquez, *Disp.* 62. c 7; and Sanchez, n. 29."

"O my good Father," said I, "how admirable are the regulations you have adopted! No reason remains for future apprehension, no confessor will ever dare to disobey. But I had no idea before of your power to enjoin upon pain of damnation; but imagined you were only capable of taking away sins, not thinking that you could *introduce* them. Now, I perceive you can accomplish every thing." "You are not correct," said he; "we cannot introduce sins, we can only point them out: I have more than once observed that you are not well versed in scholastic theology." "Be that as it will, Father," returned I, "my doubts are thus far removed; but I have another perplexity; what do you do when the Fathers of the church are in direct opposition to any one of your casuists?" "Surprising ignorance! The Fathers were good authority for the morals of their age, but they lived at too remote a period for us. They can no longer regulate our principles; it now belongs to the new casuists. Attend to Father Cellot, *de Hier*. l. 8. cap. 16. p. 714, who follows our celebrated Father Reginaldus: 'In questions of morality, the new casuists are preferable to the ancient Fathers, although they lived nearer the apostolic times:' and in conformity with the same sentiments, Diana inquires, p. 5. tr. 8. reg. 31. 'Are the clergy obliged to make restitution for revenue which has been improperly applied? The ancient Fathers reply in the affirmative, but the modern ones in the negative; let us then adhere to that opinion which dispenses us from the obligation of making restitution.'"

"Oh," said I, "what charming maxims, and how replete with comfort!" "We leave the Fathers," returned he, "to those who treat of *positive* divinity; but we who guide the consciences of men, read them but little, and quote no writings but those of the new casuists. Consult Diana, in the beginning of whose numerous works is inserted a list of two hundred and ninety-six authors, the most ancient of whom is about eighty years old." "Is not this the period of the foundation of your society?" "Thereabouts, that is to say, as soon as you made your appearance in the world. St. Augustin, St. Chrysostom, St. Ambrose St. Jerom, and others were obliged to withdraw. But may I at least be informed of the names of their successors? Who are these new authors?" "Who? —able and celebrated men; such as Villalobos, Conink, Llamas, Achokier, Dealkozer, Dellacrux, Venacruz, Ugolin, Tambourin, Fernandez, Martinez, Suarez, Henriquez, Vasquez, Lopez, Gomez, Sanchez, de Vechis, de Grasses, de Grassalis, de Pitigianis, de Graphæis, Squilanti, Bizozeri, Barcola, de Bobadilla, Bisbe, Simancha, Perez de Lara, Aldretta, Lorca, de Scarcia, Quaranta, Scophra, Pedrezza, Cabrezza, Dias, de Clavasis, Villagut, Adam à Manden, Tribarus, Binsfeld, Volfangi à Vorberg, Vostheri, Strevesdorff—" "O my Father," exclaimed I, in great alarm, "were all these people Christians?" "How do you mean, Christians? Did I not state that by these men alone we at this moment govern all Christendom?" —I really felt extreme pity, but did not express it, contenting myself with asking if all these authors were Jesuits. "No," was his reply, "but that is of no consequence; they have, notwithstanding, written many excellent things. Most of them, indeed, have borrowed from our authors, or have been copied from ours, but we are not punctilious: besides, they constantly quote and eulogize our authors. Thus Diana, who is not of our fraternity, in speaking of Vasquez, calls him *the phœnix of wit*, and elsewhere says, ' that Vasquez alone is as good authority as all the world besides—*instar omnium*: on which account our Fathers frequently make use of this good

Diana: for if you understand our doctrine of probability, you will see that their belonging to another society is of no consequence; we are, on the contrary, gratified with others besides Jesuits, being able to render their opinions probable, so that all is not imputed to us. On this principle, whenever any author advances a probability, we have a right to avail ourselves of it, if we think proper, by the doctrine of *probable opinions*, or we may reject it if the author be not attached to our society." "Oh, I understand it all," said I: "all are welcome but the ancient Fathers, and you remain in full possession of the field; you may take any direction, and ramble wherever you please. But I foresee three or four prodigious inconveniences, barriers of the most formidable description, to obstruct your progress." "And pray," said the Father, all astonishment, "what are they?" "The Holy Scripture, the Popes, and Councils,—whom you cannot contradict, and who all agree with the Gospel." "Oho! is that all? You really terrified me. Do you imagine that so obvious a case as this has not been foreseen and provided for? I am really astonished that you should think we are opposed to Scripture, to Popes, and to Councils. You shall have perfect demonstration to the contrary. I should be excessively chagrined that you should suppose we are deficient in our duty; but you have doubtless adopted this idea from certain opinions of our Fathers, which *seem* to controvert their own decisions, though it is not so in reality. But to explain this agreement, requires more leisure than I can at present command. I trust you will not be unedified by what has passed; if you will return to-morrow, I will undertake to furnish you with complete information on the subject."

Thus ended the conference, and here I close my letter. I flatter myself you will find enough to afford you amusement till my next communication.

I am, &c.

LETTER VI.

The different Artifices of the Jesuits to evade the Authority of the Gospel, the Councils, and the Popes. Consequences which follow from their Doctrine of Probability. Their Abatements in favour of the Clergy, Monks, and Servants. History of John d'Alba.

Sir,   *Paris, April* 10, 1656.

At the close of my last letter, I informed you that the good Father Jesuit promised to show me the manner in which the casuists reconciled the contradictory aspect of their opinions, and the decisions of Popes, Councils, and Scripture. The following is a recital of his statements. He began thus :

" One method of reconciling these apparent contradictions is, by the interpretation given to a term. For example ; Pope Gregory XIV. declares, that assassins are unworthy of enjoying the protection of a church, and that they ought to be dragged out by force : our twenty-four elders say, tr. 6 ex. 4. n. 27 : ' Whoever kills another in a treacherous manner, does not incur the penalty of this bull.' This, you perceive is contradictory, but by interpreting the word *assassin*, the passages are made to agree : thus, 'Are not assassins unworthy of enjoying the privilege of church protection ?' Yes, by the bull of Gregory XIV But, by the term *assassins*, we understand those who have received money to kill another in a treacherous manner. Hence those who have not committed murder for hire or reward, but only to oblige their friends, are not called *assassins*." Thus we are exhorted in the Gospel, "to give alms out of our abundance;" but many casuists have discovered a mode of exonerating even the most opulent persons from the obligation of alms-giving. This will, perhaps, appear to you a contradiction; but it is easy to reconcile it, by an interpretation of the term *abundance* or *superfluity*, so that it can scarcely ever be shown that a person possesses it. The learned Vasquez has done this in his treatise on alms-giving, c. 4 " That which is accumulated for the purpose of aggrandizing our own condition, or that of relatives, is not called *superfluity*; for which reason people can seldom be said to possess superfluity, not even kings themselves.' Diana, in quoting these words, (for he usually builds upon the foundation of our Fathers,) deduces this strong conclusion: 'that as to the question whether the rich are obliged to give alms out of their superfluity, although the affirmation be theoretically true, it will scarcely, if ever happen to be necessary in practice.'"

"This," I observed, "is certainly a fair inference from the doctrine of Vasquez; but if it be objected that, according to Vasquez, salvation would be as sure in refusing to give alms and retaining a moderate degree of ambition, as, according to the Gospel, it is in renouncing ambition in order to be capacitated to dispense alms, what reply is to be given?" "That both these ways are equally sure according to the same Gospel; the one, in the most literal and the most obvious sense, the other, according to the same Gospel, as interpreted by Vasquez. Hence you perceive the utility of the interpretative system. But when the terms are so plain as to admit of no such explanation, we make use of the consideration of *favourable circumstances*; as, for example, the Popes have excommunicated all monks who leave off their habit, but our twenty-four elders speak in this manner, tr. 6. ex. 7. n 103 : ' Upon what occasions may a monk quit his habit without incurring excommunication ?' Many are stated amongst others, this one : ' if he quit it for any disgraceful reason, as to turn pick-pocket, to go *incog.* to places of ill fame, intending speedily to resume it.' It is obvious that the papal bulls do not refer to cases of this description."

I was scarcely able to give credit to this representation, and requested to have it pointed out in the original title, where I noticed "The Practice according to the School of the Society of Jesus—*Praxis in Societatis Jesu Scholâ*"—where it was written, *Si habitum dimittat ut furetur occultè vel fornicetur.* He showed me the same thing in Diana, *Ut eat incognitus ad lupanar.* "And how is it, Father," proceeding with my inquiries, "how is it that they are released from excommunication in this particular instance?" "And do you not really comprehend this?" replied he. "Do you not see how scandalous it would be to surprise a monk in such a situation in the habit of religion? Have you never heard of the answer to the first bull, *contra sollicitantes?* And in what manner the twenty-four elders in a chapter of the school praxis of our society explain the bull of Pius V. *contra clericos,*" &c. ? "No—really I know nothing of it." "Then you have not read Escobar?" "I never could meet with him, Father, till yesterday, and that after great inquiries." "I know not," said he, "how it happens; but of late every body is in search of Escobar. What I mentioned is in tr. 1. ex. 8. n. 102. Examine it at your leisure, and you will find a splendid specimen of the manner of interpreting bulls favourably."

I perused the subject that very evening, but the statements are so revolting that I dare not repeat them.

The good Father proceeded—"You are now aware of the use we make of *favourable circumstances*: but some are so precise, that it is impossible to reconcile contradictions by means of them, so that you are ready to believe they do in some degree exist. For instance—three Popes have decided, ' that the monks, who are obliged, by a particular vow, to a life of abstinence, cannot be dispensed from it, though they become bishops;' yet Diana states, ' that, notwithstanding these decisions, they are dispensed.' " "Well, Father, how is this made to accord ?" By the most acute of all the new methods, and the most ingenious—*probability!* I will explain it. The affirmative and negative of most opinions, as you were shown the other day, have each some probability; and enough in the judgment of our doctors to be followed with a safe conscience. It is not that the *pro* and the *con* can be at the same time true, and in the same sense; this is manifestly impossible; but it is only that they are at the same time *probable* and consequently safe. On this principle, our good friend Diana speaks in p. 5. tr. 13. r. 39: 'I reply to the decision of the three Popes, which is contrary to my opinion, that, by adhering to the affirmative, they have given a statement which is in fact *probable* according to my judgment; but it does not follow that the negative may not *also* be *probable;* and in the same treatise, r. 65 on another point, in which he again differs from a Pope, he says, 'the Pope affirms this as head of the church, I admit; but he does so only within the sphere of the probability of his own opinion.' You perceive that this is no disparagement to the sentiments of the Popes, otherwise it would not be tolerated at Rome, where Diana is in the utmost credit. For he does not affirm that the decision of the Popes is not probable, but, allowing their opinion the utmost extent of probability, he only maintains that the contrary is also probable." "This is very respectful," observed I. "Yes; and it is far more subtle than the reply of Father Bauny, when a censure was passed upon his books at Rome; for he was provoked by the furious persecution of Mr. Hallier, to say, 'What has the censure of *Rome* to do with that of *France?*' Hence it is sufficiently clear, that either by the interpretation of terms, by the observation of favourable circumstances, or by the double probability of *pro* and *con*, all these pretended contradictions which so alarmed you, may always be reconciled without injury to the decisions of Scripture, Councils, or Popes."

"Reverend Father," said I, "how happy is the world to be blessed with such guides as you! How useful are these probabilities! I never discovered till now, the reason of your taking so much pains to inculcate, that a single doctor, *if he be grave*, can make an opinion probable; that the contrary may also be probable; and then *pro* or *con* may be chosen as is most *agreeable* to the individual, though he do not believe it to be true, and with such a safe conscience that a confessor who should refuse absolution upon the credit of these casuists would be in a state of damnation. Hence I understand that a single casuist may, at his pleasure, construct new rules of morality, and dispose of every thing relative to moral conduct according to his own fancy." "No," said he, "what you state must be taken with some restriction. But observe this. It is our method by which you will trace the progress of a new opinion from its birth to its maturity. The *grave* doctor who invented it, ushers it into the world, dispersing it abroad as a seed which is to take deep root. In this state it is tender, but time ripens it by degrees. On this account Diana, who has introduced many sentiments of this nature, says, in one passage, 'I advance this opinion; but because it is new, I leave it to the operation of time to ripen,—*relinquo tempori maturandam*. Thus, in a few years, it insensibly gains strength, and after the lapse of a considerable period, it becomes authorized by the tacit approbation of the church, according to that grand maxim of Father Bauny, ' when an opinion is advanced by some casuists, and not opposed by the church, it is an evidence that the church approves it.' Upon this very principle he gives authority to one of his own sentiments, in his treatise 6. p. 312." "What, Father, is the church to be responsible for all the abuse she suffers and all the errors which pervade the volumes which she does not formally censure?" "Oh, you must contend that point with Father Bauny: I merely," said he, "recite his words: you must not make *me* the party in the debate. It will be of no avail to dispute against *fact*. I stated that when time had so matured an opinion, it becomes completely probable and sure. Hence the learned Caramuel, in a letter in which he dedicates his fundamental theology to Diana, says, ' that this great man has made many opinions *pro*-

bable which were not so before,' *quæ antea non erant*, and therefore it is no sin to follow them, though once it was sinful—*jam non peccant licet ante peccaverint.*" " Really, Father, there is much to be obtained from you doctors. What then, of two persons who do the same things, shall the one who is unacquainted with your doctrine, commit sin, while the other who knows it, is innocent? Does your doctrine justify at the same time that it instructs? The law of God, according to St. Paul, included all under sin, yours makes them almost all innocent. Pray, Father, do give me minute and full information, for I cannot leave you till you have explained the principal maxims which your casuists have established."

" Alas!" exclaimed the Jesuit, " our chief design was to authorize no other maxims than those of the Gospel in their utmost strictness: and it is sufficiently evident by the regulation of our own conduct, that if we allow of any remissness in others, it is rather attributable to our condescension than to our plan. We are in fact compelled to it: mankind are now so corrupt, that being unable to bring them to our principles we must bring our principles to them. They would otherwise leave us, nay worse, they would become totally abandoned. Our casuists have therefore found it necessary to consider to what vices they are most inclined in every condition, that they might prescribe such agreeable rules, without offending against truth, as to render the compromise perfectly easy. The capital object which our society has in view to promote religion, is to avoid disgusting any one or producing despondency. We have maxims therefore adapted to persons of every description, to beneficiaries, priests, monks, gentlemen, servants rich tradesmen, bankrupts, poor women of piety, and the reverse, married persons and libertines; in short, nothing has escaped our foresight." " That is," interposed I. ' you have provided for the clergy, the nobility, and the commonalty. I should be happy to hear these maxims."

" Well, then," said the good Father, " let us begin with the *beneficiaries*. You are aware of the traffic in benefices, which is so prevalent at the present day; and were we to appeal to the statements of St. Thomas and the ancients we should find many Simonists in the church. On this account, it was deemed very necessary that our Father should make certain prudent abatements and qualifications, as Valentia, one of the four beasts of Escobar, has taught. It is at the close of a long dissertation where he suggests many expedients, of which, in my opinion, the following is the best, p. 2039. tom 3. · If a person give a temporal possession for a spiritual possession, that is, money for a living, and give the money as the price of the benefice it is a manifest simony; but if it be given as the motive to induce the patron to confer it, it is not simony, though he who confers it, have the pecuniary consideration alone in view.' Tannerus, who is also one of our society speaks in a similar manner in his third volume, p. 1519, though he acknowledges 'that St. Thomas is of a contrary opinion; peremptorily declaring, that it is always a simoniacal act to give a spiritual office in exchange for a temporal consideration, if the latter be the end in view.' By this means we prevent an infinity of simoniacal transactions: for who would be so wicked, when he offers his money for a benefice, to do it as the *price* and not as the motive to influence its bestowment? No one surely, can act so criminally."

"I perfectly agree with you," said I; "every body has *sufficient grace* to make such a bargain." "Yes, certainly: and you see how we have compromised the matter with regard to beneficiaries. As to the *priests*, we have a variety of maxims in their favour; for example, this of our twenty-four elders, tr 1. ex. 11 n. 96: 'Can a priest, who has received money for saying a mass, take money a second time for the same mass?' 'Yes,' says Filintius. 'by applying that part of the sacrifice which belongs to him as priest, to the person who pays the second donation, provided he does not receive the price of a whole mass, but of a part only, as for instance, one third.'" "Very good, Father; then here we have a specimen of the *pro* and *con*, where both are *probable*: for what you assert as such, cannot fail of being so upon

the authorities of Filiutius and Escobar. But leaving it within its *sphere of probability*, it appears to me that the contrary might, with very good evidence, be maintained. When the church allows the poor priests to take money for their masses, upon the principle that they who serve the altar should live by the altar, it is not meant that they should exchange the sacrifice for money, still less that they should deprive themselves of all those graces of which they ought to be the first recipients. I might go further, and say, with St. Paul, ' they are obliged to offer the sacrifice, first for themselves, and afterwards for the people:' and thus they are allowed to associate others in the benefits of the sacrifice, but not voluntarily to renounce them all for themselves, and bestow them on another for a third part of the mass; that is to say, for four or five pence. In truth, Father, however little *grave* I might be. I could make this opinion *probable.*"
" Doubtless, for there is no great difficulty in it; the thing is already evident. The difficulty is to find a *probability* in opinions manifestly contradictory to those which are true. This is the achievement for superior men to accomplish. Father Bauny excels in this, and it is truly delightful to see how this learned casuist penetrates the *pro* and the *con* of a question which relates to the priests, and finds reasons on either side, with astonishing skill and subtlety. He says in his tenth treatise, p. 474 : ' It is impossible to make a law to oblige curates to say mass every day, because such a law would undoubtedly expose them (*haud dubie*) to the danger of saying it sometimes in a state of mortal sin;' but he adds, in the same book, p. 441 : ' the priests who take money to say mass every day, ought to say it every day, and cannot excuse themselves by alleging that they are not always properly prepared for it, because they can at any time perform an act of contrition, and if they do not, it is their own fault, and not the sin of the persons who hire them to say mass.' In order further to remove every possible hinderance, he resolves this question also in the same treatise, q. 32. p. 457 : ' Can a priest say mass on-

the very day he is committing a mortal sin, and one of the worst description, if he make a previous confession?' 'No,' says Villalobos, 'on account of his impurity.' Sanchius, however, says *yes*, and without any offence, and this latter opinion I hold to be safe, and it ought to be followed in practice—*et tuta et sequenda in praxi.*"

"Do you really, Father," said I, "affirm, that this opinion ought to be followed in practice? What, ought a priest who has perpetrated such an enormity, to dare to approach the altar on the same day, because Father Bauny says so? And ought he to pay no deference to the ancient laws of the church, which interdict from the sacrifice for ever, or at least for a very considerable time, the priest that commits such iniquities, rather than attend to the novel opinions of the casuists, who re-admit him the very day of his transgressions?" "Where is your memory?" answered the Father: "did not I before state, that according to our Fathers, Cellot and Reginaldus, 'in morality we ought not to follow the ancients, but the new casuists?'" "O yes—I recollect it perfectly: but here is something more, in relation to the laws of the church." "You are right; but you have not yet discovered this beautiful maxim of our Fathers, 'the laws of the church lose their force, when they are no longer observed—*cum jam desuetudine abierunt,*' as Filiutius says, tom. 2. tr. 25. n. 33 We can surely see the present necessities of the church better than the ancients. Were we so austere as to banish our priests from the altar, you can easily comprehend we should have fewer masses; but the multiplication of masses conduces so much to the glory of God and the good of souls, that I will venture to affirm, with Father Cellot, in his work upon the hierarchy, p. 611, printed at Rouen, 'that there would not be too many priests, if not only every man and woman, were that possible, but all inanimate bodies, and even brute beasts—*bruta animalia,* could be metamorphosed into priests to celebrate mass.'"

I was so surprised at this extravagance, that I could not utter a syllable, so that he continued in a similar strain—" But enough of the priests; let us, to avoid greater prolixity, hasten to the *monks*. As their most pressing difficulty relates to the obedience they owe to their superiors, listen to the lenity of our Fathers. Thus speaks Castrus Palaüs of our society, *Op. mor.* p., 1. disp 2. p. 6: ' it is not disputed—*non est controversia* that a monk who has a *probable opinion* in his favour, is not necessitated to obey his superior, though the superior may have a *more probable opinion*: for a monk is allowed to take the opinion which is most agreeable to himself—*quæ sibi gratior fuerit*, as Sanchez observes. And though the commandment of the superior be just, this does not compel obedience; for it is not just in every particular and respect—*non undequaque juste præcipit*, but only *probably*, so that you are only engaged to obey him *probably*, and you are disengaged *probably—probabiliter obligatus, et probabiliter deobligatus*." "Good Father, one cannot estimate too highly the glorious benefits resulting from this double probability!" "Oh," said he, "they are great indeed; but to be brief, I will mention but a single passage more, from the celebrated Molina, in favour of those monks who have been expelled from their monasteries for their irregularities. Our Father Escobar quotes it, tr. 6. ex. 7. n. 111: ' Molina assures us, that a monk expelled from his monastery, is not obliged to reform in order to return, and that he is no longer bound by his vow of obedience." "So then, Father. these ecclesiastics enjoy a very fine liberty. Your casuists, I perceive, have treated them very kindly: they have really legislated as they would for themselves. I am afraid, however, that people in other situations will not be so liberally treated: every one must look to himself." "No," said he, "they could not have taken better care of themselves. The same indulgence has been extended to all, from the greatest to the least: but you lead me to point out our maxims in reference to *servants*."

" We have fully considered the distress they must feel when they are conscientious, in the service of dissipated masters: for if they do not deliver all the messages intrusted to them, they must lose their situations; and if they do, they hurt their consciences. Our twenty-four elders have thus provided for their comfort, tr. 7. ex. 4. n. 223, stating the particular services they may render with a safe conscience: 'to carry letters and presents—open doors and windows—help their masters up to a window—hold the ladder while he climbs up—all these are permitted as things indifferent. It is true, as to holding the ladder, they should only do it when they are violently threatened if they refuse, for it is doing an injury to the master of a house, to break in at the window. Is not all this very judicious?" "I expected nothing less," said I, "in a book deduced from four-and-twenty Jesuits." "But our Father Bauny," added he, "has taught servants how to render all these services very innocently, by having a view merely to the pecuniary reward they may gain, not to the sins themselves which they are required to manage. This is well explained, in his Summary of Sins, p. 710, last edition: 'Let confessors observe that they must not absolve those servants who carry indecent messages, if they consent to the sins of their masters; but they may do so if it be done for their own temporal advantage: and this is easily accomplished; for why should they obstinately consent to sins, of which they participate only the trouble?' And the same Father Bauny has established this great maxim in favour of those who are not content with their wages, in his Summary, p. 213, 214, sixth edition. 'May servants who complain of their wages, add to them, by swindling from their master's property, as much as they deem necessary to recompense their services.' They *may* do it *sometimes*, as when they are so poor in looking out for a situation, that they have been obliged to accept whatever offer was made them, whilst other servants of the same class gain more elsewhere.'" "That," I remarked, "is exactly the case with John d' Alba." "What John d'Alba? who do you mean?" "Have you then forgot, Father, what occurred in this place in the year 1647? pray, where could you have been?" "Oh, I was then a teacher of cases of conscience, in one of our colleges, at some distance from Paris." "I see then you are not acquainted with the story; allow me to tell it you; it was related to me the other day by a person of veracity. He stated that this John d' Alba, a servant of your Fathers of the college of Clermont, in St. James's street, not being satisfied with his wages, stole something to recompense himself. Your Fathers having detected the theft, they put him in prison, accused him of robbing the house, and, if my memory be correct, had him examined at Chatelet, the sixth of April, 1647. These details were mentioned in order to authenticate it. This fellow, upon his examination, confessed that he had taken some pewter plates, but maintained it was no theft justifying himself by the doctrine of Father Bauny. which he presented to his judges with a piece written by one of your Fathers, under whom he had studied cases of conscience, and who taught him the same thing. Upon this, M. de Montrouge one of the most considerable of the society said, 'that he was not of opinion that the writings of these Fathers, containing such an unlawful and pernicious doctrine, contrary to all laws divine and human, adapted to ruin families and authorize domestic thievery, were sufficient to absolve the delinquent; but that he thought this too faithful disciple ought to be whipped before the gate of the college, by the common hangman, who should at the same time, burn the writings of these Fathers relating to theft, forbidding them to teach such a doctrine, upon pain of death.' Universal attention was excited to the result of this advice. which was fully approved, when a circumstance happened to defer its execution. The prisoner disappeared, nobody knew how; not a word more was said about the affair, and John d'Alba went off without returning the plates. The narrator added, that the opinion of M. de Montrouge is registered at Chatelet, where it is accessible to any one's inspection. The company present were mightily delighted." "And pray," said the Father, "what amused them so wonderfully? What does all this amount to? I was speaking of the maxims of our casuists, and was just about to mention those which relate to gentlemen, and you must, forsooth, interrupt me with irrelevant stories!" "Oh, Father, this was only by the bye. and to intimate an important consideration attached to this subject, which I find you have forgot in settling your doctrine of probability." "What then can be omitted by such skilful casuists?" "It is this: you have indeed confirmed those who admit your probable opinions in their confidence both towards God and conscience; for, as you state, all is safe on the side of following a *grave* doctor; and you have emboldened them, as it respects confessors, because you have obliged the priests to absolve them on a *probable opinion*, upon pain of committing a mortal sin: but you have not fortified them against their judges so as to deliver them from the whip and the gallows, by following your *probabilities*. This is a capital defect." 'Thank you, Sir this is true; but we have not the same power over the magistrates as over the confessors, who are necessitated to refer to us in all cases of conscience; for we are the sovereign judges." "I understand you," said I "but if on the one side you are the judges of the confessors are you not on the other, the confessors of the judges? Your power is very extensive. Oblige them to absolve criminals that have a *probable opinion*, on pain of exclusion from the sacraments; that it may no longer happen, to the great contempt and scandal of the doctrine of probability, that those whom you make innocent in theory, are whipped and hanged in practice! How, without this measure, can you expect disciples?" "True, true, this must be considered," said he,—" I shall not forget it, but propose the subject to our Father Provincial. Still you might have reserved your advice for another opportunity, without interrupting me at the moment I was explaining our maxims in favour of gentlemen; and I shall now pass them over, unless you will engage to introduce no more stories."

Such is the whole of my communication for to-day, for one letter would be insufficient to relate all that I learned in this conversation.

I am, &c.

LETTER VII.

On the Method of directing the Attention. The Permission to kill in defence of Honour and of Property which is extended to Priests and Friars. A Curious Question proposed by Caramuel, namely, whether the Jesuits may kill the Jansenists?

SIR, *Paris, April, 25, 1656.*

HAVING pacified the good Father, who was a little disconcerted by my narrative respecting John d' Alba, he resumed the conversation, on being assured that I would introduce no more stories of the same kind : and he spoke of the maxims of his casuists nearly in the following words ;
" You know," said he, " that the ruling passion in persons of this class is *the point of honour,* by which they are perpetually impelled to those violent deeds which appear very contrary to the spirit of Christianity, so that it would be necessary to exclude almost all of them from our confessionals, unless our Fathers had a little relaxed the rigour of religious requirements in tenderness to human infirmities. But as they wished to adhere to the Gospel by fulfilling their duty to God, and to the people of the world by charity to their neighbour, it required all their penetration to devise expedients for the adjustment of these things with so much nicety, that it might be possible for a person to defend and retrieve his honour according to the usual methods of the world, but without doing violence to conscience ; and thus to preserve, in consistent union, two things apparently so opposite as religion and honour.

"But the execution of this design was as difficult as the design itself was useful; and I believe you are sufficiently aware both of the greatness and difficulty of the undertaking." "It does astonish me," said I, coldly. "It astonishes you? I believe so, indeed; and it has astonished others. Are you ignorant that on the one hand, the evangelical law commands not to render evil for evil, but to leave vengeance to God—and on the other, that the laws of the world prohibit our enduring injuries without demanding reparation, and frequently the death of one's enemies? Did you ever know any thing which appeared more contradictory? And yet, when I inform you that our Fathers have reconciled these opposites, you merely tell me you are astonished!" "Father, I did not fully explain myself. I should certainly have considered the thing impossible, if I did not feel persuaded from what I have seen of your Fathers, that they can easily accomplish what to other men *is* impossible. This induces me to believe they may have discovered some expedient, which I am disposed to admire, even without knowing it, but which I beg you to reveal to me."

"Since this is your view," said he, "I cannot refuse your request. Understand, then, that this wonderful principle, consists in our grand method of *directing the intention*, the importance of which, in our system of morality, is such that I should almost venture to compare it to the doctrine of probability. You have already, in passing, seen some features of it in a few of the maxims already mentioned; for when I showed you how servants might, with a safe conscience, manage certain troublesome messages, did you not observe that it was simply taking off their intention from the sin itself, and fixing it on the advantage to be gained? This is what we term *directing the intention*. You saw, at the same time, that those who gave money to obtain benefices, would be really guilty of simony, without giving some such turn to the transaction. But, that you may judge of other cases, let me now exhibit this grand expedient in all its glory, in reference to the subject of *murder*, which it justifies in a thousand cases."

"I already perceive," replied I, "that in this way, one may do *any thing* without exception." "You always go from one extreme to another," returned the Father; "pray stop your impetuosity. To convince you that we do not permit every thing, take this as a proof, that we never suffer the formal intention of sinning, for the sake of sinning, and whoever persists in having no other design in his wickedness than wickedness itself, we instantly discard. This would be diabolical indeed, a rule without exception of age, sex, or quality. But when this abandoned disposition does not exist, we endeavour to make use of our method of directing the intention, which consists in proposing a lawful object as the end of an action. We exert, indeed, the utmost of our power to dissuade men from doing what is forbidden; but when we cannot prevent the action, we at least aim to purify the intention, making amends for the vice of the means by the purity of the end. Thus our Fathers have discovered a method of permitting those violent methods of defending their honour, to which gentlemen resort. It is only for them to renounce the intention of desiring revenge, which is criminal, and to substitute the desire of defending their honour, which our Fathers allow. In this manner they can discharge all their duty both to God and man: for they satisfy the world, by permitting their actions, and conform to the Gospel by purifying their intentions. We are obliged to our modern Fathers for these discoveries; the ancients knew nothing about them. Do you understand me now?" "O yes, perfectly well," said I; "you allow men the external and material action, and give to God the internal and spiritual intention; and by this equitable division you aim to harmonize divine and human laws. But Father, to speak the truth, I am a little distrustful of you, and question whether your authors go the same lengths with yourself."

"You wrong me," answered he; "I advance nothing which I am unable to prove, and by such a variety of citations, that their number, authority, and arguments will fill you with astonishment. To show you the agreement which our Fathers have established between the maxims of the Gospel and those of the world, by this reference to the intention, I beg your attention to Father Reginaldus, *in Praxi*, b. 21. sect. 62. p. 260 : 'Private persons are prohibited from revenging themselves; for it is said by St. Paul, in the twelfth chapter of the Romans, 'Recompense to no man evil for evil,' and again, 'Vengeance is mine, I will repay, saith the Lord.' In addition to which, consider what is said in the Gospel on the forgiveness of offences in the sixth and eighteenth chapters of Matthew." "Undoubtedly, Father, if after this any thing be advanced besides what is contained in Scripture, it would not be amiss to know it. What is the conclusion to which he comes?" "It is this," said he; 'from all these considerations it appears, that a warrior may instantly pursue a wounded enemy, not indeed with the intention of rendering evil for evil, but to maintain his own honour: *Non ut malum pro malo reddat, sed ut conservet honorem.*"

"Do you observe, then, how careful they are to forbid the intention to render evil for evil, because Scripture condemns it? Mark Lessius *de Just*. lib. 2. cap. 9. sect. 12 : 'He who receives a blow must not indulge a spirit of revenge, but he may cherish a wish to avoid disgrace, and, for this purpose repel the assault even with his sword— *etiam cum gladio*.' We are so far from permitting the desire of revenge against our enemies, that our Fathers prohibit a wish for their death, arising merely from an emotion of hatred. Thus our Father Escobar writes, tr. 5. ex. 5. n. 145 : 'If your enemy be disposed to hurt you, you ought not to wish for his death through hatred, but you may do it to avoid injury;' and in accordance with this principle our great Hurtado de Mendoza says, 'it is proper for us to pray God speedily to inflict death upon those who are preparing to persecute us, if we cannot otherwise escape.'"

"My reverend Father," said I, "the church has forgotten to frame a petition among her prayers, suited to this motive." "O, but," he replied, "she has not introduced every thing that may become the subject of a request to God. Besides, this could not have been inserted, for the sentiment itself is of more recent origin than the Breviary. You are a bad chronologist; but not to enter upon this subject, listen to the following passage of Father Gaspar Hurtado *de Sub. pecc. diff.* 9. quoted by Diana, p. 5. tr. 14. r. 99; he is one of Escobar's four-and-twenty elders; 'An incumbent may, without being guilty of a mortal crime, wish for the death of the person who is a pensioner upon his benefice; and a son for that of his father, and rejoice in it whenever it happens, provided that it is only on account of the property that accrues to him, not from any personal hatred.'"

"O Father," said I, "what admirable fruit does this *direction of the intention* produce! Really its power is wonderfully extensive: but there are certain cases exceedingly perplexing, yet very necessary for these gentlemen." "Let us hear what they are," said he. "Show me, then, with all this direction of the intention, that it is lawful to *fight a duel.*" "Oh! our great Hurtado de Mendoza shall satisfy you in a moment, in a passage cited by Diana, p. 5. tr. 14. r. 99: 'When a gentleman who is challenged to a duel, is known to be not remarkably pious, but daily commits sins without the least scruple, plainly evincing that his refusal to accept the challenge does not proceed from the fear of God, but from timidity, he may be called a chicken, and not a man—*gallina et non vir.* He may, in order to preserve his honour, proceed to the appointed place, not indeed with the express intention of fighting, but only of defending himself, if his antagonist should unjustly attack him; and this action would be in itself altogether indifferent. For what harm would there be in going into a field and walking about, waiting for a person, and defending oneself against any attack?' Thus he does not, in any respect, commit sin. because here is no acceptance of a duel, the *intention* being directed to other circumstances: for the acceptance of a duel consists in the express intention of fighting, which is by no means the case with such an individual."

"Father," said I, " you have not kept your word : this is not properly to *permit duelling;* on the contrary, this writer so far considers it forbidden, that to render it allowable, he avoids calling it by that name." " Ho! ho! you begin to penetrate deeply into these subjects; I am quite delighted: still I may say that enough is allowed to all who wish to engage in duels. But as you require a direct answer, our Father Layman shall furnish it, who permits this practice in so many words, providing only that the person *direct his intention* solely to the preservation of his honour or his fortune : l. 3. p. 3. c. 3 n. 2 and 3 ; 'If a soldier in the army, or a gentleman at court, find that he shall inevitably lose his honour or his fortune should he refuse to accept a challenge, I do not see how a person can be condemned for accepting it in his own defence.' Petrus Hurtado speaks exactly in the same manner as quoted by our celebrated Escobar, tr. 1. ex. 7. n. 96 and 98 : ' A man may fight a duel even to defend his goods, if there be no other way of preserving them, because every one has a right to defend his goods, even by killing his enemy.' " Here I was all admiration, to see that the piety of the king was employed in prohibiting and banishing duelling out of the *state,* and the piety of the Jesuits was engaging all their subtlety to permit and authorize it in the *church!*

But the good Father was proceeding so fast, it was impossible to stop him—" Sanchez (pray observe what great authors I quote) goes still farther ; for he not only allows a man to *accept*, but to *give* a challenge, if he direct his intention aright Our Escobar agrees with him in this, n. 97." " If this be the fact, then I shall abandon his tuition ; but I can never believe he has written such a thing till I see it." " Read it, then, yourself," said the Father, pointing out l. 2 c. 39. n. 7, in the moral theology of Sanchez : 'It is perfectly reasonable to say, that a man may fight a duel to save his life, his honour, or his goods, if there be any considerable quantity of them, when it is apparent that his adversary has an evil design unjustly to rob him of them by suits at law and chicanery ; and there is no other way of preserving them. Navarrus well says, in such a case he may accept or send a challenge—*licet acceptare et offerre duellum.* A person may also kill an enemy secretly, and when this can be done, so as to get clear out of the affair, it is far better than fighting a duel; because by this means he avoids every evil consequence; on the one hand, the exposure of his own life to hazard; and on the other, partaking of the crime of his enemy, which he must do in a duel.'

"This, Father," said I, " is a sort of pious ambush; but, pious as it is, it is still an ambush, for a man is allowed to kill his enemy in a *treacherous manner*." "Did I say that one man might kill another in a treacherous manner? God forbid: I said he might kill him *secretly*, and hence you infer he may do it *treacherously*, as if these were one and the same thing? Attend to Escobar, and then give your opinion, tr. 6. ex. 4. n. 26 : ' It may be called killing treacherously, when a man slays another who had not any reason to suspect him. Hence, he who slays an enemy, cannot be said to kill him treacherously, though he perpetrated the deed by laying in wait or stabbing him—*licet per insidias, aut à tergo percutiat ;*' and in the same treatise, n. 56 : ' Whoever kills his enemy after a reconciliation, and under a promise no more to attempt his life, is not said absolutely to kill him in a treacherous manner, as there had been no very strict friendship subsisting between them—*arctior amicitia.*' You see by this explanation, that you are quite unacquainted even with the signification of the terms in use, and yet you presume to talk like a learned divine." " Well, I must acknowledge," said I, " this is new to me ; and from this definition it should seem that it is not possible to kill a man *treacherously ;* for no one surely ever thought of destroying any but his enemies! But, passing this, one may, according to Sanchez, kill a false accuser, I do not say *treacherously*, but only by *stabbing him behind!*" " Yes, but by rightly *directing your intention ;*—you always forget the main point. Molina maintains the same sentiment, tom. 6. tr. 3. disp. 12 : and our learned Reginaldus, l. 21. c. 5. n. 57 : ' It is allowaable to kill the false witnesses brought against us :' and, finally, according to our great and illustrious Fathers Tannerus and Emanuel Sa, we may not only kill the false witnesses, but the judge also, if he act in concert with them. Mark his words, tr. 3. disp. 4. q. 8. n. 83 : 'Sotus and Lessius affirm, that it is not allowable to kill the false witnesses and the judge who conspires with them to put an innocent person to death, but Emanuel Sa and other authors very properly disallow such a sentiment, at least in point of conscience.' In the same place, he states that both witnesses and judge may be killed." "Father, I am now quite sufficiently acquainted with your *principle* of directing the intention ; but I am desirous of understanding also the *consequences*, and all the instances in which this method gives authority to kill. To avoid mistakes, let us recur to what you have already stated—for all equivocation here is extremely dangerous. It is not allowable to kill another, but when it is very opportune and upon a good probable opinion. You have assured me, that by rightly directing the intention, one may, according to your Fathers, for the purpose of preserving one's honour, or even one's possessions, accept a duel, sometimes give a challenge, kill a false accuser secretly, and his witnesses with him, and even the corrupt judge who favours them ; and you have farther represented that he who receives a box on the ear, may repair the injury by the sword, but without a spirit of revenge. But, Father, you have not told me to what length he may proceed." "Oh! you can scarcely be mistaken in that point, because he may go as far as to kill another. This is fully proved by our learned Henriquez, l. 14. c. 10. n. 3 ; as well as others of our Fathers, quoted by Escobar, tr. 1. ex. 7. n. 48, in the following words : 'It is allowable to kill a person who gives you a box on the ear, though he run away, provided you can divest yourself of hatred and revenge, and do not prepare the way for murders in excessive numbers and injurious to the state :' the reason is, that one may as well run after him who has robbed us of our honour, as after him who has stolen property ; for though your honour may not be in the hands of your enemy as your clothes may be, it may nevertheless be recovered in a similar manner, by displaying such evidences of greatness and authority, as may command respect. In fact, is not he who has received a blow reputed to be without honour till he has killed his enemy?" This was so shocking, that I could scarcely contain myself; but, in order to be master of the whole subject, I permitted him to proceed thus, —" Nay, farther, you may kill the person who only intends to give you a blow, if there be no other means of avoiding it. This is one of the most common maxims in our Fathers: for example, Azor. *Inst. mor.* part 3. p. 105; he is one of our twenty-four elders: 'Is it allowable for a man of honour to kill the person who intends to give him a blow or a stroke with his cane? Some say no; and assign as a reason, that a neighbour's life is more important than personal honour; besides that, it is cruel to kill a man merely to avoid a box on the ear. But others affirm that it is allowable, and I most certainly think it *probable*, when it is the only means of escaping such an affront: otherwise the honour of the innocent would be perpetually exposed to the malice of the insolent.' Our great Filiutius advances the same opinion, tom. 2. tr. 29. c. 5. n. 50. and Father Hereau, in his writings upon the subject of homicide, Hurtado de Mendoza, disp. 170. sect. 16. § 137, and Becan, *Som.* tom. 19. 64. *de homicid.* and our Fathers Flahaut and le Court, in their writings, which the university has endeavoured, but in vain, to suppress, and Escobar, in the same place, n. 48—all agree in the same doctrine. It is indeed so generally maintained, that Lessius decides upon it as uncontested by any casuist, l. 2. c. 9, n. 70. He cites a great number who aver this opinion, and not an individual that opposes it, mentioning (n. 77) even Peter Navarre, who, speaking generally upon the subject of affronts, of which a box on the ear is one of the most insulting, declares, in conformity with the universal consent of the casuists, that *ex sententiâ omnium licet contumeliosum occidere, si aliter eâ injuriâ arceri nequit.* Are you satisfied? Will you have any thing more?"

"Thank you, Father," said I; "I have already had too much." But desirous of seeing how far this damnable doctrine would lead, I added, "Pray, would it not be allowable to kill a man for something less than a blow? Cannot you so direct my intention that I may kill another for a lie?" "Yes, surely, according to Father Baldelle, l. 3. disp. 24. n. 24, quoted by Escobar, in the same place, n. 49: 'It is lawful to kill any one who says *you lie*, if he can be stopped by no other means;' and the sentiment of our Fathers is, that you may kill a person in the same manner for *slander;* for Lessius, whom Father Hereau, with many others, follows word for word, in the place already introduced, says, 'If you aim to ruin my reputation, by calumniating me before persons of honour, and I cannot prevent it by any other means than killing you, may I do so? Yes—such is the concurrent opinion of the modern authors, even though the reports you circulate be *true,* but so secretly as to be undetected by the usual proceedings of law. Observe the proof. If when you attempt to take away my honour by giving me a blow, I may prevent it by force of arms, the same kind of defence is allowable when you aim to do me the same injury with your tongue. Moreover, we may prevent affronts—therefore we may prevent slander. Lastly, honour is dearer than life; but it is lawful to kill another in defence of life; therefore it is equally so to kill in defence of honour.' This is sound, logical argument. It is not talk and rant, but demonstration! And this great author Lessius shows, in the same place, n. 78, that it is allowable to kill a person even for a simple motion or gesture in sign of contempt. 'One may attack,' says he, 'and take away a person's honour, in a variety of ways, against which it would be highly proper he should defend himself; as when you are threatened with a stroke of a stick or a box on the ears, or if you should be insulted with opprobrious language or contemptuous gestures—*sive per signa.*"

"I perceive, then, my good Father, that you have done every thing that could be wished to shelter a man's honour from violation, but still his life is exposed, if one may kill another with a good conscience merely for slander or contemptuous treatment." "True; but the vigilance and caution of our Fathers is such, that they have discovered a method of preventing the practice of this doctrine upon insignificant occasions. They say that this must not be universally practised, *practicè vix probari potest:* and the reason is obvious"——"Yes, yes, I know the reason perfectly well," said I, "it is because the law of God forbids murder." "Oh! by no means, the reason is quite different: they feel it to be admissible in conscience and regarding truth in itself." "Why forbid it then?" "Pray," exclaimed the Father, "pray hear me: if people were allowed to kill others merely for detraction, we should depopulate kingdoms in an instant. Attend to our Reginaldus, l. 21. n. 63. p. 260: 'Although the opinion that a man may be killed for a slander, be not destitute of *probability* in theory, yet the reverse must be followed in practice: for it is always necessary to seek the welfare of a state while resorting to measures of self-defence. But it is obvious, that by killing every body in such an unqualified manner, there would be too great a number of murders.' Lessius expresses the same sentiment—'We must be careful that the practice of this maxim do not become injurious to a state; in that case it must not be allowed—*tunc enim non est permittendus.*'"

"How, Father! is your prohibition founded solely on political views, and are those of a religious kind disregarded? Few, alas! will stop here, especially when under the strong excitement of passion. For it may seem *probable*, that the removal of a wicked person from a state is by no means detrimental to its interests." "True, and our Father Filiutius assigns this very reason in conjunction with another of very considerable importance, tr. 29. c. 3. n. 51: 'A person may be capitally punished for killing others on that account.'" "I told you, Father, that you would never do any thing to the purpose, unless the judges were in your favour." "The judges," said he, "who cannot search into the heart, can give no decision but from the evidence of the outward action, whilst we chiefly regard the *intention.* Hence our maxims sometimes differ a little from theirs." "Be that as it may, Father, the inference deducible from yours is clear. that, independently of any injury to a state, one may kill slanderers without violating conscience, if it can be done without endangering one's person But after providing so well for *honour*, have you no security for *property?* I am aware this is an inferior affair; it is however of some consideration It seems to me that it would be possible to direct the intention so as to authorize the killing of a person for the sake of preserving it." "Surely," said he; "and I have already touched upon an idea that illustrates this permission. All our casuists agree in allowing you to kill a man who attempts a robbery of your goods, though you do not apprehend any personal violence from him, and though he run away. See Azor, who proves it. p. 3. l. 2. c. 19, 20."

"But, Father, what must the stolen property be worth to admit of proceeding to this extremity?" "According to Reginaldus, l. 21. c. 5. n. 66, and Tannerus in 22, disp. 49. 8. d. 4. n. 69, 'The article must be of considerable value in the opinion of a *prudent man.*' Layman and Filiutius concur in this statement." "But, Father, this is saying nothing. Where are we to find a prudent and wise man to give the required estimate? How is it they do not determine upon the exact sum?" "How?— Do you imagine it to be so very easy a thing to fix the relative value of human life, the life of a Christian too, in comparison with money? It is precisely in this particular, that I wish to show you the necessity of resorting to our casuists. Examine the ancient Fathers: inquire of them how much money is requisite to purchase permission to kill a man? What do they say? Nothing but *non occides,* 'thou shalt not kill.'" "Who then," I inquired, "has ventured to determine this sum?" "Who? Our great and incomparable Molina, the glory of our society, the man who, by his inimitable wisdom, has estimated it at 'six or seven ducats, for which he declares that it is lawful to kill the thief though he run away,' t 4. tr. 3. disp. 16. d. 6: and he adds, 'that he should not presume to condemn a man as guilty of any crime for killing a person who attempts to rob another of the value of a crown or less, *unius aurei vel minoris adhuc valoris :*' which has led Escobar to establish this general rule, n. 44 : 'that one may kill another *regularly* according to Molina, for the value of a crown.'"

"Well, Father, and how came Molina to possess such penetration as to determine an affair of this importance, without any aid from Scripture, the Councils, or the Fathers? I see he must have been endowed with most peculiar light, though very different from that by which St. Augustin wrote on Homicide and on Grace. I am really becoming quite learned upon this subject, and I perceive, with perfect clearness, that none but clergymen will henceforward abstain from killing those who shall violate their honour or steal their goods." "What do you mean?" said the Father: "would it be reasonable in your opinion, that the persons to whom the greatest respect is due, should alone be exposed to the insolence of the wicked? Our Fathers have anticipated this evil ; for Tannerus, tom. ii. d. 49. 8 d. 4. n. 76. says 'it is allowable for ecclesiastics and even monks to kill, not only in defence of their lives, but also their goods, whether belonging to themselves or the community.' The very same words are used by Molina, as quoted by Escobar, n. 43. Becan in 2. 2. t. 2. 9. 7 *de Hom.* concl. 2. n. 5, Reginaldus, l. 21. c. 5. n. 68. Layman, l. 3. tr. 3. p. 3. c. 3. n. 4: Lessius, l. 2. c. 9 d. 11 n. 72. According to our celebrated Father Launy, it is lawful for priests and monks to kill others to prevent their design of injuriously calumniating them ; but always under the influence of a *well-directed intention.* See t. 5. disp. 36. n. 118 : 'A priest or monk is allowed to kill a calumniator who *threatens* to publish scandalous crimes of their society or themselves, if there exist no other means of prevention; as when just ready to propagate his malignities, if he be not instantly killed. For in such a case, as it would be lawful for a monk to kill the person who was desirous of taking away his life, so is it to kill him who wishes to take away his honour, or that of his fraternity, in the same manner as it is for the people of the world in general.'"

"Really, Father," said I, "this is what I never knew before; I have always been simple enough to imagine just the reverse, having constantly heard that the church was so averse to the shedding of blood, that she would not even permit the ecclesiastical judges to attend when the verdict was pronounced upon criminals." "Oh, Sir," replied he, "you need not perplex yourself; our Father Launy proves this doctrine, but with a modesty worthy of so great a man, submits it to the *prudence* and *discretion* of the reader: and Caramuel, our illustrious defender, in his *Fundamental Theology*, p. 543, considers it as so certain, that he maintains, 'the contrary is not *probable*,' and deduces many admirable inferences; one of which, especially, he calls 'the conclusion of conclusions, *conclusionum conclusio*, 'that a priest not only *may*, on certain occasions, kill a calumniator, but there are cases when he *ought* to do it; *etiam aliquando* DEBET *occidere*.' He enters into the examination of many new questions resulting from this principle; as, for example, WHETHER THE JESUITS MAY KILL THE JANSENISTS?" "Alas! Father," I exclaimed, "this is a most surprising point in theology! I hold the Jansenists already no better than *dead men* by the doctrine of Father Launy." "Aha, Sir, you are caught; for Caramuel deduces the very opposite conclusion from the same principles." "How so?" said I. "Because," replied he, "they cannot injure our reputation. Observe his words, n. 1146 and 1147, p. 547 and 548: 'The Jansenists call the Jesuits Pelagians: may they be *killed* for doing so? No—for this plain reason, that the Jansenists are no more able to obscure the glory of our society, than an owl is to hide the sun: in fact, they promote it, though certainly against their intention—*occidi non possunt, quia nocere non potuerunt.*'"

"Alas, Father, and does the existence of the Jansenists depend solely upon their capacity of injuring your reputation? If that be the case, I am afraid they are not in a very good predicament: for if the slightest *probability* should arise of their doing you any hurt, they may be despatched at once. You can perform the deed logically and in form: for it is only to *direct your intention* right, and you ensure a quiet conscience. What a blessedness for those who can endure injuries to know this charming doctrine! But, on the other hand, how miserable is the condition of the offending party! Really, Father, it would be better to have to do with people totally destitute of all religion, than with those who have received instructions so far only as to this point, relative to directing the intention. I am afraid this *intention* of the murderer is no consolation to the wounded person. He can have no perception of this secret *direction:* poor man! he is conscious only of the *blow* he receives; and I am not certain whether he would not be less indignant to be cruelly massacred by people in a violent transport of rage, than to be devoutly killed for conscience sake."

"But, joking apart, I am a little surprised, my good Father, at all this; and the questions proposed by Father Lamy and Caramuel, I confess, displease me." "Why so?" said he; "are you a Jansenist?" "I have a reason," said I, "quite of a different description. I am in the habit of writing, from time to time, to a friend in the country, all the information I can obtain respecting your maxims; and although I simply and faithfully report your words, I cannot by any means be certain but that some strange and fanciful mortal, imagining I am inimical to your society, may deduce some extravagant inferences from your principles." "Oh," said the Father, "you need not cherish any apprehensions: I will ensure you; our Fathers have printed nothing but with the approbation of their superiors. No danger can therefore result from any kind of publicity."

Guaranteed, therefore, by this good Father, I send you this communication; but I find my *paper* is failing, not my *subject*, which it would absolutely require volumes to exhaust.

I am, &c.

LETTER VIII.

Corrupt Maxims of the Casuists respecting Judges, Usurers, the Contract Mohatra, *Bankrupts, Restitutions, &c.— Various other extravagant Notions.*

Sir,   *Paris, May* 28, 1656.

You did not perhaps imagine, that any person would have the curiosity to inquire who we were; there are, however, people who attempt to guess it, but without success. Some suppose that I am one of the doctors of the Sorbonne, others attribute my letters to four or five persons, who, like myself, are neither priests nor ecclesiastics of any description. All these erroneous conjectures tend to convince me, that my plan is not a bad one to conceal myself from every one excepting yourself and the good Father who bears with my visits, while I bear with his conversation, but not, I assure you, without some degree of punishment. It is necessary, however, to impose some restraint upon my own feelings, for he would not utter another syllable, were he to perceive my real disgust, in which case I should not be able to perform my promise of giving an account of Jesuitical morality. You ought, indeed, to set some value upon the violence I am obliged to do to my own feelings. It is truly distressing to see the whole system of Christian morals overturned by such extravagances, without daring pointedly to contradict them. But after having endured so much for your pleasure, I verily believe I shall at last blaze out for my own satisfaction, when he has finished all he has to say. Still, I shall refrain as long as possible; for, the more silent I am, the more communicative is he. At the last interview, he gave me so much information, that I shall be scarcely able to detail it all. You will, however, find some very convenient principles to oppose restitution: for, in whatever manner he may qualify his maxims, they, in fact most evidently favour corrupt judges, usurers, bankrupts, thieves, prostitutes, witches; all of whom are sufficiently dispensed from the obligation of making restitution of what they gain in their respective trades. This was fully explained in the following discourse.

"I promised," said he, "at our first conversation, to state the maxims of our authors respecting every class of mankind. You have already heard those which relate to the beneficed clergy, priests, monks, servants, and gentlemen: let us hasten to others, and begin with the judges.

"Allow me to point out one of the most important and most advantageous maxims which our Fathers have promulgated in their favour. It is that of our learned Castro Palao, one of the twenty-four elders. His words are, 'May a judge, in a question of right, decide according to one *probable opinion*, and abandon another which is *more probable?* Yes; though it be contrary to his own sentiments—*imo contra propriam opinionem:*' with this our Father Escobar perfectly concurs, tr 6. ex. 6. n. 65."

"Well, Father, this is a noble beginning! The judges are extremely obliged to you, and I do think it is very strange that they should oppose your doctrine of probability, as they sometimes plainly do, since it is so completely in their favour. You have given them the same power over the fortunes of mankind as you have yourselves over their consciences." "You see, then," returned he, "we are not acting from motives of self-interest, but solely from a regard to the peace of their consciences; and it is on this account that our great Molina has laboured so assiduously and usefully respecting the presents which are sent them. In order to relieve them from those scruples which they might otherwise feel in certain cases, he has taken care to enumerate all the cases in which they may conscientiously receive such presents, unless there should exist any particular law to prohibit them, t. 1. tr. 2. d. 88. n. 6: 'Judges may receive presents from parties, when they are given either from friendship or from gratitude, in consideration of the justice which has been rendered them, or in order to induce them to render it, or to excite them to pay particular attention to their business, or to engage them to expedite it.' Our learned Escobar says, tr. 6. ex. 6. n. 63: 'If there should be many persons who possess an equal right to have their cause promptly investigated, and the judge should take any thing from one upon condition (*ex pacto*) of despatching him first—is he doing wrong? No, certainly not, according to Layman; for by the law of natural right, he does not injure others, by granting to one in consideration of his present, that which he might have granted to any other if he chose; and, being equally obliged to do justice to all, as they have an equal right, he becomes placed under a greater obligation to him who has made the present to procure a preference, and this preference seems to be a worthy equivalent for the reward—*quæ obligatio videtur pretio æstimabilis.*'"

"Reverend Father," exclaimed I, "this permission, of which the first magistrates in the kingdom are at present ignorant, really astonishes me: for the first president has introduced an order into parliament for the purpose of preventing secretaries from taking bribes to procure such preferences, which shows that he was far from thinking it allowable for judges to do it, and all the world has applauded a reformation in this department so important to all parties."

Surprised at this, the good Father exclaimed, "Is that a fact? I never heard of it. Our opinion indeed is only *probable*, the contrary is *probable* also." "Why, truly," said I, "it is believed that the president has more than *probably* done well, for he has by this means arrested the progress of public corruption, which had but too long been tolerated." "I am of the same opinion," said he; "but passing that, let us leave the judges." "Agreed:

you are quite right: they are very ungrateful, considering what you have done for them." "Oh! it is not on that account; but there is such a variety of topics before us, that we must be brief upon each.

"Let us now speak about *men of business*. You are aware that our greatest difficulty with them is to prevent usury, for which purpose our Fathers have exerted the utmost care: for such is their utter detestation of this vice, that Escobar says, tr. 3. ex. 5. n. 1, 'that to affirm of usury it is no crime, is to be guilty of heresy;' and our Father Bauny, in his Summary of Sins, ch. 14, has filled a number of pages with an account of the punishments due to usurers. He pronounces them 'infamous when alive, and unworthy of burial when dead.'" "Indeed!" said I, "is Father Bauny so severe? I could not have imagined it." "It is so, however," said he, "when it is necessary; but then this learned casuist, observing that men are only induced to usury by the desire of gain, adds, in the same place, 'the world would be very much obliged, if guaranteeing them against the bad effects of usury, and at the same time against its guilt, some expedient could be adopted of legally procuring as much or more pecuniary profit than is obtained by usurious practices.'" "Undoubtedly, Father; then we should not have any more usurers." "This he has accomplished by furnishing 'a general method for persons of every description, gentlemen, presidents, counsellors,' &c.—and so easy, that it consists simply in pronouncing certain words when the money is lent, in consequence of which the profit may be taken without being guilty of a usurious transaction, which it would be without such a precaution." "Pray, what are these mysterious words?" "Not at all mysterious: they are his own words, for you know that he wrote his Summary of Sins in French, as he says in his preface, *to be understood by all mankind*. The person of whom you wish to borrow shall answer thus: 'I have no money to *lend*, though I have some, to be sure, to place out for an *honest and lawful profit*. If you wish to improve the sum you request by honest industry, by a copartnership of half and half, possibly I might be induced to accommodate you. But as it is a troublesome affair to settle the profits of trade, if you will ensure me a certain gain and my whole principal, without any hazard, we shall agree the sooner; and, in fact, you shall have the money immediately.' Is not this an admirable method of acquiring money without committing sin? And has not Father Bauny good reason for saying in conclusion, ' By this means, in my opinion, a great number of people who, by usury, extortion, and illegal contracts, provoke the divine indignation, may save themselves, and acquire good, honest and lawful profits."

"Father," said I, "these are most powerful words! They must certainly possess some secret charm to drive away usury, with which I am unacquainted, for I have always supposed, that this sin consisted in taking back more money than was lent." "This shows," said he, "how little you understand it. Usury, according to our Fathers, consists in little or nothing more than the intention of taking an advantage merely as usurious. Hence our Father, Escobar, points out the method of avoiding usury, by simply diverting the intention, tr 3. ex. 5. n. 4, 33, 34: 'It would,' says he, 'be usurious, to take a profit from those to whom money is lent, if it were exacted as a just debt; but if, as a debt of gratitude, it is not usury;' and, n. 3, 'it is not lawful to have an intention of profiting by the loan of your money directly, but to expect it from the goodness of the person who has borrowed it, (*mediâ benevolentiâ*) is not usury.' Such are the subtle and admirable methods we have adopted! But, after all, one of the very best in my judgment, (for we have a great variety of them,) is that of the contract Mohatra." "The contract *Mohatra*, Father!" "Oh! I see very well you don't understand it. The name, indeed, seems a little strange, but Escobar shall explain it, tr. 3. ex. 3. n. 36: 'The *contract Mohatra* is that by which one purchases cloth at a dear rate, and upon credit, in order to resell it immediately to the same person for ready money and cheap.' This is the nature of the contract referred to, by which you perceive that a certain sum is received in hand by remaining debtor for more."

"But, Father, I believe that Escobar is the only writer that ever made use of this term: is not that the fact?" "How strangely ignorant you are," said he; "the very last book of Moral Theology, printed at Paris, this year, treats of Mohatra in the most learned manner. It is entitled, *Epilogus Summarum:* an abridgment of all the bodies of divinity deduced from our Fathers Suarez, Sanchez, Lessius, Fagundez, Hurtado, and other celebrated casuists.' In page 54, you have these words: 'Mohatra is, when a man, who has occasion for twenty guineas, purchases cloths of a tradesman for thirty, at a bill payable in twelve months, and resells them to him immediately for twenty guineas down.' You see, by this quotation, that Mohatra is no new invented term." "But, Father, is this a lawful contract?" "No; for Escobar informs you, at the same place, that 'there are laws which prohibit it under the severest penalties.'" "It is useless, then." "Not at all; for Escobar, in the same passage, states some expedients to render it lawful, 'even though,' says he, 'the person who purchases and resells, fixed his intention chiefly upon nothing but the profit, provided only that he do not, in selling, exceed the highest price of articles of this description, and that in purchasing, he do not give less than the lowest, excepting it had been before agreed upon, in so many express terms, or otherwise." "But Lessius *de Just.* l. 2. c. 21. d. 16. says, 'that even though the person had sold his goods with the intention of re-purchasing them at an inferior price, he is not obliged to return the profit, except, perhaps, out of charity, supposing the individual from whom he exacts it be in indigent circumstances, and then provided he can do it without any personal inconvenience— *si commodè potest.*' This is saying as much as *can* be said." "Indeed, Father, a greater indulgence would, I think, be the extreme of vice." "Yes, yes: our Fathers well know where to stop; and you now see sufficient evidence of the utility of Mohatra. I might point out a variety of other methods, but these are sufficient. I now propose to speak of those whose *affairs are in a ruined state.*"

"Our Fathers dispense comfort suited to every one's condition; for if persons do not possess enough to live genteelly, and discharge their debts, they are allowed to become bankrupts, and conceal a part of their property from their creditors. Our Father Lessius has settled this point, and Escobar confirms his decision, tr. 3. ex. 2. n. 163 : 'May a bankrupt retain, with a good conscience, as much of his property as is necessary for the support of his family with credit—*ne indecorè vivat?* I maintain, with Lessius, that he may, even though he had gained it by injustice, and notorious crime—*ex justitia et notorio delicto :* in this case, however, he cannot retain quite *so much* as he otherwise might." "How, Father? What a strange kind of charity is this, to allow of the retention of property which has been acquired by robbery for the subsistence of a family, to the detriment of creditors to whom it properly belongs ?" "Oh!" said he, "it is impossible to give universal satisfaction, and our Fathers have been particularly solicitous of comforting the miserable and indigent, and it is for their benefit that our Father Vasquez, quoted by Castro Palao, tom. 1. tr. 6. d. 6. p. 6. n. 12, says : 'If you see a thief ready and determined to rob a poor person, you may, in order to prevent him, point out some other individual who is rich, whom he may attack instead." If neither Vasquez, nor Castro Palao happen to be in your possession, you will find the same doctrine in Escobar; for, as you are aware, he has scarcely advanced any thing but what is taken from our twenty-four most celebrated Fathers. See tr. 5. ex. 5. n. 120. "*The practice of our Society respecting Charity towards a Neighbour.*"

"Father," said I, "this is really a most extraordinary kind of charity, to save one by sacrificing another! But charity should not be partial, and he who has given such advice, should be afterwards obliged in conscience to repay the rich man whatever he lost." "Not at all, not at all: he was not the thief; he simply advised another to do it. But hear the wise decision of our Father Bauny upon a much more astonishing case, and in which you would be ready to believe, that restitution was still more obligatory. It is in ch. 13. of his Summary: 'A person desires a soldier to beat his neighbour, or burn the barn of a man who has given him some offence. The question is, whether in case the soldier absconds, the person who employed him to commit these injuries, ought to make reparation for the damage that has ensued. My opinion is, that he ought not: for no one is bound to make restitution, if he have not violated justice; and pray, where is any such violation in requesting another to do one a favour? Whatever demand you were induced to make, the man was always at liberty to grant or refuse it. To whichever side he inclines, he is influenced by his own free will, nothing compels him but his own obliging disposition and temper. If, therefore, the soldier make no compensation for the mischief he has done, it would not be obligatory on him to do it who employed the delinquent."

This passage nearly put an end to our conversation, for I was on the very point of bursting into a fit of laughter at the *obliging disposition* and *good temper* of an incendiary, and at the extravagant reasons adduced to exempt the real culprit from the duty of making reparation for the damages he inflicts, when the judges would not have reprieved him from a sentence of death; but if I had not checked my risibility, the good Father would have been completely offended, for he spoke with great seriousness, and continued in the following strain :—

"You ought now to be convinced, from such a variety of proofs, that your objections are quite nugatory, though they are perpetually diverting us from the subject. Let us then return to these wretched individuals, for whose consolation our Fathers, and among them Lessius, declare, l. 2. c. 12. n. 12, 'they are allowed to commit theft not only in cases of extreme necessity, but when their afflictions, though heavy, are not extreme.' Escobar states the same in tr. 1. ex. 9. n. 29." "This is very surprising, Father! Because there is scarcely any person in the world who cannot plead this kind of necessity, and who may not therefore commit robbery with a safe conscience; and though you should restrict this permission to those only who are *bonâ fide* in that condition, it would be opening the gates to an infinity of thefts, which the judges will punish notwithstanding this *heavy* necessity, and which you have the best possible reason to suppress—you, whose duty it is not only to maintain *justice* amongst mankind, but *charity* also, which is annihilated by such a principle. For, is it not violating charity and injuring your neighbour, to destroy his property to enrich yourself? This is what I have hitherto been taught to believe." "Perhaps so," said he, "but it is not always the fact: for our great Molina says, t. 2. tr. 2. disp. 328. n. 8, 'that the rule of charity does not require any one to deprive himself of an advantage for the purpose of screening his neighbour from a loss.' This is stated in illustration of what he had undertaken to demonstrate, namely, 'that we are not in conscience under an obligation to restore the property which another has put into our possession in order to swindle his creditors.' Lessius maintains the same opinion, and confirms it by the same principle, l. 2. c. 20. disp. 19. n. 168.

"You really do not cherish sufficient compassion for people in distressed circumstances; our Fathers evince far greater charity. They do justice to the poor as well as the rich: nay, more, they render justice even to the guilty: for though they denounce such as commit great crimes, yet they teach us that property acquired by the perpetration of them may be lawfully retained. Lessius gives this general rule, l. 2. c. 14. d. 8: 'We are under no obligation, either by the law of nature, or by any positive laws, that is to say, by *any law*, to restore what we have acquired by having committed a criminal action, as adultery, even though this action be contrary to justice;' for, as Escobar states, in quoting Lessius, tr. 1.

ex. 8. n. 59, 'the property which a woman acquires by adultery, though gained indeed in an illegitimate manner, yet may be lawfully kept, after possession is once obtained—*quamvis mulier illicitè acquirat, licitè tamen retinet acquisita.*'

"On this account, our most celebrated casuists formally decide, that what a judge takes from parties whom he has favoured by an unjust sentence, what a soldier receives for having killed another, and what any one obtains for the most infamous crimes, may be lawfully retained. Escobar has accumulated abundant evidence upon the subject from our Fathers, tr. 3. ex. 1. n. 23, where he establishes this general rule: 'Property acquired by iniquitous methods, as by murder, by an unjust sentence, by lewdness, &c. may be lawfully possessed, without any necessity of making restitution;' and again, tr. 5. ex. 5. n. 53: 'A person may dispose of what he receives for murder, an unjust decree, and infamous sins in general, &c. as he pleases, because the possession of it is just, and he acquires a right and title to whatever he gains by such means.'" "Oh, Father," exclaimed I, "this mode of acquiring I never heard of before! I doubt, moreover, whether it be authorized in law or justice, or that it is possible to obtain right and title to commit assassination, injustice, and adultery!" "I know nothing," returned he, "of what books of law say upon the subject; but this I well know, that *our* writings, which constitute the true guides of conscience, speak as I do; one case excepted, in which restitution is required, namely, 'when money is received from persons who have no power to dispose of their property; such as children under age and monks'—these our great Molina expressly exempts, tom. 1 *de Just.* tr. 2. disp. 94 : ' *Nisi mulier accepisset ab eo qui alienare non potest, ut à religioso et filio familias.*' In this case the money must be restored. Escobar quotes this passage, tr. 1. ex. 8. n. 59, and confirms it in another place, tr. 3. ex. 1. n. 23."

Here I could not help remarking, that the monks seemed to be much better treated in this instance than others. "By no means," said he; "are not all minors generally placed in the same situation, amongst whom the monks may be considered as classing all their life-time? It is therefore proper, that they should be excepted; with regard to others, there is no obligation to return to them what has been received for any iniquitous action: this is satisfactorily demonstrated by Lessius, l. 2. *de Just.* c. 14. d. 8. n. 52: 'A wicked action may be estimated at a certain price, in proportion to the advantage resulting to the individual who has caused it to be perpetrated, and the trouble it occasions him who engages in it; on which account the restitution of the reward is by no means obligatory, whatever the crime may be, as murder, unjust judgment, impurity (for these are the instances he adduces,) unless the reward be taken of those who had no power or means to give it. You may perhaps say, that he who receives money for perpetrating a wicked deed, commits sin, and therefore ought not either to take or to keep it; I answer, that after the execution of the project, it is no sin either to pay or to receive payment.' Our great Filiutius enters into a still more detailed statement. He remarks, 'that a person is obliged in conscience, to pay for actions of this nature in different proportions, according to the different circumstances of the persons who commit them, and some merit more than others.' This he establishes on the most solid reasoning, tr. 1. c. 9. n. 231: '*Occultæ fornicariæ depetur pretium in conscientia, et multò majore ratione quam publicæ. Copia enim quam occulta facit mulier sui corporis, multò plus valet quàm ea quam publica facit meretrix; nec ulla est lex positiva quæ reddat eam incapacem pretii. Idem dicendum de pretio promisso virgini, conjugatæ, moniali, et cuicumque alii. Est enim omnium eadem ratio.*'"

After this, he pointed out such infamous passages in his authors, that I dare not venture to introduce them, passages with which he would have been disgusted himself, (for he is a good man,) were it not for the reverence he entertains for his Fathers, which induces him to receive, with the utmost deference, every thing they choose to dictate. I continued silent, less however for the purpose of procuring a continuance of his discourse, than in consequence of the astonishment I felt to see books replete with such horrible, unjust, and altogether extravagant decisions, written by persons professing religion!

He pursued his topic without interruption, concluding thus: " For this reason our illustrious Molina (and I hope after this you will be satisfied) settles the question in the following words: ' Is the person who has received a reward for a criminal action obliged to return it? Why—some distinctions must be made—if the action for which the compensation was paid be not done, the money must be refunded; but if it be, there is no obligation to return it—*si non fecit hoc malum, tenetur restituere; secus, si fecit*.' This is cited in Escobar, tr. 3. ex. 2. n. 138.

" Such are some of our principles respecting restitution. You have received a great deal of information to-day: let me see how you have profited by your instructions. Now, Sir, answer me this question: ' When a judge has taken money from one of the parties in a law-suit to pronounce a sentence in his favour, is he under any obligation to return it?' " " The answer as you have taught me, is plainly *no*." " There now—I thought how it would be—did I make no *exceptions*? Did I not expressly state, that restitution is not necessary, *if* he pronounced a sentence in favour of the party which had no right; but otherwise, would you have a person purchase a decision which is legally due to him? Unreasonable, most unreasonable! Are you not aware that a judge *owes justice* to all, and therefore cannot sell it? But he does not owe *injustice*, and therefore he may sell *that*. Our most approved authors, as Molina, disp. 94 and 99. Reginaldus, l. 10. n. 184, 185, and 187: Filiutius, tr. 31. n. 220 and 228: Escobar, tr. 3. ex. 1. n. 21 and 23: Lessius, l. 2. c. 14. d. 8. n. 52; concur in this, ' that a judge is under an obligation to restore whatever he may have received for doing *justice*, unless it were given him purely from a motive of liberality; but he is not at all obliged to return what he has received of a man in whose favour he has passed an *unjust sentence.*'"

I was dumb, absolutely dumb, at these fantastical distinctions; and while reflecting upon their pernicious consequences, my worthy catechist had prepared another question. "Pray," said the Father, "answer me next time with a little more circumspection—'Is a conjurer obliged to restore the money he gains by his trade?'" "Just as you please, reverend Father." "As I please? Admirable indeed! It should seem from your way of talking, that truth depended upon every one's caprice. I see, however, this is too puzzling a question for you, and I readily concede some assistance; Sanchez shall resolve the difficulty—who but Sanchez?—First he distinguishes (Sum. l. 2. c. 38. n. 94, 95, and 96) between this conjurer 'making use of astrology and other natural methods, and his employing the diabolical art of necromancy; for in one case he is obliged to make restitution, in the other not.' Now pray tell me in which case?" "Oh," said I, "there can be no difficulty here." "Ah! I know what you mean: you would reply that he is obliged to make restitution, if he made use of diabolical agency. But you understand nothing about the matter; it is quite the reverse. Listen to the decision of Sanchez in the same passage: 'if the conjurer have not taken the pains and care to know, by means of the devil, what could not otherwise be known—*si nullam operam apposuit ut arte diaboli id sciret*—restitution must be made; but if he have taken the requisite pains, it is not obligatory.'" "How so, Father?" "What!" replied he, "is this so incomprehensible to you? The reason obviously is, that by diabolical aid, divination may probably be accomplished? but astrology is fallacious." "But, Father, suppose the devil should not give a true answer, for he is scarcely more to be depended upon than astrology, must not the conjurer then, for the same reason, make restitution?" "Not always. *Distinguo*—says Sanchez: 'For if the conjurer be an ignoramus in the diabolical art—*si sit artis diabolicæ ignarus*—he is obliged to make restitution: but if he be a skilful sorcerer, and have used every means to discover the truth, he is not obliged, because the care and diligence of such a sorcerer may be estimated at a certain pecuniary value—*diligentia a mago apposita est pretio æstimabilis.*'"

"There is some sense, Father," said I, "in this; for here is a method of inducing sorcerers to make themselves learned and expert in their art, by presenting the hope of gaining money in a lawful way, according to your maxims, and moreover serving the public." "I am afraid," said he, "this is nothing but banter; but let me assure you, it is very wrong; for, if you speak in this manner, in places where you are a stranger, it is likely people would be exceedingly displeased at your language, and censure you severely for turning religious subjects into ridicule." "Oh, I could easily defend myself; for, I believe, whoever takes the trouble to investigate the true sense of my expressions, will find just the contrary, and, perhaps, an opportunity of showing this may occur in some of our future conversations." "Ho, ho!" returned the good Father, "you are serious now, however." "I confess," said I, "that the suspicion of being capable of ridiculing sacred things, would make me very unhappy, and would be equally unjust." "Nay, my dear Sir, I was only joking with you; but to be serious." "I am quite disposed to be so, Father, if such be really your intention; but, I must acknowledge, that I was surprised to observe, that your Fathers extended their care to every class of mankind, so far as even to regulate the legitimate pay of a sorcerer." "One cannot write," said he, "for too many, or particularize cases with too much exactitude, or even repeat the same things too often in different books. You shall see this confirmed by a quotation from one of the gravest of our Fathers, Cellot, l. 8. ch. 16. § 2. *on the Hierarchy.* 'We know a person who was going to restore a considerable sum of money, by order of his confessor, and, stopping on his way at a bookseller's, asked if he had any thing new—*numquid novi?* He was shown a new treatise on Moral Theology: when carelessly turning over the leaves, without any particular view, he happened upon his own case, and found he was not obliged to make restitution; so, being discharged from his burdensome scruple, but very well content to carry the burden of his money, he returned home light at heart—*abjectâ scrupuli sarcinâ, retento auri pondere, levior domum repetiit.*'

"After all this, will you doubt the utility of our maxims? Will you ridicule and banter them now? Or, will you not rather concur with Father Cellot in his pious reflection on the happiness of such a coincidence? Incidents of this nature, are, in God, the effects of his providence; in our guardian angel, the effect of his guidance; and in those to whom they happen, the effect of their predestination. God, from all eternity, resolved that the golden chain of their salvation should depend on that very writer, and not upon a hundred others who have all stated the same thing; but they did not chance to meet with them. If this very author had not written, that individual would not have been saved. Let us then, by the bowels of Jesus Christ, implore those who censure the number of our authors, not to begrudge people writings, which the everlasting election of God, and the blood of Jesus Christ, has procured for them.

"Such, then, are the beautiful expressions which this learned man employs to prove the proposition he had advanced, ' that it is extremely useful to have a great variety of writers on Moral Theology—*quam utile sit de theologiâ multos scribere.*' "

"Father," said I, "with your permission, I will defer giving my opinion of this passage to a future opportunity, and will only at present speak to another point—whether, since your maxims are so useful, and their publication is of such consequence, you ought to continue giving me such minute information. The person to whom I transmit them, I can assure you, shows them about; not that we have any other intention in making use of them, than to serve the public by giving them information." "Well," said he, "you are aware that I conceal nothing; and the next time we meet, I shall fully state those comforts and

11*

indulgencies which our Fathers allow to facilitate the services of religion, and smooth the path to heaven; so that, having already learned what respects the particular condition and circumstances of mankind, you shall be informed of every thing relating to them generally, and thus your knowledge upon this subject will be complete.

Here we parted.

I am, &c.

P. S. I have always forgot to say, that there are different editions of Escobar. If you purchase his works, be sure to have that of *Lyons;* at the beginning of which, you will find the figure of a lamb on a book, sealed with seven seals, or the editions published at Brussels in 1651. As these are the latest, they are better and more ample than the earlier editions of 1644, and 1646, at Lyons.

LETTER IX.

The false worship of the Virgin Mary, which the Jesuits have introduced. The various facilities they have invented to procure Salvation without any trouble, and amidst the indulgences of life. Their maxims respecting Ambition, Envy, Gluttony, Equivocation, mental Reservations, the Liberty which young Females enjoy, the Habits of Women, Gaming, and the Manner of hearing Mass.

Paris, July 3, 1656.

Sir,

I shall begin unceremoniously, as the good Father did at my last interview. No sooner did he perceive me, than looking at a book which he had in his hand—" Would not you," says he, " be extremely obliged to any person who should open to you the gates of Paradise? Would not you give millions of gold and silver for a key to enter in whenever you please? But you need not purchase an admission at so dear a rate ;—here is one, nay a hundred, to be easily obtained."

Whether the good Father was reading or speaking to me, I could not tell; but it soon became apparent, by his saying, " This is the commencing paragraph of a beautiful work of Father Barry, of our society; for I never speak without authority." " May I ask," said I, " what book it is?" " The title is, '*Paradise opened to Philagic by a hundred devotions to the mother of God, of easy performance.*" " And pray, Father, will each of these devotions suffice to open heaven?" " Yes, surely—mark what follows: ' As many separate devotions to the mother of God as you find in this book, are so many keys of heaven, which will open all Paradise to you, provided you only practise them :' this is the reason, he says at the conclusion, ' it is sufficient to practise *any one* of them.'" "Teach me, then, good Father, one of the easiest of that number." "They are all easy: for example, ' Salute the holy Virgin whenever you meet her image; repeat the little chaplet of the ten pleasures of the Virgin; often pronounce the name of Mary; commission the angels to give your duty to her; cherish a desire to build more churches to her than all the kings of the world put together; wish her a good day every morning, and a good night every evening; say the *Ave Maria* every day in honour of the heart of Mary.' This last devotion he affirms will ensure the heart of the Virgin." "But, Father, is it not upon the supposition of giving her our own?" "Oh, no; that is not at all necessary, when one is too much attached to the world. Observe what he says: ' Heart for heart is what should be; but yours is a little too much captivated, and devoted to creatures; on which account, I dare not at present write you to offer this little slave called your heart;' so he remains satisfied with the *ave Maria* which he required. These are the devotions of pages 33, 59, 145, 156, 172, 258, and 420 of the first edition." "A very comfortable doctrine indeed, Father! No one, I think, can ever be damned after this!" "Alas!" exclaimed he, "I perceive you have no idea to what extremes the obduracy of some persons will lead them. There are people who will never bind themselves even to pronounce every day these two simple phrases, *good morning, good night*, because it cannot be done without at least *some* exercise of memory. Father Barry, therefore, deemed it necessary to furnish still easier methods; as, ' to wear a chaplet night and day upon the arm, in the form of a bracelet, or to carry somewhere about one a rosary, or a picture of the Virgin.' These devotions are to be found in pages 14, 326, and 447, ' and say,' adds Father Barry, ' whether I have not furnished devotions sufficiently easy, to gain the good graces of the Virgin.'" In this idea of *facility*, I most fully concurred. "It is," continued he, "all that can possibly be done, and will, no doubt, prove sufficient : for how dreadful it would be for an individual not to devote a single moment of his whole life, to put a chaplet upon his arm, or a rosary of beads into his pocket by which he might so indubitably secure his salvation, that those who have made the experiment, have never failed, whatever has been their conduct; though we admonish them to live virtuously. Allow me to quote only one example from page 34, of a woman, who, devoutly saluting images of the Virgin every day, constantly lived, to her dying day, in the practice of a mortal sin, but was, nevertheless, saved by the merit of this devotion." "But how," said I, "pray how can you know that?" "How, Sir? Because our Saviour raised her from the dead for the express purpose. Such is the complete certainty, that no one can perish who performs any of these devotions!" "True," answered I. "they are, I know, very powerful means of salvation, and the least of them are extremely meritorious, when they originate in the principle of faith and charity possessed by real saints; but to make one believe that without any change of character, they are available to conversion in the hour of death, or that God will raise such persons again, is a doctrine very well adapted, doubtless, to encourage sinners in their iniquities, by imparting a false peace, but not to effect that genuine conversion which divine grace can alone produce." "Pshaw," said the Father, "what does it signify by *what means* we obtain admission to Paradise, if we do *but obtain it?* as our late celebrated Father and provincial Binet says, speaking on a similar subject, in his excellent book, ' on the mark of predestination,' n. 31. p. 130, *fifteenth edition:* ' Whether by storm or stratagem, hook or crook, never mind—let us rejoice, so that we do but take the city of glory.' " " Agreed—but the main question is, whether we shall ever enter into it ?" " The Virgin will answer for that. Observe the closing paragraph of Father Barry's book : ' If it should happen at the hour of death, that the enemy should have any claim upon you, and any disquiet should arise in the little republic of your thoughts, you have only to say, that *Mary answers for you, and to her he must make his application.*'"

Here I remarked, that this subject might be pursued to a very embarrassing point, for "who has assured us that the Virgin engages to answer for us?" "Father Barry," replied he, "promises on her behalf, p. 465: ' As to the advantage and happiness accruing, I take upon me to answer for them, and pledge myself that the good mother will procure them.'" "But, who will answer for Father Barry?" "Who?—Pray remember he is one of our society; and are you ignorant that we answer for all the writings of our members? If you do not know this, it is time you should. A rule exists in our society, which prohibits all booksellers printing any work of our Fathers without the approbation of our divines and the permission of our superiors. It was made by Henry III., on the tenth of May, 1583, and confirmed by Henry IV., on the fourteenth of February, 1612, so that our whole fraternity is responsible for the publications of each of our Fathers. This is a peculiarity attaching to our society, on which account no work originates with us, but what expresses the spirit of the whole body. I thought it proper to give you this information."

Acknowledging my obligation, I expressed myself extremely sorry that I did not know this circumstance before, as I should certainly have paid more attention to these authors. "Nothing," he remarked, "but a want of opportunity had prevented his mentioning it; but the advantage of it will be felt in future; in the mean-time let us pursue our subject. I believe that I have explained certain means of salvation that are sufficiently easy, sure, and numerous: but our Fathers would be extremely glad, if people would not stop at this point, where nothing is required excepting what is absolutely necessary for salvation. As they are incessantly solicitous of promoting the glory of God in the highest degree, they wish to raise mankind to the noblest elevation of piety: and as people of the world are generally diverted from religion by their strange notions respecting it, we have deemed it of the greatest importance to remove this first obstruction, in which Father le Moine has acquired great reputation, by his book of 'Easy Devotion,' written with that express design. It contains a most charming picture of devotion. Never did any one know the subject so well as himself. Observe the first sentence: 'Virtue has never yet shown herself to any one, nor has any good resemblance of her been drawn. It is not surprising that so few attempt to climb up her rock. She has been painted as morose, loving solitude, associating only with grief and toil—in short, as an enemy to pleasure and merriment, which constitute the very essence of enjoyment and the sweetest relish of life, p. 92.'"

"But, Father, there have been great saints who have passed a life of extreme mortification." "True," said he, "but we have always seen saints polite, and devotees courteous, p. 191. In page 86, you will perceive that the difference in their manners proceeds from the difference of their tempers. I do not deny that you may see devotees of a pale and melancholy complexion, who love silence and retirement, who have nothing but dulness in their veins, and fasting upon their countenances; but there are many others who wear a happier appearance, having an abundance of those sweet and warm humours, and of that pure blood in which the sources of joy originate.

"Hence you may notice that the love of retirement and solitude does not attach to every devotee, and, as I said, is rather constitutional than the effect of piety: but those austerities to which you referred are characteristic of a savage and a brute. Father le Moine, in the seventh book of his *Moral Pictures*, classes them in the ridiculous and debased order of melancholy madmen. To give you a specimen of his figures: 'Such a person has no eyes for the beauties of art and nature. Any kind of pleasure he considers as an insufferable burden; he spends the festival days in a burying ground, and takes more delight in a hollow tree or in a cavern, than in a palace or on a throne. As to insults and injuries, he is as insensible to them as a statue. Honour and glory are idols he knows nothing about, and to whom he has no incense to offer. A beauty is to him a spectre, and those lofty and commanding looks, those tyrant eyes which lead captive and enslave the world, are as displeasing to *him* as the sun is to an owl."

"Reverend Father," I exclaimed, "if you had not declared that Father le Moine drew this picture, I assure you that I should have considered it as the production of some wicked fellow who meant to render saints ridiculous; for if this be not the representation of a man totally detached from those sentiments which the Gospel requires us to renounce—really I cannot understand what is."

"Ignorance! This is but 'the outline of a weak and savage character, who possesses none of the honourable and natural passions which he ought to have,' as Father le Moine expresses it. In this manner he teaches 'virtue and Christian philosophy,' conformably with the design of his publication, as stated in the advertisement. And, in fact, it cannot be denied that this method of treating upon devotion is far more agreeable to the world than any one previously adopted." "Surely, surely," said I, "there can be no comparison between them, and I begin to hope you will fulfil your promise."

"This," he replied, "will be more obvious presently; I have hitherto only spoken of piety in general. But to show you in detail how our Fathers have disburdened the practice of it from every difficulty, is it not unutterably consoling to the ambitious, to learn that they may have real religion while they indulge an inordinate love of glory?" "What, Father, however excessive it may be?" Yes; for it would always be a venial sin, unless this glory were desired merely to oppose, with the better prospect, both God and his country. Venial sins are no impediments to piety, since the greatest saints are not exempt from them. Listen attentively to Escobar, tr. 2. ex. 2. n. 17:—' Ambition, which is an inordinate appetite for power and glory, is of itself a venial sin; but when greatness is desired in order to injure the state or to offend God the more readily, these external circumstances render it mortal.'" "This, Father, is a very *comfortable* doctrine," said I, "I believe so, indeed; but not more so then what relates to avarice." 'I know,' says Escobar, tr. 5. ex. 5. n. 154, ' that the rich do not commit a mortal sin if they refuse to bestow alms out of their abundance upon the neccessitous poor—*scio in gravi pauperum necessitate divites non dando superflua, non peccare mortaliter.*'" "If that be the case, Father—really I know nothing about the nature of sin." " Pray then—to instruct you a little further—do not you suppose that a good opinion of one's self, and a perfect complacency in one's own works, is one of the most dangerous of sins ? And should not you be astonished, were I to show you, that though this good opinion be without foundation, so far from being sinful, it is on the contrary a gift of God ?" " Astonishing indeed, Father ! Is it possible ?" " Certainly it is, and our great Father Garasse, in his book, entitled *A Summary of the Capital Truths of Religion*, p. 2. p 419, says, Retributive justice demands that every good work be rewarded either by applause or compensation. When a celebrated genius produces any performance, it is duly rewarded by public approbation ; but when one of an inferior class labours hard to write something of no value, and therefore cannot obtain general applause, in order that he might not be without any recompense, God bestows upon him self-satisfaction, which it would be unjust and barbarous in the extreme to envy him. Thus God, who is perfectly just in all his proceedings, has capacitated even frogs to enjoy their own croaking."

" These," said I, " are admirable decisions in favour of vanity, ambition, and avarice ; but have you any apology for *envy ?*" " Why, this is a delicate point. We must advert to the distinction of Father Barry in his Summary of Sins. His opinion is, c. 9. p. 123, *fifth and sixth editions.* That to envy the spiritual good of a neighbour is a mortal sin, but to envy his temporal good is venial."—" Pray, Father what is his reason for this ?" " You shall hear—the good which is found in temporal things, is so trifling, and of so little consequence to heaven, that it is of no consideration at all in the view of God and saints.'" " But, Father, if this good be so *trifling,* and of such little value, how is it that you allow mankind to kill each other for the sake of it?" "Ah! you always take things so perversely; this good, it was stated, is of no consideration in the sight of God, but quite otherwise before men." "True, I did not think of that; and, I trust, by means of these distinctions, we shall have no mortal sins in the world." "Oh! don't flatter yourself; for some are always mortal in their very nature, as, for instance, *Idleness*." "O Father, are all the comforts of life to be lost at once, then?" "Hold, Sir— when you have heard the definition which Escobar gives of this vice, you will alter your opinion, tr. 2. ex. 2. n. 81: 'Idleness is a grief that spiritual things should be spiritual, as if it should be regretted that the sacraments are the source of grace; and it is a mortal sin." "O Father! I cannot imagine that any one can be *idle* in such a sense." "So Escobar says a little onward, n. 105: 'I confess it is very seldom that any person falls into the sin of idleness.' Now, surely, you must see the necessity of a good definition!" "I do, Father; and I well remember your other definitions of *assassination*, *ambush*, and *superfluities*. But how is it you do not extend this method to cases of every description, and define every kind of sin in such a manner that indulgence may *never* be a crime?" "It is not always requisite to alter definitions, as you will perceive on the subject of *good cheer*, one of the greatest pleasures of life, and which Escobar allows in the following paragraph, n. 102, of the *Practice of our Society:* 'Is it lawful to eat and drink inordinately, and without necessity, for the mere gratification of a voluptuous appetite? Yes, undoubtedly, says Sanchez, if it do not injure your health, because it is allowable for the natural appetite to enjoy all proper indulgence—*an comedere, bibere, usque ad satietatem absque necessitate ob solam voluptatem, sit peccatum? Cum Sanctio negativè respondeo, modo non obsit valetudini, quia licitè potest appetitus naturalis suis aetibus frui.*'"

"O Father," said I, "this is the most complete passage, the most finished principle in all your system of morals, and the one of all others from which the most *comfortable conclusions* may be deduced! What, then, is not gluttony even a venial sin?" "No—not as I have stated the case: but, according to Escobar, it may become so, n. 56, 'if, without any necessity, you stuff yourself with eating and drinking, till you vomit—*si quis se usque ad vomitum ingurgitet.*'

"But enough on this subject:—I proceed to the facilities we have invented for the avoidance of sin in the conversation and intrigues of the world. One of the most embarrassing things to provide against is *lying*, when it is the object to excite confidence in any false representation. In this case, our doctrine of *equivocals* is of admirable service, by which, says Sanchez, ' it is lawful to use ambiguous terms, to give the impression a different sense from that which you understand yourself,' *Op. Mor.* p. 2. l. 3. c. 6. n. 13." "This I am well aware of, Father." "We have," continued he, "published it so frequently, that in fact every body is acquainted with it: but pray, do you know what is to be done when no equivocal terms can be found?". No, Father."—"Ha, I thought this would be new to you—it is the doctrine of *mental reservations.* Sanchez states it in the same place: ' A person may take an oath that he has not done such a thing, though in fact he has, by saying to himself, it was not done on a certain specified day, or before he was born, or by concealing any other similar circumstance, which gives another meaning to the statement. This is in numberless instances extremely convenient, and is always very just when it is necessary to your health, honour, or property.' "

"But, Father, is not this adding perjury to lying?" "No—Sanchez and Filiutius show the contrary, tr. 25. ch. 11. n. 331: because ' it is the *intention* which stamps the quality of the action :' and the latter, in page 328, furnishes another and surer method of avoiding lying. After saying in an audible voice, *I swear that I did not do this,* you may add inwardly *to-day;* or after affirming aloud *I swear,* you may repeat in a whisper *I say;* and then resuming the former tone—*I did not do it.* Now this you must admit is telling the truth." "I own it is," said I; "but it is telling truth in a whisper, and a lie in an audible voice : besides, I apprehend that very few people have sufficient presence of mind to avail themselves of this deception." "Our Fathers" answered the Jesuit, "have in the same place given directions for those who do not know how to manage these niceties, so that they may be indemnified against the sin of lying, while plainly declaring they have *not* done what in reality they *have*, provided that, in general, they intended to give the same sense to their assertion which a skilful man would have contrived to do.'

"Now tell the truth, have not you sometimes been embarrassed through an ignorance of this doctrine?" "Certainly."—" And will you not admit too that it would often be very convenient to violate your word with a good conscience?" "Surely, one of the most *convenient* things in the world!" "Then, Sir, listen to Escobar, tr. 3. ex. 3. n. 48 ; he gives this general rule : 'Promises are not obligatory when a man has no intention of being bound to fulfil them; and it seldom happens that he has such an intention, unless he confirms it by an oath or bond, so that when he merely says *I will do it*, it is to be understood, *if he do not change his mind* : for he did not intend by what he promised to deprive himself of his liberty.' He furnishes some other rules which you may read for yourself, and concludes thus : 'Every thing is taken from Molina and our other authors—*omnia ex Molina et aliis :*' it is, consequently, indisputable."

"Father," exclaimed I, " I never knew before that the direction of the intention could nullify the obligation of a promise." "Now, then," said he, "you perceive this very much facilitates the intercourse of mankind. Our greatest difficulty, however, has been to regulate the conversation between men and women, for our Fathers are more reserved on the subject of chastity. They treat of questions indeed sufficiently curious and indulgent, but principally in relation to persons married or betrothed."

Here I was informed of some of the most extraordinary questions imaginable. They would absolutely fill many letters, but I refrain from even pointing out the citations.

because you show my letters to people of every description, and I should not wish to gratify those whose only object is amusement.

The only thing I can mention amongst the numberless passages he pointed out in their writings, is that which you may find in the Summary of Sins by Father Bauny, p. 165. referring to certain little intimacies which he excuses, provided the *intention* be rightly directed—as, *how to pass for a gallant;* and you will be surprised to find, p. 148, a principle of morality stated relative to the power which he says that daughters possess of disposing of themselves without the consent of their parents. " When this is done with the daughter's own consent, though the father has reason for complaining, yet neither the daughter, nor the person to whom she has prostituted herself, have done the father any injury, or violated justice with respect to him, because the daughter's purity is as much her own possession as her body, and she may do whatever she pleases with the latter, except committing suicide or cutting off a member." From this specimen you may form a judgment of the rest.

Here a passage from a heathen poet occurred to me, who was a much better casuist than these divines, for he says, "The virginity of a daughter does not belong entirely to herself, but partly to the father and partly to the mother, without whom she cannot even dispose of herself in marriage :" and I exceedingly doubt whether there be any judge who would not refuse to take the maxim of Father Bauny for a law.

This is all I am able to relate of this conversation, which lasted so long that I was at length obliged to request the good Father to change the subject; which he did, and entertained me with their regulations for female dress in the following manner : " We will not speak of those whose direct purpose is immodest, but as to others, Escobar says, tr. 1. ex. 8. n. 5 : ' If they dress without any base intention and solely to gratify the natural taste they have for display—*ob naturalem fastus inclinationem* it is either a venial sin or no sin at all ;' and Father Bauny, in his Summary of Sins, c. 46. p. 1094, declares, 'Although a woman felt aware of the bad effect which her studious care in adorning her person would produce on the bodies and souls of those who should observe her thus ornamented with costly decorations, she nevertheless would commit no sin by making use of such attire ;' and he cites our Father Sanchez as of a similar opinion."

"But what answer do your authors return to those passages of Scripture which so severely reprebend the smallest inconsistencies of this nature?" 'Lessius,' said he, "has very learnedly replied to this, *De Just*. l. 4. c. 4. d. 14. by stating, that ' those precepts of Scripture regarded only the ladies of that age who were required to furnish an edifying example of modesty to the heathen.'" "Pray, Father," inquired I, "whence did he obtain that information?" "Pshaw! It signifies nothing where he obtained it ; the sentiments of these great men are always *probable* in themselves. But Father le Moine suggests a limitation of this general license, for he would not allow it to old women. This occurs in his Easy Devotion, p. 127, 157, 163 : ' Young ladies have a natural right to adorn their persons. It is allowable at a time of life which is the very flower and bloom of existence. But at that period they must stop : it would be strange and unseasonable to seek for roses in the snow, and stars should only appear constantly at a ball, because they have the gift of perpetual youth. It is best, therefore, to consult reason and a good looking-glass to yield to decency and necessity, and retire at the approach of night." "Very judicious." "But," continued he, " that you may see how careful our Fathers have been upon every point, I must state, that permitting women to practise gaming, and perceiving that such an allowance would be often useless, if they were not also supplied with pecuniary resources for the purpose, they have established another maxim in their favour which is to be found in Escobar in the chapter on *Thieving*, tr. 1. n. 13 : 'A woman may game, and for this purpose take money secretly from her husband.'"

"This is noble, Father," said I. "Oh, but there are many other things to be said—we must, however, omit them for the sake of mentioning maxims of still greater importance, which very materially facilitate the practice of piety; for instance, the *manner of attending upon mass.* Our great divines Gaspar Hurtado *de Sacr.* t. 2. d. 5. disp. 2. and Coninck, q. 83. a. 6. n. 197. state, that ' it is sufficient to present the body at mass, though the spirit be absent: provided the coumtenance indicate a respectful gravity.' Vasquez goes further, by saying, ' It is enough to hear mass, though you have no intention of really performing any thing.' All this is likewise to be found in Escobar, tr. 1. ex. 11. n. 74 and 107, and again, tr. 1. ex. 1. n. 116. where he explains the subject by the example of those who are compelled to go to mass, but who resolve to pay no attention to it." " Truly, Father, I could never have believed this, if I had heard it from any other quarter." "Undoubtedly," said he, " it does require the authority of these distinguished writers, as well as that of Escobar, who says, tr. 1. ex. 11. n 31 ; ' A wicked intention, such as unchaste desire, united with the hearing of mass as it ought to be attended, is no prevention of the due fulfilment of the duty—*nec obest alia prava intentio, ut aspiciendi libidinosè fœminas.*'

"Turrianus, one of our learned authors, suggests, however, a still more agreeable sentiment, *Select.* p. 2. d. 16. dub. 7: ' You may hear half a mass of one priest and another half of another; indeed you may hear first the end of one mass, and afterwards the beginning of another' —nay more, he adds, ' You may hear two halves of a mass at the same time of two different priests, when one begins a mass, and the other is at the elevation of the host, because the attention may be given to both at the same time, and two half masses make one whole one—*duæ medietates unam missam constituunt.*' Our Fathers Bauny, tr. 69. 9. p. 312 ; Hurtado *de Sacr.* t. 2. *de Missa,* d. 5.

diff. 4 ; Azorius, p. 1. l. 7. cap. 3. q. 3. have given a similar opinion ; and Escobar affirms the same in his chapter respecting 'the Practice of hearing Mass according to our Society,' tr. 1. ex. 11. n. 73 ; and you will see the consequences he deduces in the same book in the several editions printed at Lyons, in the years 1644 and 1646 ; ' Hence I conclude that mass may be heard in a very short time ; as, for example, if you happen upon four masses at once, so arranged, that when one begins, another may be at the Gospel, another at the Consecration, and the last at the Communion.' " " True, true, Father ; and one might hear mass in Notre Dame by this means in an instant." " You perceive then, I trust, that nothing could be better managed to facilitate the duty of hearing mass.

" But I wish to show you in what manner the use of Sacraments is smoothed, especially that of *Penitence*. It is in this particular that you will discover the extreme kindness of our indulgent Fathers ; and you will be astonished that the devotion which strikes the whole world with wonder, has been treated with such prudence and sagacity by our Fathers, ' that having destroyed that scarecrow which devils had placed at the gate, they have rendered penance more easy than vice and voluptuousness ; so that, to use the language of Father le Moine, p. 244 and 291 of his Easy Devotion—' simply to live is incomparably more difficult than to live piously.' Is not this a marvellous change ?" " Upon my word, Father, it is ; but I cannot forbear expressing my mind. I am very apprehensive that you are taking bad measures, and that this indulgence will disgust more than it will gratify the world. Mass, for instance, is so great and so holy a thing, that your authors would suffer materially in the estimation of a great many people, were they to see the manner in which they speak of it." " This, to be sure, is true enough respecting some ; but are you not aware that we accommodate people of every description ? It seems that you do not remember what I have so frequently mentioned ; but I propose to renew the subject the very first opportunity, deferring at present our conversation upon the mitigating expedients with regard to confession. I shall make this so plain, that you will never forget it."

We now parted; and our next conversation will, I presume, relate to their politics.

I am, &c.

LETTER X.

Mitigating Expedients of the Jesuists, with regard to the Sacrament of Penitence. Their Maxims respecting Confession, Satisfaction, Absolution, Occasions of Sin, Contrition, and the Love of God.

Paris, Aug. 2, 1656.

SIR,

I am not yet come to the investigation of the politics of the society, but I proceed to one of its great principles. You will now have an opportunity of seeing those allowances in reference to confession, which most certainly constitute the very best expedient the Jesuits could have devised to conciliate all and offend none. It was necessary to know this, before we advanced further; for which reason, the Father considered it proper to give me the following instructions:—

"You have seen, by what I have already stated, how successfully our Fathers have laboured to show, by their superior wisdom, that many things are permitted now which were formerly deemed forbidden; but as some sins are still indefensible, and the only remedy for them is confession, it has been thought necessary to obviate the difficulty in the manner I am about to mention. And, after showing you, in our past conversations, how certain conscientious scruples may be removed, by proving that what was once supposed to be sinful, really is not so, it only remains for me to point out the mode of expiating real sins with facility, by making confession easy, which was formerly so difficult."

"Pray, Father," said I, "how is this accomplished?"
"By those admirable subtleties," said he, "which are

peculiar to our society, and which our Flemish Fathers call (in a book entitled, 'The Image of the Primitive Age,' l. 3, or, 1. p. 401, and l. 1. c. 2.) '*pious and holy frauds, and a sacred artifice of devotion—piam et religiosam calliditatem et pietatis solertiam*—in l. 3. c. 8.' It is by these inventions that 'crimes are now expiated *alacrius*, with more gladness and zeal than they were once committed; so that many persons remove the stain of guilt as soon as it is perpetrated—*plurimi vix citius maculas contrahunt, quam eluunt*'—as it is stated in the same passage." "Oh, I beseech you, Father," said I, "teach me some of these useful pieces of finesse." "Well, sir, there is a considerable number of them; for, as there are many painful things in confession, we have applied lenitives to each of them: and, as the principal difficulties consist in the shame of confessing certain sins, the careful particularity with which the circumstances must be explained, the penance which must be done, the resolution not to return to the commission of the sin, the avoidance of occasions that lead to it, and the sorrow for the offence, I hope to show you that there is now nothing vexatious in all this, in consequence of the extreme care which has been taken to extract all the unpalatable bitterness out of so needful a remedy.

"To begin with the pain which the confession of some kinds of sin must occasion. As it is frequently very important as you know to preserve the esteem of your confessor, is it not a fortunate circumstance that our Fathers, amongst whom are Escobar and Suarez, tr. 7. a. 4. n. 135. admit of having two confessors, 'the one for mortal and the other for venial sins, for the purpose of maintaining a good reputation with your ordinary confessor—*ut bonam famam apud ordinarium tueatur*—provided only that advantage be not taken from this circumstance to continue in a state of mortal sin.' Another ingenious contrivance is afterwards suggested for confessing to your ordinary confessor without his perceiving whether the sin was committed previously or since your last confession: 'this,' says he, 'is managed by means of a general confession, and confounding your last sin with others, to which your self-accusation refers in the aggregate.' See also *Princ.* ex. 2. n. 73. and you will be convinced that the decision of Father Bauny, *Theol. Mor.* tr. 49. 15. p. 137. is still more consolatory to those who are ashamed of acknowledging their relapses: 'The confessor, excepting in certain cases, which rarely occur, has no right to inquire whether the sin of which the individual accuses himself be habitual, nor is the penitent obliged to answer such a question; because he has no right to put the person confessing sins to the shame of divulging his frequent relapses and falls.'"

"How can this be, Father? I should as soon be disposed to say that a physician has no right to ask his patient respecting the time he has been afflicted with a fever. Do not all sins differ from each other according to the diversity of circumstances? And ought not a genuine penitent to disclose to his confessor the whole state of his conscience, with the same sincerity and frankness as if he were speaking to Jesus Christ, whose place is held by the priest? But is not that person very far from cherishing such a disposition who conceals his frequent relapses for the purpose of veiling the enormity of his transgressions?"

I saw that the good Father was prodigiously embarrassed; and he thought of evading the difficulty instead of resolving it, by urging upon my consideration another of their rules which only establishes a new disorder without in the least rectifying Father Bauny's decision, and one which in my opinion is one of their most pernicious maxims, the most directly adapted to encourage sinners in their vices. "I admit," said he, "that habit increases the malignity of sin, but does not change its nature; for which reason the penitent is not obliged to confess according to the law established by our Fathers and cited by Escobar, *Prin.* ex. 2. n. 39: 'No one is obliged to confess more than the circumstances which change the species of his sin, not those which render it more odious.' Hence Father Grenados says, in 5. *part.* cont. 7. t. 9. d.

9. n. 22 : 'that if any one has eaten flesh in Lent, it is sufficient to accuse himself of having broken his fast, without saying whether it was by eating flesh or making two meagre meals :' and, according to our Father Reginaldus, tr. 1. l. 6. c. 4. n. 116 : ' A sorcerer who should make use of the diabolical art, is not obliged to avow this circumstance ; it is enough simply to declare that he deals in divination, without explaining whether it be by chiromancy or by covenant with the devil ;' and Fagundez, of our society, p. 2. l. 4. c. 3, n. 17. states, that 'a man is not required to confess the circumstances of a rape, if a degree of consent were obtained.' Our Father Escobar introduces these statements in the same place, n. 41, 61, 62, with many other very curious decisions respecting the circumstances one is not necessitated to confess, which you may read at your leisure."

"Very accommodating," said I, " very accommodating *artifices* of devotion indeed!" " Yes ; but all would signify nothing if we had not contrived to mitigate the severity of *penance* which is very much opposed to confession. But now the most delicate have nothing to apprehend, since we have maintained in our theses in the College of Clermont, ' that if the confessor impose a *convenient* and suitable penance—*convenientem*—and yet he should not choose to accept it, he may withdraw and renounce both the absolution and the penance imposed.' Escobar further states, in his Practice of Penance according to our society, tr. 7. ex. 4. n. 188, that, ' if the penitent declare that he will defer his penitence to a future world, and suffer in purgatory all the punishment due to his offences, then the confessor is to impose a slight penance to preserve the Sacrament entire, especially if he knew that the penitent would not submit to a heavier one.' " " If this be the case," observed I, " confession should not be called the sacrament of penance." " There," returned he, " you are wrong ; for it is proper to enjoin some one at least for the sake of the form." " But, Father, do you conceive that a man deserves absolution, when he objects to the least painful service to expiate his offences? And when people are in such a disposition of mind, ought you not rather to retain than remit their sins? Have you a correct idea of the extent of your ministry, and are you not aware that you possess the power of binding and loosing? Do you suppose it is lawful to bestow absolution indifferently upon all who demand it, without previously knowing whether Jesus Christ looses in heaven those whom you loose upon earth?"

"Fine talking, truly, Sir! What! do you think we are so ignorant as not to know, that 'the confessor is to make himself the judge of the disposition of his penitent, both because he is under an obligation not to dispense the Sacraments to those who are unworthy of them, Jesus Christ having commanded him to be faithful to his charge, and not to give the children's bread to dogs; and because he is to be judge, and it is the duty of a judge to judge justly, by releasing those who are worthy of it, and binding those who are unworthy, and also because he ought not to absolve those whom Jesus Christ condemns?'" "Pray, Father, whose words are these?" "I have been quoting Filiutius, tom. 1. tr. 7. n. 354." "You surprise me; I concluded they were the expressions of one of the Fathers of the church. But this passage ought deeply to impress confessors, and make them extremely cautious in dispensing this Sacrament to ascertain whether the sorrow of their penitents be sufficient, and whether their promises to avoid future transgressions be really admissible." "There is no difficulty here," said the Father; "Filiutius has taken care to prevent the confessors suffering any embarrassment; for, after the words I have cited, he suggests this easy expedient—'The confessor may make himself quite easy about the disposition of his penitent; for if he do not discover sufficient indications of grief, the confessor has only to ask if he do not detest sin in his heart, and if he reply in the affirmative, he is obliged to believe him. The same may be said respecting his resolution for the future, unless he is under an engagement to make any restitution, or to avoid the next temptation.'" "This passage, Father, I see plainly enough is from Filiutius." "There again you are deceived, for he has taken it word for word out of Suarez, in 3 par. to 4. disp. 32. sect. 2. n. 2." "But, Father, this last quotation nullifies the former ; for confessors will no longer have it in their power to judge of the disposition of their penitents, since they are obliged to take their own assertion, even when they give no sufficient evidence of repentance. Is there so much certainty in these affirmations, that no further evidence can be requisite ? I question whether your Fathers have found, by experience, that all those who have given them promises have kept them faithfully. I am, indeed, much mistaken if they have not frequently found the very reverse." 'Pshaw," said he "that signifies nothing ; the confessors are nevertheless obliged to believe them. Father Bauny, who has thoroughly investigated this subject in his Summary of Sins, c. 46. p. 1090, 1091, 1092, concludes, that 'at all times when those who have often relapsed into sin without manifesting any signs of amendment, shall present themselves before a confessor, and tell him that they repent of what they have done and resolve to be better in future, he ought to believe their declaration, though it be presumed that such resolutions only proceeded from the lips and not the heart : and though afterwards such persons plunge into the same excesses and even with greater licentiousness, they may, notwithstanding, in my opinion, receive absolution.' Now, I trust, all your doubts are removed."

"But, Father," continued I, "you impose, I think, a very serious responsibility upon the confessors, by requiring them to believe the very contrary of what they see." "You do not understand the matter ; I mean to say, they are obliged to act and to absolve, as if they believed the resolution to be firm and constant, though they do not, in point of fact, believe one syllable of it. This is what our Fathers Suarez and Filiutius proceed to explain ; for, after saying that 'the priest is obliged to believe his penitent upon his word,' they add, "it is not necessary that the confessor should be convinced that his penitent will execute his good determination, nor even that it is probable; but it is sufficient that he thinks the general purpose exists in his mind at the moment, though in a very little time he is likely to relapse.' In this all our authors concur—*ita docent omnes autores*; and will you doubt of any thing under these circumstances?" "But pray, good Father, what will become of the acknowledgment which Father Petau himself was obliged to make in his preface to *Pen. pub.* p. 4. 'That the holy Fathers, Doctors, and Councils agree in this, as an undoubted truth, that the repentance which is preparatory to the Eucharist ought to be sincere, constant, courageous, not indolent and sluggish, nor subject to relapses?'" "But do you not perceive," said he, "that Father Petau is speaking of the *ancient church?* And this is now so *out of date*, to use the phraseology of our society, that, according to Father Bauny, tr. 49. 15. p. 95. the contrary alone is true. He remarks, 'There are some authors who affirm that absolution ought to be refused to such as often relapse into the same sins, especially if after being frequently absolved no sign of amendment appears—others negative this sentiment. But the only true opinion is, that it is not necessary to refuse absolution; and though they do not profit by the good advice so often given them, though they pay no regard to their repeated promises to change their manner of living, though they take no pains to reform and purify themselves— no matter—the true opinion and what ought to be followed, whatever others may allege, is, that in all these cases absolution ought to be conferred:' and tr. 49. 22. p. 100: 'Absolution ought neither to be refused nor delayed to such as are in the habit of sinning against the laws of God, of nature, and of the church, though no one can see any hope of amendment—*etsi emendationis futuræ nulla spes appareat.*'"

"But, Father," returned I. "might not this assurance of always gaining absolution induce sinners"—"I understand you," interrupting me—"but listen to Father Bauny, 9, 15; 'It is proper to absolve the person who avows that the expectation of being absolved induced him to sin with more readiness than he should have otherwise done without such an expectation;' and Father Caussin, in support of this proposition, says, p. 211 of his reply to *Theol. Mor.* that, ' If this representation were not true, the use of confession would be nullified to the majority of mankind, and sinners would have no other remedy but a cord and a gallows.' " " Oh, Father, how these maxims will attract people to your confessionals!" "Yes," said he, " you cannot imagine the numbers that come—' we are loaded and pressed down with a crowd of penitents—*pœnitentium numero obruimur*,' as it is expressed in the Image of our first age, l. 3. c. 8." " I know," said I, " an easy method of affording you some relief; it is simply to oblige sinners to avoid the immediate occasions of sinning; you would be amazingly eased only by this single device." " Oh Sir, we are not so anxious respecting relief; on the contrary, as it is stated in the same work, l. 3. c. 7. p. 374 ' Our society has for its object to labour in establishing virtue, to make war against vice, and to save a multitude of souls;' but as few souls are willing to abandon the immediate occasions of sin, we have been obliged to define what is intended by *immediate occasions.*' This may be found in Escobar on the Practice of our Society, tr. 7. ex 4. n. 226 : ' That occasion is not called *immediate*, when the sin is but rarely committed, such as a sin perpetrated through a sudden transport of passion, three or four times a year in the house where you reside;' or, according to Father Bauny, ' once or twice a month,' p. 1082, and again p. 1089, of his French publication, where he proposes this question, ' What ought to be done with masters and servants and cousins of both sexes living together, who from this cause mutually induce each other to sin?' " " Separate them, said I, " surely." " True, and our authors say the same *if they transgress often and almost daily;* but if they offend but seldom, as once or twice in a month, and they cannot be parted without great inconvenience and detriment, they may receive absolution according to these authors; and among them we find Suarez, provided the firmly promise to sin no more, and are truly sorry for the past."

I understood his meaning perfectly; for he had before assured me that the confessor ought to be satisfied with a verbal regret.

He continued—" Father Bauny, p. 1083 and 1084, allows such as are engaged in these more immediate occasions, ' to remain in them when they cannot be abandoned without becoming the subjects of public scandal, and thus suffering great inconvenience.' He advances the same idea in his Moral Theology, tr. 4. *de Pœnit*. q. 13. p. 93, and 9. 14 p. 94 : ' A priest may and ought to give absolution to a woman who has a man in her house with whom she often sins, if she cannot handsomely get rid of him, or has some reason for keeping him—*si non potest honestè ejicere, aut habeat aliquam causam retinendi*—provided only that she proposes to have no more criminal connexion with him.' "

" Oh, Father, the duty of abandoning these occasions of sinning is charmingly softened down, if persons be dispensed from it as soon as it is inconvenient ; but, I suppose they are at least obliged to separate when it is attended with no trouble or difficulty." " Yes ; though there are some exceptions ; for Father Bauny says in the same place, ' It is lawful for any person to go into a house of ill fame to convert dissolute women, though it be very probable he fall into sin himself ; as, if he have on former occasions been frequently left to sin by their seductions ; and though some doctors do not approve of this opinion, and do not consider it proper voluntarily to endanger one's own salvation to save a neighbour, I confess myself disposed to embrace the sentiment which they oppose."

" This is a new order of preachers, Father ! But pray, what authority has Father Bauny to send persons on this kind of mission ?" " On one of the principles of Basile Ponce," returned he, " quoted in the same place. I spoke of it before, as I think you may remember ; ' An occasion of sin may be sought directly and by itself, *primò et per se,* for the temporal or spiritual good of oneself or neighbour.' "

I was now struck with such horror, that I was on the point of breaking off the conversation, but managed to restrain my feelings in order to see the end of it, and contented myself with asking, ' What agreement subsists between this doctrine and that of the Gospel, which requires us to pluck out our eyes, and debar ourselves even of necessaries, when prejudicial to our salvation ? And how can you conceive that a man who indulges in these occasions of sin, can sincerely detest it ? Is it not, on the contrary, too visible, that he is not affected with its enormity as he ought to be, and that he is far from that true conversion of heart which would make him love God as much as he had before loved creatures ?"

" How surprisingly you talk!" said he : " that would be *true contrition :* you do not seem to know, as Father Pintereau says in the second part of Abbé de Boisic, p. 50, that ' all the Fathers unanimously teach that it is an error, amounting almost to a heresy, to represent contrition as necessary, or to affirm that attrition alone, arising *solely* from the fear of hell, which preserves the will from sinning, is not sufficient with the Sacrament." " How, Father! is it almost an article of faith that attrition alone, originating merely in the fear of punishment, suffices with the Sacrament? I believe this doctrine is peculiar to your Fathers : for others who believe attrition to be sufficient with the Sacrament, maintain, that it should at least be mixed with some love to God. And, moreover, it seems to me, that even your own authors did not formerly regard this doctrine as so certain ; for your Father Suarez speaks of it in this manner, *De Pœn.* q. 90. art 4. disp. 15. sect. 4. n. 17 : ' Though it be a probable opinion, that attrition is sufficient with the Sacrament, yet it is not certain, and perhaps is false—*non est certa, et potest esse falsa.* If it be false, attrition is not sufficient to save a man ; he, therefore, who dies knowingly in that state, voluntarily exposes himself to the moral danger of eternal damnation. This opinion is neither very ancient, nor very common—*nec valdè antiqua, nec multùm antiquis.*' Sanchez intimates a similar uncertainty in his Summary, l. 1. c. 9. n. 34 : ' A sick man, and his confessor, who should satisfy himself in the hour of death with attrition and the Sacrament, would both commit a mortal sin, on account of the great danger of damnation to which the penitent would expose himself, if the opinion that attrition suffices with the Sacrament should not be true.' To the same purpose Comitolus, *Resp. Mor.* l. 1. q. 32. n. 7. 8 : ' He is not too sure that attrition is sufficient with the Sacrament.' "

Here the worthy Father stopped me, exclaiming, " Do you read our authors, then? Very good—but you will do better not to read them, without some one of us : for, by reading them alone, you see that you are ready to infer that these passages are opposed to those who, at present maintain our doctrine of attrition, whereas we could have shown, that nothing tends more to promote it. How glorious is it for our Fathers, to see their opinion so universally diffused, that, excepting divines, there is scarcely any person but believes our doctrine of attrition to have been the uniform sentiment of the church! When, therefore, you prove from our own Fathers, that only a few years ago, this opinion was held uncertain, what is it but to allow our modern authors all the honour of its establishment ?

" On this account, our intimate friend, Diana, believed he was obliging us by pointing out its gradual progress to perfection, which he has done, p. 5. tr. 13. by saying, ' that formerly the ancient scholastics maintained that contrition was necessary immediately after committing a mortal sin ; but since that period, it was not thought obligatory, except on festival days, and afterwards, when some extraordinary calamity threatened a whole nation; and, according to others, it ought not to be long deferred when death was evidently approaching. However, our Fathers Hurtado and Vasquez, have given an admirable refutation of all these opinions, proving that contrition is necessary only when a person cannot be absolved any own power, it would leave nothing to be done by the Sacrament. Thus our Father Valentia, the celebrated Jesuit, tom. 4. disp. 79. 8. p. 6: 'Contrition is not at all necessary to obtain the principal effect of the Sacrament, but, on the contrary, is rather an obstacle—*imò obstat potiùs quo minùs effectus sequatur.*' Nothing more can be wished in favour of attrition." "I am of the same opinion, Father," said I; "but allow me to express my sentiment, and to show you to what extravagances this doctrine leads. When you say that attrition, *arising solely from the fear of punishment,* is sufficient with the Sacrament for the justification of sinners, does it not follow that a person may expiate his sins, and be saved without ever loving God in the whole course of his life? But will you, Fathers, venture to maintain this principle?"

"I see," said he, "by your question, that you want to know the doctrine of our Fathers respecting the love of God. It is the last and most important point in their morality, which you might have perceived by the quotations I have introduced upon the subject of contrition. But pray do not interrupt me while I am furnishing some others of a more precise nature upon the love of God, for the consequences resulting from them are considerable. Attend to Escobar, who relates the different opinions of our authors on this subject, in 'the Practice of the Love of God according to our Society,' tr. 1. ex. 2. n. 21. and tr. 5. ex. 4. n. 8: 'When' he asks, 'is a person obliged to cherish a real affection for God? Suarez says, 'it is sufficient to love him a little previous to the moment of death,' without fixing the precise time:—Vasquez, 'that it is enough to love him in the very moment of dying:'—others, 'at Baptism;' others again, 'at seasons of contrition;' and some, 'upon festival days:' but our Father Castro Palao opposes all these opinions and with good reason—*meritò*. Hurtado de Mendoza states, that 'we are under an obligation to love God once in a year, and that we are kindly treated in not being obliged to it more frequently:' but Father Coninck that we are under an obligation to do so 'once in three or four years'—Henri quez, 'every five years;' and Filiutius says, 'it is probable that we are not rigorously obliged to it every five years.' When then?—This question he refers to a wise man's own judgment."

I allowed him to proceed with this nonsense, which was a surprising display of the insolence with which the human mind can sport with the love of God:—" But," continued he, " our Father Anthony Sirmond, who excels upon this subject, in his admirable book on the 'Defence of Virtue,' where, as he tells the reader, *he speaks in plain terms*, expresses himself thus,—tr. 2. sect. 1. p. 12, 13, 14, &c. ' St. Thomas says, we are under obligation to love God as soon as we acquire the use of reason;' but that is a little too soon. Scotus mentions every Sunday; but on what authority? Others, in seasons of grievous temptation: *right*, in case this is the only way of avoiding temptation. Sotus states, that when some great benefit has been conferred by God, it is well to thank him for it. Others speak of the hour of death: that is too little. Nor do I believe it to be necessary on every sacramental occasion: attrition will suffice with confession, if it be convenient. Suarez says that we are obliged to love God some time: but at what time? You are to be the judge of that; he professes to know nothing about it. But if such a doctor as this does not know, I am at a loss to conceive who does.' And he concludes at last, that, in strict propriety, we are only obliged to observe the other commandments without cherishing any affection to God, and without having any inclination of mind towards him, provided we do not hate him: this is illustrated throughout his second treatise. You will see it in every page, particularly in p. 16, 19, 24, 28, where the following passage occurs: 'God, in commanding us to love him, is satisfied if we obey him in his other commands. If God had said, · I will consign you to perdition, whatever obedience you render to me, unless you also give me your heart, would this motive, think you, have been well suited to the end which God has in view?' It is said, therefore, that we shall love God by doing his otherwise, or is at the point of death.' But, to proceed, respecting the wonderful progress of this doctrine, I must add, that our Fathers Fagundez, *Præc.* 2. t. 2. c. 4. n. 13., Granados, in 3 par. contr. 7. d. 3. sect. 4. n. 17., and Escobar, tr 7. ex. 4. n. 88. in the 'Practice of our Society,' have decided 'that contrition is not necessary even in dying moments, because if attrition with the Sacrament be not sufficient at the point of death, it will follow, that attrition would not be sufficient with the sacrament.'—— And our learned Hurtado *de Sacr.* d. 6. quoted by Diana, par 5. tr 4. *Misal.* r 193. and by Escobar, tr. 7. ex. 4. n. 91, goes still further; only listen: 'Is the sorrow for sin which arises entirely from its temporal consequences, as the loss of health, or property, sufficient?—Here, a distinction is requisite: if it be thought that the evil is not sent immediately from the hand of God, this sorrow is not sufficient; but if it be believed that it is so sent, and in fact every evil, as Diana says, excepting sin proceeds from him, this sorrow is sufficient.' Escobar states the same in his 'Practice of our Society,' in which Father Francis Lamy concurs, tr. 8. disp. 3. n. 13."

"You really surprise me, Father; for I see nothing in all this attrition but what is merely natural; and thus a sinner may render himself worthy of absolution, without any supernatural grace: but every one knows that was condemned as a heresy by the Council of Trent" "I should have thought the same," said he, " but yet it must be otherwise; for our Fathers of the College of Clermont, maintained, in their theses of the 23d of May, and the 6th of June, 1644, col. 4. n. 1. 'that attrition may be holy and sufficient for the Sacrament, though it be not supernatural;' and in that of August, 1643, 'That attrition which is only natural, is sufficient for the Sacrament, provided it be honest—*ad sacramentum sufficit attritio naturalis, modò honesta.*'

"This is all that can be said, unless an obvious inference be deduced from these premises, that contrition is so little necessary to the Sacrament, that, on the contrary, it would be detrimental to it, because, as it effaces sin by its will, as if we loved him with the affections of the soul, and as if we were excited by love itself. If this should really be the case, so much the better; if not, we do not, however, strictly disobey the commandment of love, while performing these works; so that we are not so much commanded to *love him*—(pray observe the goodness of God!) as *not to hate* him.'

"Thus have our Fathers discharged mankind from the *painful* obligation of actually, and with all the heart, loving God: and so advantageous is this doctrine, that our Fathers Annat, Pintereau, Le Moine, and A. Sirmond himself have strenuously defended it whenever opposed. You have only to examine their replies to the Moral Theology, and that of Father Pintereau in p. 2. of Abbé de Boisic, p. 53, where you may judge of the value of this dispensation by the price it cost, the price of the blood of Jesus Christ. The very crown and perfection of this doctrine, is its releasing from the *troublesome* obligation of loving God, which is the privilege of the evangelical as distinguished from the Jewish law. 'It was reasonable,' says he, 'that by the law of grace in the New Testament, God should remove the irksome and difficult duty which was attached to the rigorous law of exercising an act of perfect contrition in order to justification, and that he should institute Sacraments to supply our defects, and to facilitate obedience; otherwise Christians, who are the children, could not recover the good graces of their Father, any more readily than the Jews, who were slaves, could obtain mercy from their God.'"

"Oh, Father," exclaimed I, "you make me out of all patience; I am struck with perfect horror at these statements." "It is not I that am responsible," said he. "I know very well," said I, "they are not your own words, but you cite them without any sign of disapprobation; nay, so far are you from detesting the authors of these maxims, you hold them in the highest esteem for promulgating them. Have you no apprehension that your concurrence renders you a partaker of their crimes?

Can you be ignorant that St. Paul judges worthy of death. not only the originators of wickedness, but those who consent to it? Was it not sufficient to allow mankind so many prohibited things by your palliatives and apologies? Must you also furnish them with the opportunity of perpetrating crimes which you admit to be inexcusable, by that assurance and facility of obtaining absolution which you offer them, though for this purpose you destroy the power of the priests, and oblige them to absolve, rather like slaves than judges, the most abandoned transgressors, without any change of life, without any sign of repentance but promises a thousand times violated, without penance, *unless they choose it*, and without avoiding occasions of sin, *if such avoidance be attended with any inconvenience?*

"But you advance a step further, and the liberty you take of corrupting the most holy rules of Christian conduct, extends even to the entire subversion of the divine laws. You violate *the great commandment which contains both the law and the prophets*—you stab piety to the very heart—you take away and quench the spirit which gives life—you affirm that the love of God is not necessary to salvation, and even assert, that 'this exemption from loving God is the grand benefit which Christ has conferred upon the world;'—all which is the very acme and perfection of impiety.

"What!—The price of the blood of Jesus Christ obtain an exemption from loving him!!—Previous to the incarnation mankind were obliged to love God, but since *God so loved the world that he gave his only begotten Son*, shall the world thus redeemed, be discharged from the duty of loving him? Strange divinity of our days! Marvellously strange! You dare to take away the anathema which St. Paul pronounces against those who *love not the Lord Jesus Christ!* You destroy what St. John says, that *he that loveth not abideth in death!* and even the declaration of Christ himself—*he that loveth me not, keepeth not my commandments.* In this manner you make those worthy of enjoying the presence of God for ever, who never once loved him in all their lives! This surely is the mystery of iniquity complete! Oh, my good Father, at length open your eyes; and, if not properly affected with the other monstrous doctrines of your casuists, let these latter specimens withdraw your confidence by their excessive extravagance! With all my heart I cherish this wish for you and all your fraternity, and pray God that he would condescend to show them how false-that light is which conducts to such precipices and dangers, and to fill the hearts of those with his love, who dare to dispense others from the obligation."

After some further considerations of the same kind, I left the Jesuit; and it is scarcely probable I shall renew my visit. It need not, however, be any subject of regret to you; for if it were necessary to explain any more of their maxims, I have read a sufficient number of their writings to be able to tell you almost as much of their morality, and perhaps more of their politics, than he would have done himself.

I am, &c.

LETTER XI.

ADDRESSED TO THE REVEREND FATHERS OF THE JESUITS.

Ridiculous Errors may be refuted by Raillery. The precautions it is necessary to use, which the Author has observed, but which have not been regarded by the Jesuits. The impious buffooneries of Fathers le Moine and Garasse.

REVEREND FATHERS,   Aug. 18, 1656.

I HAVE seen the letters you have circulated in opposition to those I wrote to one of my friends upon the subject of your morality, in which one of your principal points of defence is, my not having spoken of your maxims with sufficient seriousness This you repeat in all your communications, and go so far as to say, "that I have turned sacred things into ridicule."

This reproach, my good Fathers, is very astonishing, and very unjust. In what passage have I turned sacred things into ridicule? You notice particularly the *contract Mohatra* and *the story of John d'Alba*: but do you call these sacred things? Is Mohatra something so venerable that it would be blasphemous to speak disrespectfully of it? And are the lectures of Father Bauny upon thieving, and which induced John d'Alba to practise it against yourselves, so sacred that you have a right to represent it as an act of impiety to ridicule them?

What! Fathers, are the fancies of your authors to pass for articles of faith? And may not some passages in

Escobar be laughed at, as well as the fantastic and unchristian decisions of some of your writers, without incurring the charge of making a jest of religion? Is it possible that you can so often venture to repeat such absurd representations? Are you not seriously apprehensive, that, while censuring me for ridiculing your extravagances, you will furnish me with a new subject of mockery, namely, *that very censure itself?* that I shall retort it upon yourselves, by showing that I have ridiculed nothing in your writings but what was really ridiculous? and thus, by making a jest of your morality, I have absolutely been as far from ridiculing sacred things, as the doctrine of your casuists is remote from the holy doctrine of the Gospel?

There is a wonderful difference, my good Fathers, between laughing at religion, and laughing at those who profane it by their extravagant opinions. It would, indeed, be impious to disregard the truths which the Spirit of God has revealed; but it would be impious also not to treat with merited contempt the falsehoods with which the vain spirit of man has opposed them. For, since you compel me to enter upon this subject, I beg you to consider, that as the great principles of Christianity deserve our love and respect, those errors which are diametrically opposite to them, merit contempt and hatred. There are two things sufficiently obvious in the truths of our religion, a divine beauty which renders them lovely, and a holy majesty which makes them venerable; and there are two observable peculiarities in errors, an impiety which renders them horrible, and an impertinence which makes them ridiculous. For this reason the saints always cherish these two sentiments of love and fear for truth, and their wisdom is comprised in fear, which is the principle, and love, which is the end; and on the other hand, they have always entertained feelings of hatred and contempt for error, and their zeal is equally engaged in vigorously resisting the malignity of the wicked, and in putting their extravagance and folly to the blush by ridicule.

Do not then, good Fathers, pretend to make the world believe that it is unworthy of a Christian to laugh at your errors, since it would be very easy to convince those who do not know the fact, that this practice is just, that it is common with the Fathers of the church, and that it is authorized by Scripture, by the example of the most eminent saints, and even by God himself.

Have you not observed that God both abhors and despises sinners at the same time? And even at the very hour of their death, a time when their state is most deplorable and wretched, divine wisdom will unite mockery and ridicule with the anger which consigns them to everlasting punishment—*in interitu vestro ridebo et subsannabo*. Acting upon a similar principle, the saints will do the same, since David intimates, that when they witness the condemnation of the wicked, " the righteous shall see and fear, and shall laugh at him—*videbunt justi et timebunt et super cum ridebunt.*" Job speaks to the same purpose: " the righteous shall laugh them to scorn—*innocens subsannabit cos.*"

But it is very remarkable on this subject, that the very first adddress of God to man, after his fall, was according to the Fathers, ironical—*a poignant sarcasm*. After Adam had transgressed, through the hope which the devil had excited that he should be as God, the sacred writings state that the Divine Being subjected him to the punishment of death, and after inflicting this melancholy mark of the displeasure due to his offences, he derided him in the following words: " Behold the man is become as one of us!—*ecce Adam quasi unus ex nobis!* which is, according to St. Chrysostom and other expositors, *a keen and obvious irony*, by which he *cut him to the heart.* " Adam," says Rupert, " deserved to be thus ridiculed, and was made much more sensible of his folly by this ironical expression, than he could have been by any serious address. Hugh of St. Victor, after stating a similar idea, adds, " This irony was due to his sottish credulity. and this kind of raillery is an act of justice, when the individual against whom it is directed really deserves it."

You see then, Fathers, that ridicule is, sometimes, best adapted to reclaim men from their wanderings, and is in that case an act of justice; because, as Jeremiah remarks, " The works of those that go astray are worthy of laughter, because they are vanity—*vana sunt et risu digna;* and it is so far from being wicked to laugh at such persons, that, according to St. Augustin, it is an effect of divine wisdom ; " The wise laugh at fools, because they are wise, not indeed, from any wisdom of their own, but from that divine wisdom which will laugh at the death of the wicked."

The prophets under immediate inspiration made use of the same kind of irony, as we see by the examples of Daniel and Elijah. Specimens may be found also in the discourses of Christ himself; St. Augustin remarks, that he chose to humble Nicodemus, who conceived himself a very skilful lawyer. Perceiving how much he was inflated with pride as a doctor of the Jews, he tried and astonished his presumption by the profundity of his inquiries, and having completely perplexed and confounded him, asked, " Art thou a master in Israel and knowest not these things ?" As if he had said, " Proud ruler ! acknowledge that thou knowest nothing !" Upon which St. Chrysostom and St. Cyril agree in remarking, " That Nicodemus deserved to be so jeered."

You see then, Fathers, if at this day persons were to set up to teach Christians as Nicodemus and the Pharisees did the Jews, and were ignorant of the principles of religion, maintaining, for instance, " that it is possible to be saved without ever loving God in the whole course of life," we should only be imitating the example of Jesus Christ by making a jest of their vanity and ignorance.

I persuade myself that these holy examples will suffice to show, that ridiculing the errors and extravagances of mankind, is not acting contrary to the general conduct of the saints, and that the censure you pronounce is no less directed against the great doctors of the church—as St. Jerome, in his letters and writings against Jovinian, Vigilantius, and the Pelagians—Tertullian in his Apologetic against the follies of idolatry—St. Augustin against the monks of Africa, whom he calls the *Hairy*—St. Irenæus against the Gnostics—St. Bernard and the other Fathers of the church, who, having been the imitators of the apostles, ought to be imitated by Christians in all succeeding ages; since, whatever may be said, they alone constitute the true models for the present times.

I cannot, therefore, think I have erred in following them; and having sufficiently explained this point, I shall do no more than quote the admirable language of Tertullian, which justifies my whole procedure. "What I have done is only a skirmish before the battle. I have rather pointed out the wounds which may be inflicted, than actually inflicted them myself. If there be citations which excite ridicule, it is because the subjects themselves lead to it. There are many things which deserve to be derided and jeered in this manner, lest they should acquire any kind of importance by a serious attack. Nothing is more worthy of laughter than vanity, and it belongs to truth to laugh because she is gay, and to sport with her enemies because she is certain of victory. It is true we should be careful that our raillery is not low and unbecoming; but when it can be adopted with propriety and address, it is our duty to avail ourselves of it." Is not this passage, Fathers, extremely appropriate to our subject? The letters I have hitherto written are but preludes to the battle. I have done nothing at present but play, and " pointed out rather the wounds that may be given you than inflicted them myself." I have merely cited passages from your authors, without making scarcely any remarks. So that, " if they excite ridicule, it is because the subjects themselves lead to it." For really is any thing better calculated to excite laughter, than to see so grave a subject as Christian morality filled with the grotesque fancies of your Fathers? Such a high conception was formed of those maxims, which, it was said, " Jesus Christ himself revealed to the Fathers of your society, that when it is found, that " a priest who has received money to say mass, may besides take more of others by giving up all his share in the sacrifice—that a monk is not excommunicated for relinquishing his habit when it is done to dance, to pilfer, or to frequent *incog.* houses of ill-fame—and that the precept of hearing mass is obeyed by hearing the four parts from as many different priests at the same time"—when, I say, these and similar decisions are made public, it is impossible not to be surprised into a fit of laughter, because nothing produces it sooner than a wonderful disproportion between what we expected and what we behold. And how was it possible to treat the great majority of these subjects otherwise, since, as Tertullian remarks, " to treat them seriously would be to authorize them."

What! is it necessary to employ the authority of Scripture and of tradition, to show that to stab an enemy behind his back and in ambush is treachery! And that to give money as a motive to induce the resignation of a benefice is simony? These are contemptible practices in themselves, which deserve to be jeered at and ridiculed In short, what this ancient writer says, that " nothing is more worthy of laughter than vanity," and the rest of the same passage, applies here with such just and convincing force, that one cannot hesitate in deciding whether folly may be ridiculed without violating decorum.

Allow me to say, Fathers, that irony may be resorted to without any breach of charity, though this is one of the sins you charge upon me: for " charity obliges us sometimes to ridicule the errors of men that they may be induced to laugh at them themselves." As St. Augustin observes *Hæc tu misericorditer irride, ut eis ridenda ac fugienda commendes.* And the same charity sometimes requires us to retort with indignation, as we are taught by Gregory Naziangen, " the spirit of charity and meekness has its seasons of emotions and anger." In fact, to quote from St. Augustin, " Who will venture to affirm that truth ought to remain unarmed against falsehood, and that our adversaries may be allowed to terrify the faithful by their threatening words, or triumph over them by witticisms ; but that the Catholics must only reply with a dull coldness and formality calculated to lull the reader asleep! Upon this principle, is it not obvious, that the most extravagant and pernicious errors may be introduced into the church, if they must not be treated with derision, through an apprehension of offending against decorum, or repressed with zeal, through fear of being accused of uncharitableness?

And will you really admit, Fathers, that one man may murder another to avoid a box on the ear, or any similar affront, and not allow a refutation of a public error of such consequence? You assume the liberty of saying, that "a judge may conscientiously retain the gains of injustice," and the world must not contradict you. You print, with the privilege and approbation of your doctors, that "a man may be saved without ever having loved God," and will you interdict those who shall defend the true faith, by declaring that an attack upon you is an offence against charity, and ridiculing your maxims is irreconcileable with Christian modesty? I really question whether any persons can be found to believe you; nevertheless, if there be individuals who imagine that I have violated the charity I owe you, by decrying your morality, I only wish them to examine attentively how they came by such an idea: for they may suppose that it results from their zeal, which cannot without scandal endure to witness the accusation of a neighbour; I would beseech them to consider that at least it is not impossible it may proceed from some other cause, and probably from a secret dislike, often concealed from our own perceptions, which an unholy principle within us never fails of exciting against those who oppose moral irregularities.

In order to supply a rule for ascertaining the true principle of this zeal, I would inquire, whether at the time they are complaining of the treatment endured by a religious order, they are still more distressed that this same religious body treat truth in such a manner? If indignant not only at my letters, but much more at the maxims they quote and expose, I should admit that their resentment partakes of something of zeal, though of a nature not very enlightened, and then the passages here introduced will be sufficient to open their eyes. If displeased, however, at the reproofs, and not at the things against which they are levelled; really, my Fathers, I cannot help repeating they are grossly deceived, and their zeal is miserably blind.

What, I demand, can be a more strange kind of zeal than to be irritated against those who prosecute public crimes, indeed, but not the persons who commit them? What new order of charity is this, which takes offence at the exposure of glaring errors, but is not at all affected to see the total subversion of morality by the propagation of these errors? Were these persons in danger of assassination, would they be offended at the conduct of an individual who should step forward to forewarn them of their danger, and instead of going out of their way to avoid it, trifle away time in complaining of his want of charity who had ventured to expose the criminal intention of the assassins? Are they enraged when desired not to eat of a poisoned dish, or not to enter a town where the plague is raging?

How then is it that they consider it as uncharitable to expose those maxims which are injurious to religion, and on the contrary they believe it uncharitable not to discover what is prejudicial to health and life? Unless the reason be that their attachment to life induces them to receive every thing well which conduces to its preservation, while the indifference they feel respecting truth not only occasions their taking no zealous part in her defence, but makes them displeased at the efforts of others to demolish falsehood.

Let such persons, therefore, consider as before God, how shameful and how dangerous to the church are the principles of morality which your casuists industriously circulate—how scandalous and licentious is the liberty which they have introduced into the system of morals—and how obstinate and violent is the hardihood with which you maintain them: and if they do not believe it is time to resist the progress of such disorders, their blindness will be as deplorable as yours, for both you and they have equal reason to fear the language of St. Augustin on the words of Jesus Christ: " Wo unto you, ye blind guides!"—*Væ cæcis ducentibus.*

But that you may no longer give or receive false impressions, allow me to state,—though, Fathers, I am ashamed to undertake to inform you, what it is in fact your duty to teach—but I beg leave to state some of those marks which the Fathers have specified, for judging whether rebukes proceed from a pious and charitable motive, or from a spirit of impiety and resentment.

The first of these evidences is, that a spirit of piety invariably prompts a man to speak with truth and sincerity: but envy and hatred resort to falsehood and calumny; *splendentia et vehementia sed rebus veris*, says St. Augustin. Whoever makes use of falsehood is actuated by a diabolical influence. No possible mode of *directing the intention* can sanction calumny, and though you were to gain over the whole world by such a proceeding, it cannot be allowable to vilify the innocent, because we must not perpetrate the least evil for the sake of acquiring the greatest good: for, as Scripture asserts, " the truth of God does not stand in need of our lie." St. Hilary also says, " It is the duty of the advocates of truth to advance nothing but what is true." I can say, Fathers, as in the sight of God, that I detest nothing so much as offending against truth, even in the slightest degree; and I have always taken very particular care, not only not to falsify, which would be horrible indeed, but not in the least to alter or distort the sense of a passage; so that if I might venture on this occasion to adopt the words of St. Hilary, I could say, " if the things we affirm be false, let our words be accounted infamous; but if we prove that our representations are public and notorious, it is not departing from apostolic modesty and liberty to inflict censure."

It is not sufficient however, Fathers, to utter only what is true, we must not even state *all* that *is* true: for it is proper to record only what it is useful to disclose, and not those circumstances which merely tend to wound without producing any salutary effect. Hence, as the first rule is to speak the truth, the second is to speak it with becoming discretion. " The wicked," says St.

Augustin, "persecute the good by suffering themselves to be hurried forward by the blind impulse of passion, whereas the good pursue the wicked with a wise discretion, in the same manner as a surgeon will consider what he lances, while the murderer is perfectly regardless where he strikes." You, my good Fathers, well know, that I have avoided citing some maxims of your authors which would have deeply wounded you, though I might have introduced them without sinning against discretion any more than many learned Catholics themselves have done before. Every person who is at all conversant with your writers, must be aware how much I have spared you; moreover, I have not uttered a syllable against any individual in particular, for I should be extremely sorry to expose secret and personal faults, whatever proofs I might have in my possession; this would be an unjustifiable piece of malignity, and what ought never to be done unless the good of the church rendered it absolutely necessary. It is obvious, then, that I have not been wanting in discretion, while I have felt obliged to animadvert upon your maxims and morality, and that you have much greater reason to praise my reserve than to blame my indiscretion.

The third rule is, that when it is requisite to employ raillery, piety demands that it should be employed only against errors, not against sacred things: but a spirit of buffoonery, impiety, and heresy ridicules even what is most sacred with indiscriminating severity. I have already justified myself in reference to this particular, and one is indeed far enough from being liable to this fault (ridiculing *sacred things*), when animadverting upon the maxims quoted from your authors!

Lastly; for I will mention but one more rule, which is the principle and end of all the rest—the spirit of charity produces an ardent desire for the *salvation* of those whom she reproves, and prays for the the blessings of God at the same time that she addresses her censures to men. "We ought always," says St. Augustin, "to preserve charity in the heart, even when it is necessary to act outwardly in a rough manner, and to lash them with a severe, but it should be with a kind-intentioned violence;—their *benefit* ought always to be preferred to their *gratification.*"

I believe, Fathers, there is nothing in my letters to evince any contrariety of feeling to this desire, and charity requires you to believe that this is in reality my wish, when you can see nothing contrary to it. You cannot, therefore, it seems, point out any violation of this rule, or of any other which charity obliges me to follow; and for this reason you have no right to say that I have offended in any thing I have done against this heavenly principle.

But if you feel desirous of seeing in a few words a specimen of that conduct which offends against these rules, and which bears the genuine marks of a spirit of buffoonery, envy, and hatred, I will furnish you with some examples; and that they may be the better known and the more familiar to you, I shall extract them from your own writings.

I shall begin with the unbecoming manner in which your authors treat of sacred subjects, in their railleries, their gallantries, and their serious discourses. Do you imagine that the ridiculous stories of your Father Binet, in his *Consolation for the Sick*, are adapted to the professed design of affording Christian consolation to those whom God afflicts? Will you affirm that the profane and coquettish manner in which your Father le Moine speaks of piety in his *Easy Devotion*, is more adapted to excite respect, or to produce contempt for the idea which he suggests of Christian virtue? Does his book of *Moral Pictures* breathe any thing, whether in prose or verse, but a spirit of vanity and worldliness? Is the ode in the seventh book entitled *The Praise of Modesty*, where he shows that "every thing beautiful is red, or liable to become so," worthy of a priest? This ode was composed for the purpose of comforting a lady whom he calls Delphina, because she was very apt to blush. In every stanza he says that some of the most valuable things are red, as roses, granites, the mouth, the tongue; and amongst these gallantries so disgraceful to a monk, he dares with

15

inexpressible insolence to join those blessed spirits that stand in the presence of God, of whom no Christian ought to speak but with the utmost respect.

>The glorious cherubs of the sky,
>Who wave their golden wings on high,
>Whom God enlightens with his eyes,
>And with his breath their zeal supplies:
>These splendid spirits, as they tread
>Celestial fields in flaming red,
>Or to themselves or God they owe
>The immortal blaze in which they glow,
>And fan with mutual wings and love
>Each other in the realms above:
>But, oh *Delphina*, in thy face,
>We see a still diviner grace!

What say you to this, my good Fathers? What think you of the preference given to Delphina's blush above the ardors of those blessed spirits who breathe nothing but charity? And of the comparison of a lady's fan with those mysterious wings? Does it not appear exceedingly *christian* in the mouth of a priest who consecrates the body of Jesus Christ? I know that this is nothing but a gallant rhodomontade, and he is only laughing; but is not this making a jest of sacred things? And is it not a fact that if he were to have justice done him, he could not escape a censure? even though he should plead, which is not less censurable, the reason which he assigns in his first book, " that the Sorbonne possesses no jurisdiction over Parnassus, and the errors of that part of the world are not subject either to censure or inquisition;" as if nothing could be blasphemous or impious but in prose! But even this will not avail to defend another passage in the preface to the same book:—" The water of the river on whose banks he composed his verses, is so adapted to make poets, that though it should be changed into holy water, it could never cast out the demon of poetry;" nor can any apology be offered for your Father Garasse in his *Summary of the principal Truths of Religion*, p. 649, where he adds blasphemy to heresy in speaking of the sacred mystery of the incarnation: " The human personality was grafted or mounted upon the personality of the word"—not to mention many other things—such as respecting the name of Jesus, usually represented thus—✝ IHS, "Some," says he, "take away the Cross, in order to read the simple characters IHS, which is Jesus stripped and robbed."

Thus unbecomingly do you treat the truths of religion, contrary to that inviolable rule which requires every one to speak of them with reverence. But you offend no less against that rule which demands truth and discretion upon this subject. What is more common than calumny in your writings? Are those of Father Brisacier sincere? And does he speak the truth when he says, p. 4, par. 24 and 25, that "the nuns of Port Royal do not pray to the saints, and have no images in their church?" Are not these most outrageous falsehoods, when the contrary is seen by all Paris? And does he speak with discretion when he attacks the pure and austere innocence of those virgins, whom he calls "girls without penitence, disregardful of the sacraments, living without the holy communion, foolish, fantastic, calagans, desperate, &c. or what you please," blackening them by so many other contemptuous terms, as to draw down upon his head the ecclesiastical censure of the archbishop of Paris? What do you think of the calumnies he circulates against priests of the most irreproachable morals in the first part of his work, p. 22, asserting that "they practise novelties in confession to entrap the beautiful and the innocent;" and that "he should be terrified to mention the abominable crimes which they perpetrate?" Is it not an insufferable piece of rashness to advance such odious impositions, not only without proof, but without the least shadow or appearance of it? I shall refrain from any further illustrations at present, deferring it to another opportunity, when I can be more diffuse; for I have more to say upon this subject, but I have now given sufficient specimens of your violations both of truth and discretion.

It may perhaps be said, that at least you do not transgress the last rule, which demands a desire for the salvation of those who are the objects of reprehension, and that you cannot be accused of it without violating the secret of your heart, which is known only to God. It is indeed strange, Fathers, but nevertheless it is a fact, that while your hatred against your adversaries has led you to wish their everlasting perdition, your blindness has been such as to discover to view such an abominable desire, and so far from secretly forming any wish for their salvation, you have made public vows for their damnation. The city of Caen can testify this to the great scandal of the church, and you have since dared to defend this diabolical conduct even at Paris, and in your publications. Nothing surely can add to these monstrous impieties—to mock and speak contemptuously of the most sacred things—to calumniate virgins and priests by the most daring and scandalous falsities, and then to form desires and utter vows for their damnation! Whether this confounds you I cannot tell, nor do I know how you came to think of accusing me of a want of charity—me, who have spoken with so much strictness and moderation as not to make a single reflection upon the horrible violations of charity of which you have yourselves been guilty in your deplorable transports of rage.

I shall conclude, by referring to one other charge you have preferred against me; it is, that amongst the numerous maxims I have cited, there are some which have already been objected against you, whence you complain of my "repeating to your disadvantage what has been said before." I answer, the reason of this recurrence to the objections already made, is that you have not in the least profited by the statement of them. What good has resulted from the representations of so many learned doctors and the whole university? What did your Fathers Annat, Caussin, Pintereau, and le Moine, do in their replies, but accumulate reproaches upon the heads of those who gave them salutary advice? Have you ever suppressed the volumes which contain such infamous maxims? Have you reprimanded their authors? Are you become more circumspect? Is it not since that time that Escobar has been so often reprinted in France and the Low Countries, and that your Fathers Cellot, Bagot, Bauny, Lamy, le Moine, and others, continue to publish the same things every day, and even new ones in as licentious a manner as ever? Complain no more then, my good Fathers, I beseech you, either of my reproaching you with maxims which you have not yet relinquished, or of my objecting against your new ones, or of my holding them all up to ridicule together. You have nothing more to do than to reflect upon them, to produce your own confusion and my vindication. Who can, without laughing, look at Father Bauny's decision upon the burning of barns? or that of Father Cellot upon restitution? or the rule of Sanchez in favour of conjurers? or the manner in which Hurtado proposes to avoid the sin of duelling, by only walking in a field and waiting for somebody? or the compliments of Father Bauny to varnish over usury—to sanction simony by a turn of the intention— to avoid falsehood by speaking alternately in a whisper and in an audible voice—with the other opinions of your *gravest* doctors? Have I need of any further vindication? And can any thing better be devised than, as Tertullian says, "to laugh at the vanity and weakness of such opinions?"

But, my good Fathers, that corruption of morals which your maxims superinduce, merits a different treatment, and we may very well inquire with Tertullian, "Am I to laugh at their folly or to reproach their blindness—*rideam vanitatem an exprobrem cœcitatem?*" I am inclined to think one may either laugh or cry as we choose—*Hæc tolerabilius vel ridentur vel flentur,* says St. Augustin. "There is," to quote from Scripture, "a time to laugh and a time to mourn:" and I sincerely wish, Fathers, that I were unable to prove in your example, the truth of the following words in the book of Proverbs: "If a wise man contendeth with a foolish man, whether he rage or laugh there is no rest."

LETTER XII.

Refutation of the Quirks and Turns of the Jesuits on the Subjects of Almsgiving and Simony.

REVEREND FATHERS,   Sept. 9, 1656.

    I was about to write to you respecting your injurious treatment of me in your publications, in which you have been so long bestowing upon me the epithets of "impious—buffoon—ignoramus, merry-andrew, impostor, calumniator, knave, heretic, disguised Calvinist, disciple of du Moulin, possessed with a legion of devils."
    I wished that the world should understand the reason you had for treating me in this manner: for I should be sorry that all this guilt should be laid to my charge; and I felt resolved to complain publicly of your calumnies and misrepresentations—when behold, I received your answers, in which I am accused to my face. This has obliged me to alter my design, but not entirely to relinquish it; since, in the course of my defence, I hope to convict you of more *real* impostures than you have imputed to me of *false* ones.
    In truth, Fathers, you are more to be suspected than I am; for is it at all probable that I, standing alone, feeble and destitute of all human support, should oppose so large a body, and that I should expose myself to total ruin, by being detected of imposture, with no other assistance than truth and sincerity? It is abundantly easy to discover where the falsehood lies in questions of this description. I should have plenty of accusers, and they would not be refused justice. But you, Fathers, are quite differently

circumstanced : you can say whatever you please against me, and I can have no appeal.

From this difference in our respective situations, I ought to be extremely cautious, even though I had no other inducements to be so ; but by treating me as a notorious impostor, you compel me to reply : and yet you must be perfectly aware this cannot be done, without exposing anew and revealing the foundation of your points of morality ; so that I question whether your proceeding be quite politic. The war is at your doors, and you must be at the expense of it ; for though you expected, by perplexing the subjects of dispute with scholastic terms, the replies would necessarily be so long, so obscure, and so intricate, as to spoil their relish ; perhaps this will not be altogether the case, for I shall endeavour to introduce as little as possible of that jargon. I know not how it is, but the fact seems to be, that your maxims are so excessively diverting, every body is delighted. Remember, however, that it is yourselves who provoke me to this ; and we shall see who is the most successful combatant.

The first of your impostures relates to the opinion of Vasquez, respecting almsgiving. Allow me to be perfectly explicit here, in order to remove all obscurity from our disputes. "There are two precepts in the church with regard to almsgiving ; the one to give out of one's superfluity to the ordinary necessities of the poor—the other to give what may be necessary according to one's condition of life, in cases of extreme necessity." This is what Cajetan says after St. Thomas ; so that to show the opinion of Vasquez, I must state the rule by which he directs us to dispose of what is superfluous as well as what is necessary.

The supply of superfluity, which is the most usual means of assisting the poor, is totally abolished by that single maxim, c. 4. n. 14. to which I have referred in my letters, " That which people accumulate to exalt their own condition or that of their parents, cannot be termed superfluity ; and therefore you will scarcely ever find superfluity in the world, not even amongst princes." You perceive, Fathers, by this definition, those who are ambitious cannot have any thing superfluous; and thus the charity of the greatest part of the world is at once annihilated." But even supposing this abundance should be possessed, the individual is dispensed from the obligation of giving it in cases of ordinary necessity, according to Vasquez, who opposes those who wish to impose charity upon the opulent. These are his words, ch. 1. n. 32; " Corduba teaches us, that when we have any thing superfluous, it must be given to those who require the common necessities of life, at least some portion of it, that some kind of obedience may be rendered to the precept—*but this doctrine is not quite satisfactory to me—sed hoc non placet*—for I have shown the contrary against Cajetan and Navarre." Thus, Fathers, the obligation of almsgiving is absolutely nullified, at the good pleasure of Vasquez.

In cases of extreme and urgent necessity, it is our duty to do something for the poor; but you will see, by the conditions with which he connects this obligation, the richest person in Paris is perfectly released from contributing any thing as long as he lives. To mention only two—

1. "*When you know* that the poor person will not be assisted by any other individual—*hæc intelligo et cætera omnia, quando* scio *nullum alium opem laturum,*" ch. 1. n. 28. What say you to this, Fathers? Is it likely to happen in Paris, where there are so many charitable people, that it can be certainly known no person will be found to relieve the poor petitioners of our bounty? Yet, according to Vasquez, without this knowledge, they may be dismissed without help.

2. The other condition is, that the necessity of the poor man be such, that "he is in danger of his life or of losing his reputation," n. 24 and 26, which is very uncommon; and that which evinces its infrequency is his representation in n. 45., that a poor man who is in such circumstances that he says we must afford him relief, " may *rob* the rich with a safe conscience." This must be a very extraordinary case, unless he will assert that it is usual to

permit this theft: so that, after destroying the obligation of almsgiving out of our superfluity, which is the greatest source of charity, he does not oblige the wealthy to assist the poor out of their necessaries, but when he permits the poor to rob the rich. Such is the doctrine of Vasquez, whom you are in the habit of recommending to your readers for their edification.

I now proceed to your impostures. And here, in the first place, you expatiate upon the obligation which Vasquez imposes on all ecclesiastics to give alms: but I have never yet spoken of them, though I am ready to do so whenever you please: at present they are out of the question. With regard to the laymen, who alone are concerned, you seem to be desirous of making us believe that Vasquez only gives us the opinion of Cajetan in the passage I have quoted, not his own. Nothing, however, can be more false; but as you have not absolutely asserted this, I am willing to save your honour, by supposing you did not intend it.

You complain, that after quoting the following maxim of Vasquez, "it is scarcely possible to find superfluity in the world, even amongst kings;" I infer, that "the rich, upon this principle, cannot be obliged to give alms out of their abundance." But what can you mean, Fathers? If it be true that the rich seldom have any superfluity, is it not certain that they can scarcely ever be under any obligation to give alms out of their superfluity? I would prove this by an argument in detail, but that Diana, who thinks so highly of Vasquez that he calls him "the phœnix of wits," has deduced the same inference from the same principle. After quoting this maxim of Vasquez, he adds: "In the question, whether the rich are obliged to give alms out of their superfluity, although the opinion which obliges them to it be true, it would never or seldom happen that they are obliged to it in practice." I quote Diana *verbatim*. What then can he meant, when Diana cites the opinions of Vasquez with great approbation, when he represents them as probable and "very accommodating to the rich?" It is not said that he is either calumniator or falsifier, and you make no complaints of any misrepresentation; but when I introduce the very same sentiments from Vasquez, but without dignifying him with the name of *phœnix*, I am an impostor, a liar, and a corrupter of his maxims!

Certainly, my good Fathers, you have reason to apprehend that the difference of your treatment towards those who differ nothing in their statements, but solely in their estimation of your doctrines, will discover the real feeling of your hearts, and make it evident that your principal object is to uphold the credit and glory of your society; since as long as your accommodating theology passes for a wise condescension and compliance, you will not disavow those who divulge it. but praise them as your auxiliaries: but so soon as it is exhibited in the light of a pernicious relaxation, then the same interest of your society requires a disavowal of those doctrines which injure your credit with the world. Thus you admit or renounce opinions, not according to truth, which is immutable, but in conformity to the various changes of the times, as an ancient writer says, *omnia pro tempore, nihil pro veritate*. Take care. Fathers,—and, that you may no longer accuse me of deducing from Vasquez an inference which he had disavowed, know that he has deduced it himself, c. 1. n. 27: " Scarcely is any one obliged to give alms, if the obligation respect his superfluities only, according to the opinion of Cajetan, and *my own opinion also—et secundum nostram*." Confess then. Fathers, from the testimony of Vasquez himself, that I have exactly stated his own idea. and consider with what kind of conscience you can venture to assert, that " if the original were consulted, it would be seen with astonishment that he teaches the very reverse."

In short, this is your grand argument, that if Vasquez do not oblige the rich to bestow alms out of their superfluity, he obliges them however to give out of their necessaries. But you have forgot to point out the multitudinous conditions which he states to be requisite, and which so fetter and restrict the obligation, that it is almost annihilated: and, instead of explaining his doctrine, you only state in general terms, that he obliges the rich to give even that which is necessary to their rank. But this, my Fathers, is going too far : the rule of the Gospel does not extend to such lengths, and Vasquez is far enough from promulgating or patronizing this new mistake. In order to cover his indulgence, you attribute to him a reprehensible excess of severity, by which means you discredit your own fidelity of quotation But he does not merit this reproach ; for he has established, as I have shown, that the rich are not obliged, either in justice or charity, to give of their abundance, still less out of their necessaries, to relieve the ordinary wants of the poor, and they are only required to bestow what is necessary on occasions which seldom or never occur.

You state no further objections ; it only remains, therefore, to show the falsehood of your representations respecting Vasquez as more strict than Cajetan. This is sufficiently easy, since the cardinal himself says : " We are required in justice to give alms out of our superfluities, even in the common necessities of the poor, because, according to the holy Fathers. the rich are only stewards to distribute of their abundance to the necessitous :" and thus, while Diana says of the maxims of Vasquez, that they are very convenient and very agreeable to the rich and to their confessors, the cardinal, who has no such consolation to minister, declares, *de Eleem.* c. 6 : " he has nothing to address to the rich, but the following words of Christ : *It is easier for a camel to go through the eye of a needle, than for a rich man to enter into the kingdom of heaven ;* and to their confessors, *If the blind lead the blind they shall both fall into the ditch*" —so indispensable in his view is this obligation ! All the saints and Fathers have also established it as an unalterable truth. " There are two cases," says St. Thomas, q. 2. 9. 118. art. 4. " in which we are obliged to give alms from a principle of justice—*ex debito legali ;* the one, when the poor are in danger ; the other, when we enjoy superfluous possessions ;" and 9. 87. a. 1—" the three-tenths which the Jews were to eat with the poor were augmented in the new law, because it is the will of Christ that we give to the poor, not only the tenth part, but all our superfluity."

Vasquez, however, does not approve the imposing of an obligation to give even a part; such is his complaisance to the rich, his cruelty to the poor, and his opposition to those sweet and charitable sentiments of St. Gregory, which appear so offensive to the opulent: " When we bestow upon the poor what is necessary to their subsistence, we do not so much give them what is our own, as pay them what is theirs; and this is rather an act of justice than a work of mercy."

In this manner the ancient saints recommend to the rich to divide their temporal possessions with the poor, if they wish with them to participate the riches of heaven: and while you are endeavouring to inflame the ambition of men, which will never admit of the existence of any superfluity, and their avarice, which refuses to part with any they may possess; the saints are, on the contrary, labouring to induce mankind to give their superfluity, and show them that they may have enough to distribute, if they would measure their means, not by that cupidity which knows no bounds, but by that piety which ingeniously devises plans of retrenchment, by which persons may have it in their power to exercise charity. " We may have much to spare," says St. Augustin, " if we keep only what is necessary; but if we seek after vanities, nothing will satisfy us. My brethren, pursue only what is sufficient for the work of God, that is, to support nature, and not what will gratify concupiscence, which is the work of the devil; and remember that the superfluity of the rich is necessary and due to the poor."

I very much wish, Fathers, that what I have said, may not only serve for my justification—this is of trifling importance—but may make you perceive, and lead you to detest every corrupt principle in the maxims of your casuists, that we may be all sincerely united in the sacred rules of the Gospel, according to which we must be judged.

With regard to the second point, relative to *Simony*, previous to my giving any reply to your reproaches, I propose to explain your own doctrine upon the subject. Being extremely embarrassed with the canons of the church on the one hand, which impose tremendous punishments on Simonists; and on the other, the avarice of so many persons who follow that infamous traffic, you have had recourse to your usual method of allowing men whatever they desire, and giving mere words and forms to God. For what do these Simonists require for their livings but money? But you have exempted this from the charge of Simony. But inasmuch as the word must be retained, as well as some subject to which it must be attached, you have chosen for this purpose an imaginary idea which never came into the mind of Simonists, and which would be perfectly useless; which is, to esteem money considered in itself as equivalent to a spiritual good in itself considered. For who ever thought of comparing things so disproportionate and so different in nature? And yet, without this metaphysical comparison, a person may give his benefice to another, and, according to your writers, receive money in exchange, without committing Simony.

In this manner you make a mock of religion to gratify the passions of mankind; but see, nevertheless, how gravely your Father Valentia utters his *dreams* in the passage quoted in my letters, tom. 3. disp. 6. qu. 16. p. 3. p. 2044: "One may give," says he, "a temporal for a spiritual good in two ways: the one, by setting a higher price upon the temporal than the spiritual possession, which would be Simony; the other, by taking the temporal as the motive and end which induces the gift of the spiritual, without, however, estimating the temporal at a higher rate than the spiritual—then it would *not* be Simony. The reason is this: Simony consists in receiving the temporal as the full *worth* of the spiritual. If, therefore, the temporal be demanded, *si petatur temporale* —not as the *value*, but as the *motive* which induces the bestowment of the spiritual, it is not by any means Simony, even though the principal aim and wish be directed to the temporal possession—*minimè erit Simonia, etiamsi temporale principaliter intendatur et expectatur.*"

Has not your great Sanchez had a similar revelation, whose words are quoted by Escobar, tr. 6. ex. 2. n. 40: " If temporal possessions be given for spiritual ones, not as the *price,* but as the *motive* to induce the patron to confer it, or as a recompense for having done it, is this Simony? Sanchez assures us it is not." Your theses at Caen, in 1644, state, " It is a probable opinion, taught by many Catholics, that it is no Simony to give temporal for spiritual possessions, when not given as a *price.*"

As for Tannerus, his doctrine is the same with that of Valentia, which will prove how much mistaken you are in complaining that I have asserted his doctrine does not accord with that of St. Thomas, since he acknowledges it himself in the passage quoted in my letter, tom. 3. disp. 5. p. 1519: " There is not," says he, " properly and truly any Simony, but in taking a temporal gift as the price of a spiritual one ; but when it is taken as a motive to induce the gift of the spiritual, or as a grateful testimony of the favour, it is not Simony, at least not in conscience." A little further, he adds, " The same may be said, though the individual should regard the temporal (or money) as his principal end, and though he even prefer it to the spiritual ; however St. Thomas and others may seem to state the contrary, by assuring us that it is absolute Simony to give a spiritual for a temporal good, when the temporal is the end in view."

Such, Fathers, is your doctrine of Simony, as taught by your best authors, who in this particular follow each other very accurately. It remains for me to advert to your impostures.

The opinion of Valentia, as you have made no remarks upon it, remains as it did ; but you dwell upon that of Tannerus, asserting that he has merely decided it is not Simony by the divine law, and you wish to circulate the impression that I took care to suppress the words *divine law* in the passage. But this is unreasonable, Fathers, because this phrase was never inserted there at all! You afterwards add, that Tannerus declares it to be Simony by a *positive law*. Good Fathers, you deceive yourselves; for he does not speak generally, but only in reference to particular cases—*in casibus à jure expressis;* by which expression he furnishes an exception to his general rule, that "it is not Simony in conscience," which implies it is not so by any positive law, unless you would represent Tannerus impious enough to maintain that what is Simony by a positive law is not Simony in conscience. But these phrases, *divine law, positive law, natural law, an internal and external tribunal, cases expressed in law, external presumption,* and others alike unknown, are invented for the purpose of escaping under this veil, and diverting the mind from noticing your extravagances. You shall not, however, be sheltered by these vain subtleties, for I am resolved to propose to you such plain questions that they shall not be liable to a *distinguo*.

I ask, then, without talking of *positive law*, or *external presumption*, or *exterior tribunal* whether, according to your authors, an incumbent would be guilty of Simony by disposing of a living of 200*l*. per annum, for 500*l*. ready money, not as the value of the benefice, but as a motive which induced him to part with it? Tell me candidly, Fathers, what would your authors say to such a transaction? Will not Tannerus say at once, "that it is not Simony in conscience, because the money is not the price of the living, but only the motive for bestowing it?" Will not Valentia, your Caen theses, Sanchez, and Escobar, give a similar decision, and for the same reason? And does this patron require any other authority to apologize for his Simony? And dare you treat him as a Simonist in your confessionals, whatever might be your private opinion, when he would have it in his power to silence you by appealing to your own *grave doctors?* You must admit, then, that such a patron is free from Simony by your own confession; and now defend this doctrine if you can.

This, my good Fathers, is the proper method of treating questions, without entangling them with scholastic terms, or changing the state of the question, as you have done in your last attack. Tannerus, you say, declares that such an exchange is a great sin, and you reproach me with having maliciously suppressed that circumstance, which, as you affirm, *justifies him entirely*. But here you are mistaken in several respects: for, though your statement were true, the question was not whether there was any *sin* in it, but whether it amounted to *Simony*: this is a very different consideration: *sins*, according to your maxims, only require confession; *Simony* obliges to restitution: and there are people who are sufficiently acquainted with this difference. You have discovered expedients to render confession easy, but none to render restitution agreeable. I must say further, that the case which Tannerus accuses of sin, *is not merely* that in which a spiritual is given in exchange for a temporal possession, which latter constitutes the principal motive; but, he adds, "the temporal being more valued than the spiritual;" and this is precisely the imaginary case to which I before adverted. In fact, there is no evil in charging that with sin, since it must be a piece of prodigious wickedness, or monstrous stupidity, to incur a sin so easily avoided, by only comparing the price of these two possessions at the time when the one is allowed to be given for the other. Besides, Valentia, on the same passage, in examining whether it be criminal to give a spiritual good for a temporal, the latter being the principal motive, relates the reasons of those who decide in the affirmative, adding, *sed hoc non videtur mihi satis certum:* "this does not appear to me quite certain"

Since that, your Father Erade Bill, professor of Cases of Conscience at Caen, has decided that there is no sin in such a transaction, for *probable opinions* are always *ripening*. This is stated in his writings of 1644, against which M. Dupré, doctor and professor at Caen, made that fine oration, afterwards printed and sufficiently well known. For though Father Erade Bill admits that the doctrine of

Valentia followed by Father Millard and condemned by the Sorbonne, " is contrary to the common opinion, and in many things suspected of simony, and justly punished when the facts are discovered;" he still says it is *probable*, therefore safe in point of conscience, and consequently unconnected either with simony or sin. "It is," he says, "a probable opinion, and taught by the majority of Catholic divines, that there is no simony, and *no sin*, in giving money or any other temporal consideration for a benefice, whether as an acknowledgment, or as a motive without which it could not be conferred, provided it be not given as a price equal to the benefice."

Nothing more surely can be required : for according to all these maxims, simony is so uncommon, that Simon Magus himself, who wished to purchase the Holy Ghost, could not be convicted of it, in which he is the very model of your simonists who buy it ; and Gehazi, who took money for a miracle, is the representative of your simonists who sell it. It is indisputable that when Simon, in the Acts, offered money to the apostles to confer this power, he did not use the words *buying*, *selling*, or *price;* he did nothing more than offer some money as a motive to induce the bestowment of that spiritual gift ; which, according to your writers, being no simony, he would have been perfectly fortified against the anathema of St. Peter, had he been lucky enough to have known your modern doctrines.

This ignorance also was very unfortunate for Gehazi, when he was smitten with the leprosy by the word of Elisha ; for only taking money of the prince who was miraculously cured as an acknowledgment, and not as an equivalent for that divine virtue which had operated the miracle, he might have obliged Elisha to cure him again under pain of a mortal sin. In such a case he would only have acted in conformity to your grave doctors, who require all confessors to absolve their penitents in such circumstances, and to cleanse them from their spiritual leprosy, of which the corporeal is but a figure.

Seriously, my Fathers, nothing would be easier than to turn you and your doctrines here into ridicule. How could you so expose yourselves? I should have nothing more to do than to state your own maxims; as for instance, that of Escobar in his "Practice of Simony according to the Society of Jesus," n. 40: "Is it a simoniacal transaction when two monks enter into an engagement with each other in this manner, 'Give me your vote to procure my election to a provincial, and I will give you mine to make you prior?'—By no means." Again, tr. 6. n. 14: "It is no simony to procure a benefice, by promising money which you really never intended to pay, because it is only a mock simony, which is no more real, than a counterfeit guinea is a genuine one."

It is by such subtleties practised upon conscience, that he has discovered a method, by adding knavery to simony, of procuring benefices without either money or simony. But I have not time to proceed here, and must hasten to defend myself against your third calumny on the subject of *bankrupts*. Can any thing be more gross? You treat me as an impostor, on account of a sentiment of Lessius, which I have not quoted from him, but which was alleged by Escobar, in a passage which I have introduced; hence, though it were true that Lessius did not maintain the sentiments attributed to him by Escobar, can any thing be more unjust than to censure *me* for it? When I quote Lessius, or your other authors myself, I agree to be alone responsible. But as Escobar has collected the opinions of twenty-four of your Fathers, I ask whether I am to be answerable for any thing but what I quote from him; or, whether in addition to this, I must be responsible for the citations which he has given in the passages whence I have derived them? This would be most unreasonable; but this is precisely the case in the present instance.

I introduced into my letter the following passage of Escobar, faithfully translated; upon which, by the way, you have made no remark: "Can a bankrupt, with a safe conscience, retain as much as may be necessary to his living handsomely—*ne indecorè vivat?* I answer, with Lessius, in the *affirmative—cum Lessio assero posse,* &c." Upon which, you tell me, Lessius is not of that opinion. But consider a little what you are asserting: for, if it be true, that he is of that opinion, you will incur the name of impostors for affirming the contrary; and, if he be not, Escobar will be deemed an impostor: so that some one of your society must necessarily fall under this imputation. But what a scandal! And how strange that you should not foresee the consequences of things! You seem to imagine, that you are at liberty to circulate injurious representations without once reflecting upon whom they may fall.

Why did you not explain your difficulty to Escobar previous to its publication? He could have satisfied you. It is easy to communicate with Valladolid, where he is at present in perfect health, completing his body of Moral Theology, in six volumes; on the first of which I propose some day to offer a few observations. You sent him my first ten letters; you might, also, have sent your objection, and I feel assured he could have furnished you with a reply, for he has, no doubt, seen in Lessius the passage from which he took his *Ne indecorè vivat:* only look attentively, my good Fathers, and you will find it there as I did, lib. 2. c. 16. n. 45: *Idem colligitur apertè ex juribus citatis, maximè quoad ea bona quæ post cessionem acquirit, de quibus is qui debitor est etiam ex delicto potest retinere quantum necessarium est, ut pro sua conditione* NON INDECORE VIVAT. *Petes an leges id permittant de bonis quo tempore instantis cessionis habebat? Ita videtur colligi ex D. D.*

I will not stop to show you that, in order to authorize this maxim, Lessius abuses the law which allows a bankrupt mere subsistence, and not a genteel support. It is sufficient to have vindicated Escobar from such an accusation, which is, in fact, doing more than I ought. But you, my good Fathers, do not do so much as you ought: for the question is to reply to the passage in Escobar, whose decisions are very accommodating, being independent of what precedes or follows, and included in brief articles, are not subject to your distinctions.

I have quoted the entire passage which permits bankrupts "to retain their goods, even though unjustly acquired, for the maintenance of their families in a handsome way;" upon which I exclaim in my letters—"How, Fathers! by what monstrous charity do you concede that goods acquired in an iniquitous manner, belong rather to those who have got them, than to their lawful creditors?" To this question, it became you to furnish a reply; but it has proved so terribly embarrassing, that you endeavour, though in vain, to elude it, by flying from the question, and introducing other passages from Lessius, which have no kind of relevancy to the subject.

I demand, then, whether this maxim of Escobar can be followed with a safe conscience by persons in a state of insolvency? Be careful what you say: if you answer *no*, what will become of your doctor, and what of your doctrine of probability? If you say *yes*, I refer you to the parliament.

I must leave you, Fathers, in this dilemma; for I have not room to undertake the next subject respecting murder, but will avail myself of the very first opportunity to take this and the rest in order.

I propose to say nothing at present of the advertisements with which you finish every imposture, and which are so replete with infamous falsehoods: to all this, I shall reply in another letter, in which I hope to point out the source of all your calumnies. Really, Fathers, I pity you for having recourse to such methods: your abusive language will never elucidate our differences, and your menaces shall not prevent my defending myself. You think that you have power and impunity—I think that I have truth and innocence. It is a strange and protracted war when violence attempts to suppress truth. All the efforts of violence will prove unavailable to weaken it—truth will be the more advanced: her light can never be extinguished by violence; it will burn the brighter. When force contends with force, the strongest destroys the weakest—when reasons oppose reasons, those which are true and convincing, confound and dissipate those which are false and vain: but violence and truth can do nothing with each other. Let it not be asserted, however, they are upon an equality, for this mighty difference exists: violence has a course limited by the commands of God, who renders its efforts subservient to promote the glory of the truth it attacks; but truth subsists for ever, and eventually triumphs over all her enemies, because she is eternal and powerful as God himself.

REFUTATION

Of the Reply of the Jesuits to the last Letter.

SIR,

Whoever may be the persons that have undertaken to defend the Jesuits against the letters which have so clearly detected the irregularity of their morals, it appears by the pains you take to afford them some assistance, that you well know the weakness of their principles; and in this respect your judgment is correct: but if you really thought yourself capable of justifying them effectually, you are inexcusable.

No, no—I entertain a better opinion of you, and persuade myself that your design was merely to divert the author of the letters from keeping up this amusing game. But you are not successful; and I am extremely gratified to find that the thirteenth letter, which has just made its appearance, passes unnoticed your remarks upon the eleventh and twelfth, and does not seem to think about you at all. This leads me to hope that the author will equally neglect your other publications.

You are not to suppose, however, that he would not have found it perfectly easy to have given you a deadly thrust. Could he, who has so vanquished your whole society, have found any difficulty in conquering an individual? You may judge of this by the manner in which I am now going to reply to what you have written against his twelfth letter.

I shall pass over all your abuse. The author of the letters has promised to afford you ample satisfaction upon that subject; and he will do it, I venture to pronounce, in such a way as to cover you with shame and sorrow. He will find no difficulty in confounding such simple individuals as you and your Jesuits, who, by a criminal conspiracy, usurp the authority of the church to treat whoever you please as heretics, when you see yourselves incapable of constructing a defence against the merited reproaches incurred by their impious doctrines. For my own part, I shall confine myself to the refutation of those new impostures which you employ in justification of these casuists. To begin with the great Vasquez.

You have not given the least reply to any thing which the author of the letters has written respecting his erroneous statements on the subject of Almsgiving; and only prefer against him a charge at random of four misrepresentations, of which the first is, that in a quotation from Vasquez in the sixth letter, he has suppressed the following words; "*Statum quem licité possunt acquirere*;" and disregarded the accusation it had occasioned.

I plainly perceive, Sir, that you have implicitly believed upon the word of your good friends the Jesuits, that these words are really to be found in the passage to which the author of the letters refers. Had you known they were not there, you would of course have censured these Fathers for their false accusation, rather than have been surprised at his not deigning to answer this objection. But do not place too much reliance upon them, or you will be often entrapped. Examine the passage in Vasquez for yourselves, in the treatise on Almsgiving, c. 4. n. 14; but you will find nothing of the phrase which is said to have been suppressed, and you will be very much astonished to find them in no other situation than at the distance of fifteen pages back. I have no doubt but that, after this discovery, you will complain of these good Fathers, and will no longer deem it proper to reproach this author with having suppressed the passage in question, otherwise he must have quoted fifteen previous folio pages in a letter of only eight pages quarto, in which he is accustomed to in-

To Grand Dad

Have a Merry Christmas
& a Happy New Year!

-Kimmy

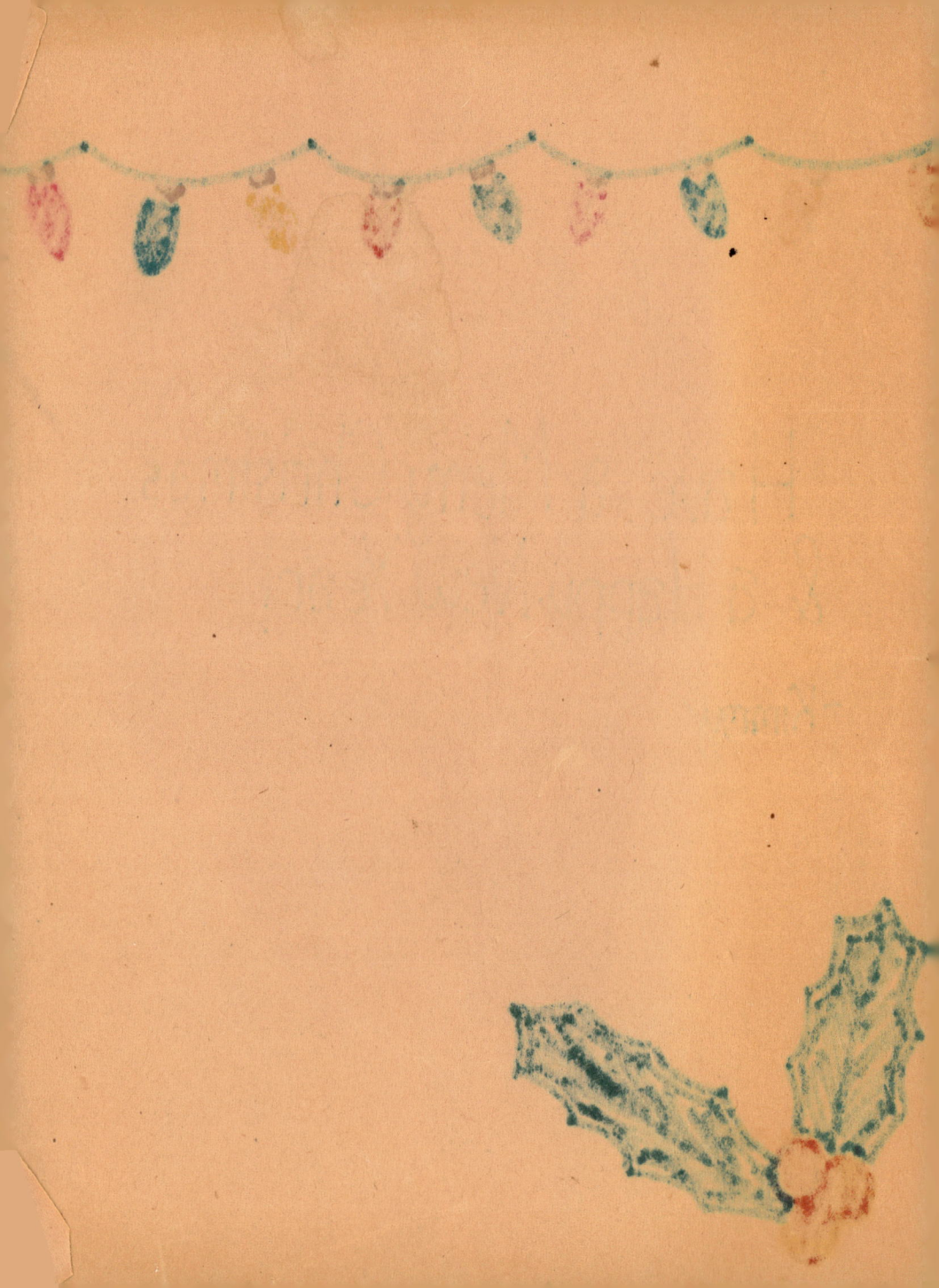

troduce twenty or thirty citations, which surely would be an unreasonable expectation.

These words, therefore, can only serve to convict yourselves of a fabrication, without justifying Vasquez. That Jesuit is accused of nullifying the precept of Christ, which obliges the rich to give alms out of their abundance, by maintaining that "what the wealthy reserve in order to assist their relations or aggrandize themselves is not superfluous; and that scarcely any such thing can be found amongst men, not even amongst kings." The inference that "there is scarcely such a thing as superfluity in the world," annuls the obligation of alms-giving. since the conclusion being that they have nothing superfluous, they are under no obligation to dispense charity. If the author of the letters had deduced this inference, you would have had some pretence for intimating it was not contained in this principle, "that what the rich lay up in order to advance their own condition or that of their relations is not to be called superfluity." But he found this consequence already stated in Vasquez, where he read these words, so remote from the true spirit of the Gospel and the moderation of a Christian; "One can scarcely find any superfluity amongst mankind, not even amongst kings." There also he read this last conclusion, supported in the twelfth letter: "One is scarcely ever obliged to give alms, if the only obligation be to do it out of one's superfluity;" and it is remarkable that this is stated in the very same place with these words, by which you pretend to elude the consequence—*Statum quem licitè possunt acquirere.* You cavil therefore about this principle very uselessly, when you are necessitated to be silent respecting the inferences formally deduced in Vasquez, and which are sufficient to nullify the precept of Jesus Christ, of which he is accused.

If Vasquez had drawn erroneous consequences from his principle, he would have superadded an error of judgment to an error in morals; but this would not have made him more innocent, nor the precept of Jesus Christ the less annihilated. But it will appear by the refutation of the second falsity, which you have charged upon the author of the letters, that these pernicious consequences are properly deduced from the erroneous principle which Vasquez establishes in the same place ; and that this Jesuit has not sinned against the rules of logic, but against those of the Gospel.

This second falsity, which you attribute to him in defiance of his own convictions, is, that he has omitted the words in question, from a malicious design to pervert the sentiment of this Father, and to draw from it this scandalous conclusion, " An ambitious man can have no superfluity." I have only to say to this, in one word, that there never was a more unreasonable accusation. The Jesuits themselves never complained of this consequence ; and yet you reproach the author of the letters for not having replied to an objection which has never been made to him. But if you suppose that in this particular you have been more sharp-sighted than all the rest of your fraternity, it will be easy to cure you of a vanity so injurious to this great body. How can you deny that the inevitable conclusion from this principle of Vasquez, " that what is treasured up to aggrandize a man's condition and that of his relations, is not called superfluity," is, that an ambitious man can have no superfluity ? I readily allow you to add the condition he specifies in another passage to improve a possession by lawful means—*statum quem licitè possunt acquirere*—but this will not prevent the correctness of the inference, which you deny.

It is true, Sir, some rich persons may enhance their fortune by lawful means ; the general good may sometimes justify such a desire, provided they do not so much regard their own honour and interest as the honour of God and the interest of the public ; but it does not often happen that the Spirit of Christ, without which no purity of intention can exist, inspires the rich of the world with desires of this nature. He rather admonishes them to lay aside the useless weight which prevents their ascent to heaven, and to tremble at the words of his Gospel, " He that exalteth himself shall be abased."

Thus the eagerness discernible in the greatest proportion of mankind, to rise to a more elevated condition, and to advance the interests of their relatives, though by lawful measures, is commonly nothing more than the effect of covetousness and ambition. It is, Sir, a gross error, to imagine there is no ambition in desiring to increase one's fortune only when illegal methods are pursued; and it is this which St. Augustin condemns in his book on Patience, c. 3: "The love of money," says he, "and the passion for glory, are follies which the world thinks allowable, believing that avarice, ambition, luxury, amusements, are innocent, so long as we do not fall into any crime or disorder forbidden by the laws." Ambition consists in seeking distinction for the mere sake of distinction, honour for the sake of honour; as avarice is the love of riches for the sake of riches. If with these you connect unjust means, you render them the more criminal; but you cannot by substituting legitimate methods, render them innocent. But Vasquez says nothing of those occasions in which certain good people desire an alteration in their condition, and, as cardinal Cajetan expresses it, are *in the probable expectation of accomplishing it;* if he had, he would have been ridiculed for concluding that superfluity is scarcely ever to be found, because such occasions are exceedingly rare, happening but once or twice in a whole life, and then only to a very small proportion of the opulent, to whom God reveals that they shall not injure themselves by rising higher to serve others, and cannot hinder most rich persons from possessing a superfluity. But he speaks of a vague and indeterminate desire of aggrandizement, of a desire which has no limits; for if it were bounded, the rich would begin to possess superfluity as soon as they attained them. In short, he believes that this desire is so generally allowed of, that it almost entirely prevents the rich from possessing any superfluities.

You may understand, Sir, by the preceding statement, the pretence for accumulation and pressing forward to a more elevated condition, though by legitimate methods—*ad statum quem licitè possunt acquirere*—which the author of the letters denominates *ambition*; because this is the name by which the Fathers, and, indeed, every one else, distinguishes it. He was not obliged to imitate one of the most ordinary pieces of finesse practised by those wretched casuists, who banish the names of vices, but retain, under different appellations, the vices themselves. If, then, the words *statum quem licitè possunt acquirere*, had really been in the passage he has quoted, there was no need to omit them, in order to render the passage objectionable. It is by adding them, he has a right to accuse Vasquez of maintaining, that if you possess ambition, you cannot have a superfluity. He is not the first who has deduced the same inference from this doctrine. Mr. Du Val had done so before in express terms, when combating this pernicious maxim, tom. 2. qu. 8. p. 576: "It will follow, says he, "that whoever desires a higher dignity, that is to say, who has greater ambition, would not have a superfluity, though he should possess much more than was necessary to his present condition—*Sequeretur cum qui hanc dignitatem cuperet; seu qui* MAJORI AMBITIONE DUCERETUR. *habendo plurima supra decentiam sui status, non habiturum superflua.*"

You have not succeeded very well, then, in the first two falsities which you have charged upon the author of the letters. Let us see if you are better grounded in the two others, of which you have accused him in his defence. The first is, that he asserts, Vasquez does not require the rich to give out of what is necessary to their own rank. The answer to this is easy, for I have only to say at once, *it is false, and he says quite the contrary*. A sufficient proof of this is, that very passage which you produce three lines after, where he states that Vasquez "requires the rich to give out of their own necessities on certain occasions."

Your last complaint is equally unreasonable. The author of the letters has objected to two decisions in Vasquez: the one is, "that the rich are not obliged, either in justice or charity, to part with their superfluities, still less their necessaries, to supply the common wants of the poor;"—the other, "that they are not obliged to part with what is necessary, but on such occasions as seldom or never occur." Having no reply to the first of these decisions, which is the most infamous, what did you do? Why, join them together, and, imputing some great error to the last you would make people believe, that you had fully replied to both. In order, therefore, to unravel what you purposely perplex, I ask you pointedly, whether it is not true that Vasquez teaches that the rich are never under any obligation to give, either out of their superfluities, or out of their necessities, in justice, or in charity, to the ordinary wants of the poor? Has not the author of the letters proved this by the following quotation from Vasquez? "Corduba teaches, that if a person possess a superabundance, he is obliged to give to those who are in circumstances of ordinary necessity, a portion, at least, in some measure, to fulfil the precept."—(Here remark, that he is not inquiring, whether he is obliged in justice or charity, but whether he is absolutely obliged at all.)—Let us see the decision of your Vasquez—"But this does not quite please me—*sed hoc non placet;* for we have shown the contrary against Cajetan and Navarre." To this you furnish no answer, but leave the Jesuits convicted of an error so opposite to the Gospel.

As to the second decision of Vasquez, which is, that the rich are not obliged to give out of what is requisite to maintain their own rank, but on occasions so rare that they scarcely ever occur; the author of the letters has demonstrated it with equal clearness, by collecting the conditions which this Jesuit requires to constitute the obligation; namely, "to be assured, that the poor person in this urgent necessity, will receive assistance from no one but ourselves; and that this necessity threatens him either with the destruction of life, or the loss of reputation." He then demands, whether such cases were of very frequent occurrence in Paris; and, lastly, presses the Jesuits by this argument—whilst Vasquez allows the poor to rob the rich in the same circumstances in which he obliges the rich to relieve the poor, he must either suppose that such occasions are very unusual, or that stealing was commonly permitted. What said you, Sir, to this? You disregarded all these proofs, and contented yourselves with citing three passages from Vasquez, who says in the first two, that the rich are obliged to help the poor in cases of urgent necessity, which is expressly acknowledged by the author of the letters: but, then, you take especial care not to state the restrictions he mentions, which so order these urgent necessities, that they seldom oblige to the duty of almsgiving; which is, in fact, the point in dispute.

The third passage simply states, that the rich are not under obligation to give alms, except in extreme necessities, as when a man is at the point of death, because they are too rare; whence you conclude, that it is false to say the cases in which Vasquez obliges to give alms are very rare. But you are joking, surely; for no other conclusion can be drawn, but that Vasquez does not admit the occasions of distributing to the poor are *very rare;* but he, in reality, makes them so by the conditions which he imposes. In this, he has only followed the example of his society. This Jesuit had at once to satisfy the rich, who are not very desirous of too frequent almsgiving, and the church, which enjoins them to do it often out of their superfluity. He was desirous, therefore, according to the usual methods of the society, to satisfy every body, and he has succeeded exceedingly well; for he requires on one side, conditions of such unfrequent occurrence, that the most avaricious ought to be satisfied; and, on the other, takes away the term *rare*, to please the church in appearance. The question is not, then, whether Vasquez calls those opportunities by the name of *rare*, in which we are obliged to alms-giving. He has never been accused of calling them rare. Oh, no; he was too skilful a Jesuit to call bad things by their proper names. The question is, to know whether they are not *rare* by the restraints he has laid upon them; and this has been so plainly shown by the author of the letters, that he has

17*

left you no other but this general answer, which never fails you—*dissimulation* and *silence.*

All you have added respecting the subtlety of Vasquez, in giving such a variety of senses to the words *necessity* and *superfluity,* is mere illusion. He never takes them but in the two significations, in which all divines concur. There are, according to him, "things necessary to nature and necessary to station ; superfluous to nature and superfluous to station." To constitute superfluity of the latter kind, he states that it must not only be so in reference to your present station or rank, but also with regard to the wealth which may hereafter be acquired either by the individuals themselves, or their relatives, by lawful methods. Hence, according to Vasquez, whatever may be stored up to enhance a man's condition in the world, is simply to be called necessary to his condition, and superfluous only to nature : moreover, he is not obliged to bestow alms out of it, excepting on those occasions which the author of the letters has shown to be so rare, as seldom or never to occur.

It is unnecessary to add any thing to what the author of the letters has said concerning the comparison between Vasquez and Cajetan. I will merely remark in passing, that you are equally unjust to them both, when you maintain that, "contrary to what he (the Cardinal) had said in his treatise on Almsgiving, he teaches us in his book on Indulgences, 'that to violate the obligation to give what is superfluous, is a venial sin.'" Now, Sir, read him yourself, and no longer place such implicit confidence in the Jesuits, living or dead. You will find that the Cardinal solemnly avows the very opposite doctrine ; and, after saying that nothing but extreme necessities, under which designation he includes most of those which Vasquez denominates urgent, constitute it a mortal sin, he subjoins an exception in reference to the possession of superfluities—*seclusâ superfluitate bonorum.*

I hasten then to accompany you to the doctrine of simony. The author of the letters had nothing in view, but to show that the society of Jesuits hold the following maxim: "that it is not simony in conscience, to give a spiritual in exchange for a temporal possession, provided the temporal be only the chief motive, and not the price;" and, to prove it, he quotes at length, in his twelfth letter, the passage from Valentia, which so clearly avows it, that you have no reply to offer; no more than to Escobar, Erade Bill, and others who maintain the same doctrine. It is quite sufficient that all these authors concur in this opinion, to show, that according to the whole society, who assert the doctrine of probability, it is safe in conscience, after so many grave authors have maintained it, and so many grave provincials have approved it Acknowledge, then, while leaving this sentiment to remain in full force, as you do, a sentiment in which all the other Jesuits concur, and adhering to Tannerus alone, you really achieve nothing against the design of the author of the letters, whom you attack, or in favour of the society which you defend.

But, in order to afford you complete satisfaction upon this subject, I aver that you have distorted the language even of Tannerus, quite as much as that of others. First, you cannot deny, that he says in general, " it is no simony in conscience—*in foro conscientiæ*, to give a spiritual possession for a temporal one, when the temporal is nothing more than the principal *motive* and not the *price*." And when he states it is no simony in conscience, the meaning is, that it is not so either by a divine or positive law; for what is simony by positive law is simony in conscience. This is the general rule, to which Tannerus produces one exception; namely, " that in cases expressed in the law, it is a simony by positive law, or a presumptive simony." But, since an exception cannot be so extensive as the rule, it necessarily follows that the general maxim, " it is no simony in conscience to give a spiritual in exchange for a temporal possession, which is only the motive and not the price," must apply to some species of spiritual things, consequently some kind of spirituals may, without simony, be given by positive law for temporals, by changing the word *price* into *motive*.

The author of the letters has chosen the sort of livings to which he applies the doctrine of Valentia and Tannerus: nevertheless, he allows you to substitute any other, and to say, that it is not livings, but sacraments or ecclesiastical preferments that may be given for money. All this he believes to be equally impious and leaves you to the choice. This, it seems, you have done, wishing it to be understood, that it is no simony to say mass, when the principal motive for it is merely to obtain money. This follows, from your account of the custom of the church at Paris. For, if you had merely stated that Christians may offer temporal things to those from whom they receive spiritual, and that priests, who serve at the altar, should live by the altar, you would have said only what nobody disputes, but which has no relevancy to the question.

The point is, whether a priest, whose principal motive in presenting the sacrifice respects the money he receives, is or is not guilty of simony in the sight of God. You may exculpate him by the doctrine of Tannerus, but can you do it upon the principles of Christian piety? "If simony," says Peter le Chantre, one of the greatest ornaments of the church of Paris, "be so shameful and so damnable in things connected with the sacraments, what must it be in the very sacraments themselves, especially in the Eucharist, in which the holy body of Christ, the fountain and origin of all graces, is taken? Simon the sorcerer," he adds, "when rejected by Peter, might have alleged, 'Thou rebukest me, but I will triumph over thee and the whole body of the church—I will establish the seat of my empire on the altars themselves; and when the angels assemble at one corner of the altar to worship the body of Jesus Christ, I will be present at the other, to cause the minister of that altar, or rather my own, to form the body for money.'" And yet this simony, so strongly condemned by this pious divine, does not consist in any thing but *cupidity*, which, in the administration of spiritual things, principally regards the temporal gain which accrues; which induces him to say, in general, c. 25, that, "when the holy offices," which he calls works of the right hand, " are exercised for the love of money, they produce simony : *opus dexteræ operatum causâ pecuniæ acquirendæ, parit simoniam.*"

What would he have said then, if he had heard of this horrible maxim of the casuists which you defend, "that it is allowable for a priest to renounce all the spiritual advantage which may result from the holy sacrament, for the sake of a little money?"

You perceive then, Sir, if this be all you have to say in defence of Tannerus, you only make him guilty of a greater impiety: but you will never be able, from his statements, to prove that it is simony by a positive law to take money as a motive for the gift of a benefice. For, please to observe, that he does not simply say, that it is simony to bestow a spiritual possession in consideration of a temporal gift, as a motive, and not as the price or value; but he subjoins this alternative, that it "either is simony by a positive law, or a presumptive simony." A presumptive simony, is no simony in the sight of God, and deserves no condemnation before the tribunal of conscience. To say, with Tannerus, that it is simony by positive law or presumptive simony, is, in fact, to say only it is simony, or it is not.

Such is the amount of Tannerus's exception, which the author of the letters need not have mentioned in his sixth letter, because, without citing any of this Jesuit's expressions, he merely says that he is of the same opinion with Valentia; but he introduces and expressly answers it in his twelfth, though you falsely accuse him of passing over it.

It was to avoid the perplexity of these distinctions, that the author of the letters proposed this question to the Jesuits, " whether, according to their authors, it was simony in conscience to give a living of 200*l.* per annum, and take 500*l.* as a *motive*, and not as a *price?*" He has urged them to give a direct reply, without speaking about positive law; that is, without making use of those terms which are unintelligible to mankind in general, but not without regarding it, as you have misrepresented him, contrary to all grammatical construction. Kindly, however, to afford us satisfaction, you have given us this brief conclusion, "that taking away the positive law, there would be no simony, as there would be no sin in not hearing mass on a holyday, if the church had not commanded it;" that is to say, it is a simony, because the church has constituted it such, but that without her positive decisions it would be indifferent. Upon which, I must observe,—

1. Yours is no reply to the question. The author of the letters demanded, if it were simony, *according to the Jesuitical authors he has cited;* and you tell us, *ex cathedrâ*, it is only a simony of positive law. But the object is not to know *your* opinion, which is of no weight. You pretend, perhaps, to be a *grave* doctor? This is rather questionable; but what say Valentia, Tannerus, Sanchez, Escobar, Erade Bill, who are indisputably grave? Your answer must be coincident with their sentiments. The author of the letters states, that, according to these Jesuits, there is no simony in conscience in these instances. As to Valentia, Sanchez, Escobar, and others, you abandon them; adhering, indeed, a little to Tannerus, but, as you see, without any substantial reason; so that, after all, the society teaches, that a spiritual may be given for a temporal consideration, without simony in conscience, provided that the temporal be only the principal motive and not the price. This was all that was demanded.

2. I maintain, that your reply contains a shocking impiety. What, sir! dare you affirm that, independently of the laws of the church, it would be no simony to give money with such a perverted intention to obtain ecclesiastical preferments?—that, previous to the existence of the canons upon this subject, it was lawful to purchase them, provided the money were not given as the value; and thus St. Peter was to be deemed rash for so authoritatively condemning Simon Magus, since it does not appear that he offered the money more as a price than as a motive?

Pray, Sir, to what *school* would you send us to learn this doctrine? Not, surely, to that of Jesus Christ, who always commanded his disciples to give freely what they had freely received; by which he excludes, as Peter le Chantre says, in *verb. Abb.* c. 36, "all expectation of presents or services, whether by agreement, or otherwise, because God sees the heart." Nor is it the school of the church, who treats those who employ money to obtain ecclesiastical offices, not only as criminals, but heretics, denominating this kind of traffic, extenuate it as you will, not a violation of her positive laws only, but a heresy—*simoniacam hæresim*.

The *school*, then, in which these maxims are learned, that it is only a simony of positive law, or only a presumptive simony, or no simony or sin at all, to give money for a living, as a motive, and not as the price, can be no other than that of Gehazi, and of Simon Magus, the sorcerer. This is the school in which these two first dealers in sacred things are to be deemed innocent, who are every where else regarded as most execrable; and where, leaving cupidity to its own desires and determination, is taught to evade the law of God, by changing a term which cannot alter the thing itself. But let the disciples of this school hear in what manner that great Pope Innocent III., in his letter to the archbishop of Canterbury, in the year 1199, has thundered against the damnable subtleties of those, "who, being blinded by the desire of gain, attempt to palliate simony under an honourable name—*simoniam sub honesto nomine palliant:* as if a change of name could change the nature of a crime, and the punishment it merits. But," he adds, "God is not to be mocked; and if these followers of Simon Magus should escape the punishment they deserve in the present life, they cannot possibly avoid, in the other world, the everlasting misery which is in reserve for them. The speciousness of a name is incapable of extenuating the malignity of the sin; it is a disguise which will not hinder a thing being accounted wicked—*Cum nec honestas nominis criminis malitiam palliabit, nec vox poterit abolere reatum.*"

The last subject of observation is bankruptcy; upon which I admire your assurance. The Jesuits, whose cause you advocate, have very improperly thrown the question of Escobar upon Lessius; for the author of the letters only quoted Lessius upon the authority of Escobar, charging the latter only with this doctrine, which has occasioned so much complaint; namely, that the bankrupts may retain a sufficiency for a genteel living, *though these goods were obtained by injustice and crimes universally notorious!* is, besides, solely on account of Escobar that he urges them either publicly to disavow this doctrine, or as publicly acknowledge it; in which case he appeals to parliament. Some *answer* is here required, and not merely the statement that Lessius, who is out of the question, is not of the same opinion with Escobar, who alone is concerned. Do you really think of answering questions by only changing them? Pray desist from such strange attempts.

You shall reply to Escobar before we come to Lessius. Not that I refuse to enter the lists, for I promise to give you a faithful and full explanation of the notions of Lessius respecting bankruptcy, which I feel persuaded will shock the parliament as much as the Sorbonne. To this then, by the help of God, I pledge my word; but you shall previously answer the contested point relating to Escobar. You must give a precise and satisfactory account upon this subject, before any new questions are investigated. Escobar is first in turn, and in spite of your evasions, shall have the first attention. Be assured Lessius shall follow immediately.

N. B. *Though this letter was the production of another and inferior writer, it seemed, upon the whole, too interesting to be omitted.*

LETTER XIII.

The Doctrine of Lessius respecting Murder the same with that of Victoria. The Ease with which we pass from Speculation to Practice. Reason why the Jesuits make use of this vain Distinction, and how unavailing it is to their Justification.

REVEREND FATHERS,   Sept. 30, 1656.

    I HAVE seen your last performance, in which you proceed with your impositions as far as the twentieth, declaring that this is the concluding part of that kind of accusation of which your first consists, from which you pass to the second, where you adopt a new method of defence, by showing that many other casuists, beside yours, are as relaxed in discipline as yourselves. I perceive, now, my good Fathers, to what a multitude of misrepresentations I have to reply; and since the fourth, where we stopped, is upon the subject of Homicide, it will be proper in answering it, at the same time to investigate the eleventh, thirteenth, fourteenth, fifteenth, sixteenth, seventeenth, and eighteenth, which are all upon the same subject.
    In the present letter, I shall prove the truth of my citations, in contradiction to the falsities with which you have charged me. But since you have ventured to assert, " that the sentiments of your authors on murder are conformable to the decisions of the Popes and to the ecclesiastical laws;" you oblige me in the following letter, to overturn a proposition so extremely rash, and so prejudicial to the church. It is of importance to show that she is free from your corruptions, that the heretics may not be able to avail

themselves of your errors, and deduce consequences of a nature dishonourable to her character. On the one hand, therefore, by surveying your pernicious doctrines, and on the other, the canons of the church, which have always condemned them, we shall at once discover what ought to be avoided and what followed.

Your fourth misstatement relates to a maxim concerning murder, which you represent me as having falsely attributed to Lessius. It is this : " He who has received a box on the ear may instantly pursue his enemy, and even strike him with a sword not out of revenge, but to make reparation to his insulted honour." This, you assert, is the opinion of the casuist Victoria. But this is not the subject of dispute; for it is not inconsistent to say it is the opinion both of Victoria and of Lessius; since Lessius himself says, it is the sentiment of Navarre and of your Father Henriquez, who teach, " that he who has received a box on the ear may pursue his man instantly, and return him as many as he may deem necessary to make reparation to his honour." The only question therefore is, whether Lessius coincides in the sentiment of these authors as well as his colleagues; and for this reason you add, " that Lessius only mentions this opinion to refute it; so that I attribute to him a sentiment which he only states to oppose, the most base and shameful action of which a writer can be guilty." But I maintain, my Fathers, that he introduces it with approbation and to follow it. This is a question of fact, which it will be easy to determine. Let us see then, how you prove your assertions, and you shall afterwards see how I prove mine.

In order to show that Lessius is not of this opinion, you say that he condemns the practice of it; to demonstrate which, you cite a passage, l. 2. c. 9. n. 82, where he has these words : " I condemn the practice of it." It is true, if these words are sought for in Lessius, n. 82, they will be found according to your quotation; but what must be said, Fathers, when we find, at the same time, that in this place he is discussing a question totally different from the one of which we are speaking; and the opinion, the practice of which he condemns in that place, is in no respect the same with what we have in hand, but one entirely distinct from it? To be convinced of this, it is only necessary to open the book itself, where we shall find all the rest of the discourse to the same purpose.

He treats upon the question at n. 79, "Whether we may kill a person for a box on the ear," and concludes it, at n. 80, without uttering a single syllable of condemnation. As soon as this question is determined, he enters upon a new one in article 81, "whether we may kill another for slander?" And upon this latter it is at n. 82, he introduces the very words you have quoted: "I condemn the practice of it."

Now, Fathers, is it not most shameful that you should dare to produce these words to make people believe that Lessius condemns the opinion of its being allowable to kill another for a box on the ear? and, having given only the proof referred to above, triumph as you do in this strain. "Many persons of honour in Paris have already detected this flagrant falsity by reading Lessius, and have thus learned what kind of dependence may be placed upon this calumniator?" What Fathers! is it thus you abuse the confidence which persons of honour have reposed in you? To make them understand that Lessius is not of a particular opinion you open his book for them in a place where he is condemning quite another opinion; and as these persons do not question your veracity, and therefore do not think of examining whether the passage really refers to the point in debate, you cheat their credulity. I am persuaded, Fathers, that in order to excuse so infamous a falsehood, you must have recourse to your doctrine of equivocation, and reading this passage *aloud*, you say in a *low inaudible tone*, this belongs to another subject. But I cannot tell whether this reason, though it may satisfy your consciences, will be sufficient to silence the just complaints of these people of honour, when they find how you have imposed upon them.

Pray do all you can, Fathers, to prevent their seeing my letters, as it is the only way which remains of maintaining your credit with them a little longer. I make a different use of yours, distributing them amongst all my friends, anxious that every body should read them. I fancy both of us act with good reason : for, after publishing this fourth imposture with such pomp, you will be in sad disgrace if it should come to be known that you have substituted one passage for another. It will be easily believed, that if you had found what you wished in the place where Lessius treats upon the subject, you would not have sought it elsewhere, and that you only had recourse to this measure, because you could not discover any thing where you were looking to answer your purpose. You were resolved to find something in Lessius to authorize your assertion, p. 10. l. 12 : " that he does *not* admit this opinion to be probable in speculation :" and Lessius expressly states, in his conclusion, n. 80, " the opinion that one person may kill another for having given him a box on the ear *is* probable in speculation." Is not this, in so many explicit words, a contradiction to your statement? And who can sufficiently admire the effrontery with which you contradict a plain matter of fact, even by using the very same terms; so that, instead of concluding from your supposititious passage, that Lessius was *not* of this opinion, he positively declares by his own expressions that he really *is*.

You were desirous, again, that Lessius should be made to affirm that " he condemns the practice of it ;" but, as I have before said, there is not a syllable of condemnation to be found in the passage. His language is, " It appears that one ought not *easily* to allow the practice of it—*in praxi non videtur facilé permittenda*." Is this, my Fathers, the mode of speaking adopted by a man who *condemns* a maxim? Would you say that one ought not *easily* to allow the practice of adultery or incest? Ought we not, on the contrary, to conclude, that as Lessius says no more, but that the practice ought not to be *easily* permitted, his opinion is that it may be *sometimes* though *rarely* permitted? And, as if he were solicitous of teaching every body when it ought to be permitted, and thus removing all scruples out of the way of persons likely to be disgusted, and that might prove unseasonably troublesome, not knowing upon what occasions they might in practice be allowed to kill others, he has been careful to point out what they ought to avoid in practising this doctrine conscientiously. Do hear him, my Fathers: "One ought not, methinks," says he, "easily to permit it, *because* of the danger of being excited by a spirit of hatred and revenge or passion, or lest it should occasion too many murders." Hence it is obvious that, according to Lessius, murder is still permitted in practice, if inconveniences be avoided, that is to say, if one can perpetrate the deed without hatred or revenge, and under circumstances which do not excite to a *too frequent repetition of murders!*

Are you desirous of an example, my good Fathers? You shall have one of recent occurrence. It is that of the box of the ear at Compeigne. You must admit that the person who received it has evinced by his behaviour, the great command he possessed over the passions of hatred and revenge. Nothing remained but to avoid too numerous murders; and you know, Fathers, that it is so very rare for Jesuits to give blows to officers of the king's household, that there was no reason to apprehend a murder on that account would have occasioned too many others. You cannot, therefore, deny but that this Jesuit might have been slain with a good conscience, and that the offended party might, in this instance, have availed himself of the doctrine of Lessius: and perhaps, my Fathers, he would have done so, had he been educated in your school, and taught by Escobar, "that a person who has received a box on the ear is reputed to have lost his honour till he has killed the person who gave it him." But you have reason to believe, that his having received quite opposite instructions from a curate, no mighty favourite of yours, contributed not a little to save the life of a Jesuit.

Pray say no more, then, of the inconveniences to be avoided on so many occasions, without which, murder is allowed in practice upon the authority of Lessius. This your writers have fully acknowledged, as quoted by Escobar in his *Practice of Homicide according to your Society.* " Is it allowed," says he, " to kill the person who gives you a box on the ear ? Lessius states it is so in speculation, but that it ought not to be advised in practice—*non consulendum in praxi*—on account of the danger which may arise from hatred or from murders prejudicial to the state. BUT THE OTHER AUTHORS HAVE DECIDED, THAT IF THESE INCONVENIENCES BE AVOIDED IT IS ALLOWED AND SAFE IN PRACTICE—*in praxi probibilem et tutam judicarunt Henriquez*, &c."

Behold how opinions advance, by degrees, to the highest probability! To what a pitch have you carried the opinion just mentioned, by admitting it without any distinction either in speculation or practice in these words: " It is lawful, upon receiving a box on the ear, instantly to return it by a stroke with a sword, not out of revenge, but for the preservation of one's honour." Your Fathers, at Caen, taught the same doctrine in 1644, in their public writings, which the university presented to parliament in their third request against your doctrine of Homicide, in p. 339 of the volume then printed.

Observe then, Fathers, that your own authors themselves destroy this futile distinction between speculation and practice, which the university has treated with ridicule, and the invention of which is one of your political secrets it is well to disclose : for, besides that the knowledge of it is requisite to your fifteenth, sixteenth, seventeenth, and eighteenth impostures, it is always very proper and necessary to discover by degrees the principles of your mysterious policy.

Whenever you have undertaken to decide upon cases of conscience in a favourable and accommodating manner, you have found some of them in which religion alone was concerned, as questions relating to contrition, penitence, the love of God, and all others which refer to the inward feelings of conscience. But you have discovered others, in which the state was as much concerned as religion; such as those which regard usury, bankruptcy, homicide, and others of a similar nature. And it is very affecting to those who cherish a genuine love to the church, to witness, in an incalculable variety of cases, in which you have only had religion to oppose, how you have, without hesitation, distinction, or fear, overthrown the laws; as appears most evidently in your presumptuous boldness, against penitence and the love of God; because you were aware this was not the appropriate place for the visible exercise of divine justice. But, where both religion and the state were interested, your apprehensions of human justice have induced you to divide your decisions, and to form two questions upon these subjects; the one you call *speculation*, in which, considering crimes in themselves, and not in reference to the welfare of the state, but solely to the law of God by which they are interdicted, you have allowed them without the slightest hesitation, thus subverting the law of God which condemns them;—the other you term *practice*, in which, considering the injury the state might suffer and the presence of the magistrates who maintain the public safety, you do not always approve of those murders and crimes in practice which are allowed in speculation, so that you contrive to shelter yourselves from the judges.

Upon that question, for example, "whether it is lawful to kill for slander," your authors, Filiutius, tr. 29, cap. 3, n. 52, Reginaldus, l, 21, cap. 5, n. 63, and others, reply, "it is allowable in speculation—*ex probabili opinione licet*—but I do not admit of it in practice, on account of the number of murders it may sanction, and which would prove detrimental to the state, if all slanderers were to be slain; and besides, such murderers would be punished by justice." In this manner your opinions begin to exhibit themselves under a distinction by which you subvert the interests of religion alone, without sensibly affecting the state. Hence you imagine yourselves to be in perfect security, supposing the credit you have obtained in the church will prevent her punishing your offences against truth, and that the precautions you have adopted, not too easily to allow those permissions in practice, will screen you on the part of the magistrates, who not being judges in cases of conscience, have not properly to do with any thing but the external act. Thus an opinion which would be condemned under the name of *practice*, shows itself in safety under that of *speculation*.

Having formed this basis, it is easy to construct the rest of your maxims. There is an infinite distance between the divine prohibition against murder, and the speculative permission given by your authors. But the distance is very trifling between this permission and the practice. It now then only remains to show, that what is permitted in speculation, is so in practice also, and for this we have ample evidence You have produced it in cases of much greater difficulty. Do you wish, good Fathers, to see how this can be? Follow the reasoning of Escobar, who has clearly decided it in the first of the six volumes of his great Moral Theology, of which I have before spoken, where he seems to have quite a different light from what he had in his collection from your four-and-twenty elders; for, at that time, he thought there might be probable opinions in speculation, which might not be safe in conscience; but he has since thought the reverse, and has strongly established it in his last work: so much has the doctrine of probability gained by time, as well as each probable opinion in particular! Attend to his language in *prolog.* n. 15, " I do not see how it can possibly arise, that what is allowed in speculation should not be so in practice, since what can be accomplished in practice depends upon what is permitted in speculation; and these things differ from each other only as cause and effect. It is speculation which determines action. *Whence it follows that one may, with a safe conscience, follow in practice the opinions which are probable in speculation; and even with more safety than those which have not been so fully examined by speculation.*"

Escobar really reasons admirably sometimes; and, in fact, there is such a connexion between speculation and practice, that when one has taken root, you make no difficulty in permitting the undisguised progress of the other. This has been seen in the permission to kill for a box on the ear, which, from simple speculation, has been boldly carried forward by Lessius into practice *that one ought not easily to grant*, and from thence by Escobar to *an easy practice;* from which your Fathers at Caen have advanced it to a *full permission*, without any distinction between theory and practice.

Thus, by little and little, you make your opinions grow. Were they all at once to appear so monstrously extravagant, the utmost horror would be excited; but this slow and imperceptible progress gradually habituates the public to them, and diminishes their offensiveness. By this means, the permission to murder, so odious to the church and state, first insinuates itself into the church, and, afterwards, from the church into the state.

Similar success has attended the opinion respecting killing for slander; for that has now obtained the same permission without any distinction. I should not have stopped to report these passages of your Fathers, had it not been necessary to abash the confidence with which you have twice asserted, in your fifteenth imposture, p. 26 and 30, "There is not one Jesuit who admits murder for slander." When you write in this manner, Fathers, you should prevent my seeing it, because it is so easily confuted: for not only your Fathers Reginaldus, Filiutius, &c., have allowed of it in speculation, as I have before stated; and not only does the principle of Escobar insensibly lead to the practice; but, I will say further, that many of your authors have allowed it in so many words; amongst others, Father Hereau, in his public lectures; in consequence of which, the king ordered him into confinement in your house, having taught, amongst many other errors, "that when he who defames us in the presence of people of honour, continues to do so, after being warned to desist, we may kill him; not, indeed, publicly, for fear of scandal, but in secret—*sed clam.*"

I have already spoken of Father Launy, and you are not ignorant that his doctrine upon this subject was censured in 1649, by the university of Louvain: nevertheless, two months have not yet elapsed since your Father, Des Bois maintained, at Rouen, this very condemned doctrine of Father Launy, teaching, "that it is lawful for a monk to defend the honour he has acquired by his virtue, even by killing the person who dares to attack his reputation—*etiam cum morte invasoris:*" which has occasioned such scandal in that city, that all the curates have united to impose silence upon him, and oblige him, by canonical means, to retract his doctrine. The affair is, at present, before the ecclesiastical court.

What can you now say, Fathers? Will you, after this, undertake to maintain, that "no Jesuit is of opinion, that one may kill another for scandal?" Was any thing more needed to convince you of this than the opinions even of your own Fathers, since they do not forbid to kill in speculation, but only in practice, "on account of the ill consequences which may accrue to the state?" I ask then, Fathers, if our disputes relate to any thing else than an examination whether you have overturned the law of God which prohibits homicide? The question is not whether you have injured the state, but religion? To what purpose is it then, in a dispute of this nature, to show that you have spared the state, when you make it evident at the same time, that you have subverted the interests of religion, by saying as you do p. 28. l. 3. "that the sense of Reginaldus, on the question relating to killing for slander is, that a private person has a right to adopt this mode of defence, considering it only in itself?" I wish for nothing more than this admission to confound you.— "A private person," say you, "has a right to adopt this mode of defence,"—that is to say, he has a right to kill for slander—"considering the thing in itself"—consequently, Fathers, the law of God which expressly forbids murder, is, by this decision, destroyed.

It is of no avail afterwards to say, "that it is unlawful and criminal, even according to the law of God, on account of the murders and disorders which would occur in the state, because we are obliged, by divine appointment, to regard the welfare of the state." This is wandering from the question; for, my good Fathers, there are two laws to be observed—the one prohibits murder, the other forbids injuring the state. Reginaldus, perhaps, has not broken the law which enjoins our doing nothing to injure the state; but he has certainly violated that which commands us not to kill; but the latter is the only one which relates to the present subject.

Moreover, your other Fathers, who have allowed these murders in practice, have nullified both commands.

But let us advance a little further. We are perfectly aware, that you do sometimes forbid doing injury to the state; and you allege, that your design is to observe the law of God, which requires us to give it our support. This may be true, though it is by no means certain, since you may do the same thing merely through fear of the judges. Let us then examine from which of these principles it proceeds.

Is it not obvious, Fathers, that if you were truly to love God, and the observance of his law were the primary and principal object in view, this regard would uniformly predominate in every important decision, and would influence you on all occasions to take the deepest interest in religion? But if, on the contrary, we see, that in so many cases, you violate the most solemn commands which God has enjoined upon man, when there is only his law to oppose; and that even on the occasions now in question, you annihilate the law of God, which prohibits these actions, as criminal in themselves, and seem to be deterred from approving them in practice, solely by a fear of the judges; do not you give us reason to believe, that your apprehension has no regard to God, and that if you uphold his law in appearance, in what respects the duty of not doing injury to a state, it does not originate in any reverence for the law itself, but merely to gain your own ends, as all other religious politicians of no piety have done?

And will you really tell us, Fathers, that the law of God which forbids homicide, will sanction murder for slander?

and after having thus violated the eternal law of heaven, can you think of removing the scandal you have occasioned, and persuade us that you pay a proper regard to it, by adding that you forbid the practice of it from considerations of state, and through fear of the judges? Is not this, in fact, raising a new scandal, not out of respect for the judges, for this is not what I reproach you for, and you are very ridiculous upon this point in page 29. I do not blame you for being afraid of the judges, but for being afraid of *them only.* This is the point—for this I censure you, because it is making God less the enemy of crimes than man. Were you to say that one may kill a slanderer according to human judgment, though not according to God, this would have been more tolerable: but, to assert that what is too criminal to be endured by men, may be innocent and just in the eyes of God who is justice itself, what do you do but show to the whole world, by this monstrous and awful perversion, which is so opposite to the true spirit of saints, that you are bold against God and timid towards your fellow-men? Had you sincerely intended to condemn these homicides, surely you would have allowed that command of God which forbids them; and had you ventured at first to permit these homicides, you would have openly permitted them in defiance of the laws of God and man. But as you have allowed them by insensible degrees, and took the magistrates by surprise, whose business it is to watch over the public safety, you have acted a wily part by separating your maxims: and, on the one side, proposing, " that it is allowable in speculation to murder for slander," (for you are left to examine things in speculation,) and, on the other side, producing this detached maxim, " that what is allowed in speculation is also in practice." What concern does the state appear to have in this general and metaphysical proposition? In this manner these two principles being received separately are little suspected, and the vigilance of the magistrates is eluded ; for it is only necessary to unite these maxims together, to deduce from them the inference to which you tend, "that one may murder in practice for simple slander."

Here we behold one of the finest specimens of your subtle policy, separating in your writings the maxims which you associate in your opinions. By these means, you have introduced your doctrine of probability, which I have so frequently explained; and this general principle being established, you advance things separately, which, though possibly innocent in themselves, become horrible when conjoined with this pernicious principle. As an example of this, turn to page 11 of your impostures, where it is incumbent upon me to answer this statement; "that many celebrated divines are of opinion that one man may kill another for having given him a box on the ear." If, indeed, a person had said this who did not maintain the doctrine of probability, he could not be subject to any reproof, since it would, in that case, be only a simple recital which could be of no consequence; but you, Fathers, and all others who hold this dangerous doctrine, "that whatever celebrated authors approve is safe in conscience," with another to this purpose, "that many celebrated authors are of opinion that one man may kill another for having given him a box on the ear," what are you doing but putting a dagger into the hands of every Christian to kill those who have offended them, by giving them an assurance that they may do it with a safe conscience, because in this they will only follow the opinion of so many *grave* authors?

What abominable language, which, while stating that some authors hold a damnable opinion, decides at the very same time in favour of that damnable opinion, and makes conscience sanction every thing it merely reports? We understand it, Fathers! This is the peculiar language of your school: and it is truly astonishing that you should be so audacious as to talk in this high strain, since it displays your sentiments in so undisguised a manner, and convicts you of holding this opinion as safe in conscience, " that one man may kill another for a box on the ear," as soon as you have said that a multitude of celebrated authors maintain it.

You can no more defend yourselves in this, than you can serve your purpose by those passages from Vasquez and Suarez which you oppose to me, in which they condemn those murders so much approved by their fraternity. These testimonies, separated from the rest of your doctrine, might dazzle people who know but little about it; but your principles and your maxims must be joined together. In this place you say that Vasquez does not allow of murders; but what do you state elsewhere? Why, truly, "that the probability of one sentiment does not prevent the probability of a contrary sentiment;" and again, "it is allowable to follow the least probable and the least sure, abandoning that which is most probable and most sure." What follows from all this put together, but that we have perfect liberty of conscience to adopt any one we please of those opposite opinions? And what becomes, Fathers, of that fruit which you expected from all these citations? It is all gone, since it is only necessary for your condemnation, to collect those maxims which you separate for your justification. Why, then, do you produce those passages of your authors which I have not quoted, to excuse those which I have cited, since they have nothing in common? What right does this give you to call me an *impostor*? Have I asserted that all your Fathers are equally depraved? Have I not said, on the contrary, that your principal interest consists in having all kinds of opinions to suit all sorts of occasions? Does any one wish to kill? Let him repair to Lessius. If the reverse, let him apply to Vasquez, that no one may be discontented at having no grave author on his side. Lessius will discourse of homicide like a heathen, and of almsgiving perhaps like a Christian. Vasquez will speak of almsgiving like a heathen, and of homicide like a Christian. But by means of probability, which both Vasquez and Lessius maintain, and which unites all your opinions in a kind of common coincidence, they will mutually blend each other's sentiments, and will be under an obligation to absolve those who have acted conformably to the opinions which each of them has condemned. You are thus perplexed by variety : whereas, uniformity would be far more tolerable ; and nothing can be more contrary to the express orders of St. Ignatius and your first generals, than this confused intermixture of all sorts of opinions. I shall, perhaps, some time say a little more upon this subject ; and people will be surprised to find how much you have degenerated from the original spirit of your institution, and how the generals of your own order foresaw that the monstrous doctrines of your morality might become injurious, not only to your society, but to the peace of the whole church.

I must, however, tell you that no advantage can be gained to your cause from the opinion of Vasquez. It would be extraordinary indeed, if among so many Jesuits who have become authors, only one or two could be found to coincide in the principles common to all Christians. There is no honour in maintaining that one cannot commit murder for a box on the ear according to the Gospel, but denying it to be shameful and horrible ; so far then is this from justifying you, that nothing can be more to your disadvantage ; since, although some of your doctors have told you the truth, you have not followed it, but love darkness rather than light. Vasquez has taught you, " that it is a heathenish and not a Christian sentiment, to say one may return a box on the ear with a blow of a stick, that it is subversive both of the law and the Gospel, to assert we may kill a man for it, and that the most abandoned of mankind acknowledge this to be the case." You, however, in contradiction to this universal admission, suffer Lessius, Escobar, and others, to decide that all the prohibitions which God has issued against homicide, do not render it improper to kill a person for giving a box on the ear. To what purpose, then, is it to produce this passage of Vasquez in opposition to the opinion of Lessius, unless it be to show that Lessius, according to Vasquez, is a *heathen and a scoundrel?* But this I should not dare to affirm. What conclusion is to be drawn, but that Lessius *destroys the law and the Gospel*—that at the last day Vasquez will condemn Lessius on this point, as

Lessius will condemn Vasquez on some other—and that all your writers will rise up in judgment against each other for mutual condemnation, on account of their dreadful, outrageous opposition to the law of Christ?

Since, then, my Fathers, your doctrine of probability renders the good sentiments of some of your authors useless to the church, and serviceable only to promote your own policy; they show by their contradictions, your duplicity of heart, which, indeed, you have fully evinced, by declaring on the one hand, that Vasquez and Suarez are opposed to homicide, and on the other, that many celebrated authors are in favour of it for the purpose of offering two ways to mankind, by perverting the simplicity of the Gospel of God, which pronounces a curse upon the double minded, and providing two ways for themselves— *Væ duplici corde, et ingredienti duabus viis!*

LETTER XIV.

Jesuitical Maxims on the subject of Homicide refuted by the holy Fathers. Reply, in passing, to some of their Calumnies, and a Comparison of their Doctrine with the Form observed in pronouncing Judgment in Criminal Cases.

Paris, Oct. 23, 1656.

REVEREND FATHERS,

If I had only to reply to the three remaining impostures on the subject of homicide, it would be unnecessary to detain your attention long—a few words would suffice, as will be soon seen, for your refutation ; but as I feel persuaded it is more important to impress the world with a just horror of your opinions than to verify my own citations, I shall be obliged to employ the greatest part of this letter in refuting your maxims, and representing how remote you are from the sentiments of the church, and even from nature.

The permission to kill, which you give on so many occasions, evinces that in this affair you have so forgotten the law of God, and so extinguished the light of nature, as to need reminding of the simplest principles of religion and of common sense. What can be more natural than the following sentiment : " One private individual has no right over the life of another. We so well know this ourselves," says St. Chrysostom, " that when God established the law against murder he did not add, it was on account of its being an evil, because the law supposes that men have already learned this truth from nature."

This commandment has been in force in all ages. The Gospel confirms the law, and the decalogue only renewed that which mankind had received from God previous to the law in the person of Noah, from whom the human race were to spring. At the renewal of the world God addressed that patriarch, "At the hand of a man, even at the hand of a man's brother, will I require the life of a man. Whoso sheddeth man's blood, by man shall his blood be shed; for in the image of God created he man."

This general prohibition deprives men of all power over the lives of others; and God has so reserved it to himself alone, that, according to the principles of Christianity, which in this entirely oppose the false notions of paganism, a man does not possess power over his own life. But, as Providence has seen fit to preserve mankind in society, and to punish the wicked who should disturb them, he has himself ordained laws for the execution of criminals; so that those murders which, independently of his appointment, would be punishable, become, in consequence of such appintment, praiseworthy and just. St. Augustin has stated this in an admirable manner in l. 1. ch. 21. of his *City of God*. "Some exceptions," says he, "are made by God himself to this general prohibition against murder, either by the laws he has prescribed for the capital punishment of the guilty, or by the particular commands he has sometimes given for the execution of certain individuals. In this case it is not man that kills, but God, of whom man is only the instrument, as a sword is in the hand of him who uses it. But, with the exception of these cases, whoever kills another is guilty of murder.

It is certain then, Fathers, that God alone possesses a right to take away life, nevertheless, having enacted laws for the execution of criminals, he has made kings or empires the depositories of this power. This is what St. Paul teaches us when speaking of the authority of potentates to put men to death, he represents it as descending from heaven, "they bear not the sword in vain, they are the ministers of God's revengers to execute wrath upon him that doeth evil."

But as God intrusts them with this power, he requires them to exercise it as he does himself, that is, with justice, as St. Paul expresses it in the same place : " For rulers are not a terror to good works but to the evil. Wilt thou then not be afraid of the power ? Do that which is good and thou shalt have praise of the same. For he is the minister of God to thee for good." And this restriction, so far from diminishing their power, on the contrary exalts and assimilates it to that of God, who is incapable of evil, but almighty in doing good ; which distinguishes it from that of devils, who are impotent to good, and powerful only in doing evil. The sole difference between God and earthly potentates is this : God being justice and wisdom itself, can destroy upon the spot whom he pleases, and in any manner he pleases ; for, besides that he is the sovereign master of men's lives, it is certain that he cannot take them away without cause or without consideration, since he is equally incapable of injustice and error. But princes cannot act in the same manner ; because, though the ministers of God, they are nevertheless men and not gods. They may be surprised by false impressions, exasperated by surmises, or transported by passion ; and this has led them to submit to plans of human arrangement in the establishment of judges in their dominions, to whom they have communicated this power, in order that the authority with which God has invested them, may be employed solely for the purpose for which it is given.

To be exempt from homicide, therefore, it is requisite to be guided by the authority and justice of God ; otherwise we commit sin if we kill another with his authority but without his justice, or without his authority though in concurrence with his justice. From the necessity of this union it is, that, according to St. Augustin, " whoever kills a criminal without authority becomes criminal himself; for this great reason, that he usurps an authority which God has not delegated to him:" the judges, on the contrary, who possess this authority, are nevertheless guilty of murder. if they cause the innocent to be put to death contrary to the laws, which they ought to follow.

Such, Fathers, are the principles which have obtained, in all ages and places, to secure the peace and safety of the community, and upon which all the legislators of the world, both sacred and profane. have founded their laws. Never did even pagan nations deviate from this rule, unless when no other way remained of preserving chastity or life: for, as Cicero states, they believed "the laws themselves seemed to offer weapons for the defence of persons in such extremities."

But this case, with which I have at present nothing to do, being excepted, there never was a law which allowed private individuals to kill others, and permitted it, as you do, to guard against an affront, or prevent the loss of honour or of property, when life is in no kind of danger: no, that is what I affirm was never done even by infidels. Indeed, they have expressly forbid it, for the law of the twelve tables at Rome enacted, "that it was not allowable to kill a robber in the day time who did not defend himself with arms." This had been before prohibited in Exodus, c. 22: and the law *Furem ad Legem Corneliam,* taken from Ulpian, "forbids the killing of robbers even in the night, who do not threaten or attempt our lives," Cujas, *in tit. dig. de Justit. et Jure ad Leg.* 3.

Pray inform me, my good Fathers, by what authority you permit that which divine and human laws concur in prohibiting? And what right has Lessius to assert, l. 2. c. 9. n. 66. and 72, "that the book of Exodus forbids our killing thieves in the day time, who do not defend themselves with arms; and they who do put them to death are punishable in justice: but, they would not be guilty in conscience when there is no certainty, or at least a doubt, of being able to recover what has been stolen. as Sotus observes, because there is no obligation to run the hazard of losing any thing to save a thief? and that all this may be done by ecclesiastics themselves?" What prodigious effrontery! The law of Moses, forsooth, punishes those who kill thieves when they do not endanger our lives, and the law of the Gospel absolves them!! What then, is Jesus Christ come to destroy the law and not to fulfil it?—" The judges," says Lessius, " would punish such as kill in such a case, but they would have no guilt lying upon their conscience." Is the morality of Jesus Christ, then, more cruel and less inimical to murder than that of heathens, whence the judges have taken those civil laws which condemn it? Do Christians place a higher value upon the possessions of this world, or less upon human life, than idolaters and infidels? Pray, Fathers, what foundation have you for this representation? You have neither the express law of God nor man, but merely this strange mode of reasoning—" The laws allow of self-defence against thieves by repelling force with force;—but defence being permitted, murder is also allowed, otherwise self-defence would be impossible."

But, my worthy Fathers, it is perfectly false to say—self-defence is permitted, therefore murder is allowed. It is the cruel mode of defence which is the source of all these errors, and which is called by the faculty of Louvain, a murdering defence—*defensio occisiva*, in their censure upon the doctrine of your Father Launy on homicide. I maintain then, according to the laws, there is so great a difference between murder and self-defence, that in those very cases where defence is permitted, murder is forbid when a man's life is not endangered. Listen to Cujas in the same place: " It is lawful to repel the man who is going to seize upon any of your property, *but it is not lawful to kill him:*" and, again, " if any one come up to strike, and not to kill you, it is indeed lawful to repulse him, *but it is not lawful to kill him.*"

Who, then, has authorized you to say, with Molina, Reginaldus, Filiutius, Escobar, Lessius, and others, " it is lawful to kill the man who is going to strike you?" and, again, " it is lawful to kill the person who *intends* to offer you an insult, according to the concurrent opinion of the casuists, as Lessius affirms, n. 74—*ex sententiâ omnium.*" By what authority do you, who are but private individuals yourselves, communicate this power of killing to other private individuals, and even to ecclesiastics? And how dare you usurp the right of life and death, which exclusively belongs to God, and is the most glorious attribute of omnipotent sovereignty? To this, your answer was required; but you fancy you have given a satisfactory reply, by merely saying, in the thirteenth imposture, "The price for which Molina allows of killing a thief, who runs away without doing any violence, is not so little as I said, and it must be greater than six ducats." What weakness is this! And what consideration would you fix? Fifteen or sixteen ducats? But you would not the less incur my censure. You cannot, however, affirm, that it exceeds the value of a horse; for Lessius, l. 2. c. 9. n. 74. positively states, "It is lawful to kill a thief who runs away with your horse;" but I tell you further, that this value is, according to Molina, settled at six ducats, as I have related; and if you will not rely on my testimony, take an umpire whom you cannot refuse. It is your Father Reginaldus, who, in explaining this passage of Molina, l. 21. n. 68, affirms, "that Molina there determines the value for which it is not lawful to kill, at three, or four, or five ducats." So, Fathers, I am not only supported by Molina, but even by Reginaldus.

It will prove no less easy to refute your fourteenth imposture, with regard to the permission of Molina, "to kill a thief who robs you of a crown-piece." This is so evident, that Escobar introduces it, tr. 1. ex. 7. n. 44. where he states, that "Molina regularly fixes the price for which a man may be killed, at a crown." All you charge upon me is, that I have suppressed the concluding words of this passage—"that in this case, the moderation of a just defence ought to be regarded." But why do you not complain of Escobar for a similar omission? Methinks you are rather deficient here. You suppose we do not understand what you mean by self-defence. Are we not aware, that it signifies a *murdering defence?* You would have us believe, that Molina merely intended, by this expression, that when a person is in danger of life by defending a crown-piece, he may kill the robber in self-defence. If so, Fathers, why does Molina add in the same passage, that *he differs in this particular from Carrerus and Bald*, who admit of killing another to save one's own life? No, no. I assure you, Molina only means, that if one could save the crown-piece without killing the thief, the murder ought not to be perpetrated; but, if this cannot be done without killing him, even though no risk of life be incurred, as when the thief is unarmed, it is lawful to kill him, in order to save the crown-piece; in doing which, he thinks a man does not exceed the moderation of a just defence! To prove this, he shall explain himself, tom. 4. tr. 3. d. 11. n. 5: "A person does not exceed the moderation of a just defence, even though he take arms against such as have none, or take better weapons. I know some are of a different opinion, but I cannot coincide with their judgment, even in the external tribunal."

Thus, Fathers, it is plain that your authors allow of murder in defence of one's goods, or honour, even when life is in no danger; and, upon this principle, duels are authorized, as I have already so often shown, without your attempting any reply. In your writings, you attack but a single passage of Father Layman, which allows killing "when a man would otherwise be in danger of losing his fortune or his honour;" and you assert, that I have suppressed the following words: "*this is a very rare case.*" I am really all admiration, Fathers! What charming misrepresentations you impute to me! As if the only question were, whether this case occurred but seldom?—whereas it is, whether duelling is not permitted in that passage? These are two very distinct considerations.— Layman, as a casuist, was to judge whether duelling is lawful; and he declares it is. We are able to judge without his aid, whether it is of rare occurrence, and hesitate not to affirm, it is extremely common. But if you would rather take your good friend, Diana's word for it, he tells you expressly, *it is very common*, part. 5. tract. 14. misc. 2. resol. 99. Common, or uncommon, however, or whether Layman, in this point, follows Navarre, as you wish us to believe, is it not abominable that he should consent to this opinion? that, in order to preserve a false honour, it should be made lawful in conscience to accept a challenge, in opposition to the edicts of all Christian states, and in defiance of all the canons of the church, while you have neither laws, canons, nor the authority of Scripture, or of the Fathers, nor the example of a single saint, to support these diabolical maxims—nothing, nothing whatever, but this impious mode of reasoning—" Honour is dearer than life: but it is lawful to kill in defence of one's life;—*therefore*, it is lawful to kill in defence of one's honour?" What, then, because the irregularities of mankind have led them to prefer this false honour to that life which God has bestowed upon us to use in his service, it is allowable to kill each other for its preservation!! It is this love of honour above life, which is of so mischievous a tendency; and yet this vicious feeling, which is sufficient to contaminate the purest actions, if referred to that end, is made to justify the most criminal ones, only because they are so referred.

What strange perversion! and to what extravagances are you leading us! It is abundantly evident, that the same principle will justify our killing others for much less things which may happen to be put in competition with honour:" as for example, on account of *an apple*.

Nay, Fathers, do not exclaim against me, and say that I am deducing pernicious consequences from your doctrine; for I am supported by the authority of the *grave* Lessius, who writes thus, n. 68: " It is not lawful to kill another for the preservation of a thing of trifling value, as a crown or *an apple, aut pro pomo*, if it were not for the shame of losing it; in that case a man may seize it again, and even kill the thief, if necessary, to regain it—*et, si opus est, occidere*, because this is not so much to defend one's property as one's honour." Now this, good Fathers, seems very plain. But to crown all by a maxim which is wonderfully comprehensive, attend to Father Hereau, who copies from Lessius—"*the right of defence extends to* EVERY THING *which is necessary to guard us from* ANY KIND OF INJURY."

What monstrous consequences are included in this inhuman principle, and how ought the whole world to oppose it, especially public men! It is not merely the general interest, but their own, which is deeply concerned; since your casuists, quoted in my letters, extend their permission to kill, even to them; and thus the factious, who apprehend punishment for their delinquences, which do not seem wicked in their own view, easily persuading themselves that they are oppressed by violence, will at the same time imagine, " that the right of defence extends to every thing which is necessary to guard us from any kind of injury." They will no longer have to strive against that remorse of conscience which stifles so many crimes in their birth, but will think only of surmounting external obstacles.

But I will say no more, Fathers, upon this point, nor of other murders which you have allowed, and which are still more abominable, and at the same time of more importance to the welfare of nations, than all those of which Lessius and other of your authors treat in so undisguised a manner; the former particularly, in the fourth and tenth *doubts*. O that these horrible maxims had never escaped out of the bottomless pit, and that the devil, who is the orignal author of them, had never found men sufficiently devoted to his service to promulgate them amongst Christians!

It is obvious, from what I have been stating, that there is a wide difference between the relaxness of your opinions and the strictness of the law of civilized and even pagan nations. How must they appear when compared with ecclesiastical laws, which are incomparably more holy since the church alone understands and possesses true holiness? This chaste spouse of the Son of God, who, like her divine Lord, could shed her own blood for others, but not theirs for her, cherishes a peculiar horror of murder in proportion to the extraordinary illumination she has received from God. She not only considers men as men, but as the image of that God whom she supremely adores, and entertains a holy and respectful regard toward every individual, as purchased by an infinite price, to be the temple of the living God. For this reason, she considers the death of a man who is executed without the sanction of his authority, not only as murder but sacrilege, depriving her of one of her members ; because, whether he be or be not a believer, she always views him either as being one of her children or capacitated to be so.

For these reasons, since God became man for the salvation of men, they are rendered so important to the church, that she has always punished murder which destroys them, as one of the greatest crimes that can be committed against God. Allow me to adduce some examples, not to intimate that all such severities ought to be continued, for I know that the church has authority to manage external discipline variously, but to elucidate her immutable opinion upon this subject. For the penance which she appoints for murder may differ according to the change of times, but her horror for this atrocity can never change under any conceivable vicissitude of circumstances.

The church would not, for a long period, be reconciled to such as were guilty of wilful murder, but at death, though you are. The celebrated council of Ancyra condemned them to penance during the rest of their days; and the church has since considered it a very great indulgence towards them, to reduce the time to an indefinite number of years. But the more effectually to deter from wilful murder, she punishes with much severity those which have occurred by accident, as may be seen in St. Basil, St. Gregory Nyssenus, and in the decretals of Popes Zachary and Alexander II. The canons cited by Isaac, bishop of Langres, t. 2, 13. ordain " seven years of penance for a murder in self-defence ;" and we see St. Hildebert, bishop of Mans, in his reply to Ives of Chartres, states, " he had done right in degrading a bishop for life who had killed a thief with a stone in his own defence."

Dare you, after this, assert that your decisions are conformable to the spirit and canons of the church? I defy you to point out one that gives permission to murder for the preservation of one's property merely; for I do not speak of those cases in which a man is forced to defend his life, *se suaque liberando.* Your own authors admit there are none; as, amongst others, Father Launy, tom. 5, disp. 36, n. 136: " There is no law," says he, " human or divine, which expressly allows of killing a thief who does not stand upon his defence." But this you permit in so many words. I defy you further, to point out a single canon which sanctions murder for honour, for a box on the ear, for an affront, and for a slander. I defy you to refer to any one that permits the killing of witnesses, judges, and magistrates, whatever injustice we may have reason to apprehend. The spirit of the church is far from these seditious maxims, which open the doors to insurrection, to which the populace is so naturally addicted. She has always taught her children not to render evil for evil, to give place to wrath, not to resist violence, to render to every one his due, honour, tribute, submission, to obey magistrates and superiors, even though unjust; because we ought always to respect the power of God who has appointed them to rule. She prohibits, even more strongly than the civil laws do, deciding in their own cause; and it is by her spirit that Christian kings avoid the punishment even of capital crimes, referring them to the judges to execute the law according to the proper forms of justice; which is so opposite to your conduct, that the comparison ought to cover you with blushes. And since I am thus led to the subject, let me beseech you to pay attention to the difference between your method of putting your enemies to death, and that of the judges in executing criminals.

Every body, Fathers, knows that private individuals have no power to seek the death of any one; and that if a person have ruined our fortune, crippled our bodies, burned our houses, murdered our father, and shown himself resolved to destroy our reputation or even to assassinate us, justice would not listen to our requisition to have him put to death. It has been necessary, therefore, to appoint public persons to demand this execution in the name of the king, or rather on behalf of God. Is it, in your opinion, Fathers, out of mere grimace and form, that judges have adopted this regulation? Have they not done it in order to make the civil laws conformable to those of the Gospel—that the external proceedings of justice might not be contradictory to the internal sentiments which Christians ought to cherish? It is obvious, how much this first mode in which justice operates, surprises you; but the rest will utterly confound you.

Suppose, then, these public functionaries should require the death of the individual who has perpetrated all these crimes, what is to be done? Will they instantly plunge a dagger into his bosom? No, no. The life of men is too important to proceed with such incaution; the laws do not dispense power to all sorts of people, but only to judges of tried probity and capacity. Do you imagine that *one* is sufficient to condemn a man to death? No, Fathers, there must be at least *seven:* and of these seven there must not be one who was ever offended by the criminal, lest passion should bias or corrupt his judgment. You know also, Fathers, that for the purpose of having the mind clear and undistracted, the *morning* is the time appointed for the discharge of these duties: such is the care taken in a proceeding of so much importance, in which they are the vicegerents and ministers of God, and bound to condemn only those whom he himself condemns.

In order, therefore, to act as the faithful dispensers of divine power in taking away human life, they are at liberty to decide only according to the depositions of witnesses and all other prescribed forms; after this they cannot in conscience pronounce sentence, but in conformity to the laws, nor adjudge any to death but whom the laws condemn. And then, my Fathers, if the command of God requires them to deliver up these miserable men to punishment, the same command obliges them to take care of their guilty souls; and it is because they are guilty that the greater attention should be manifested, so that they may not be abandoned to execution till the proper means have been used to impress their consciences. All this is very correct and very innocent; nevertheless, the church entertains such an abhorrence of blood, that she considers those unworthy of ministering at her altars who have assisted in criminal adjudications, though attended with such religious observances; from which it is easy to conceive what the church thinks of murder.

Such is the proceeding of *justice* in disposing of the lives of men: let us now examine *your* method. In the new laws you have promulgated, there is but one judge, and he is the offended person in fact, he is party, judge, and executioner. He demands of himself the death of his enemy, appoints his punishment, and executes him on the spot; and, without any regard to the body or soul of his brother, he kills and damns him for whom Christ died; and all this to avoid a box on the ear, a reproach, or an offensive word, or other minor delinquences, for condemning which to the punishment of death, a judge, invested with legitimate authority, would be highly criminal; because the laws are far from so condemning them. And, finally, to crown these extravagances, you neither impute sin nor irregularity to those who commit murder in this manner without authority and contrary to the laws, even though perpetrated by religious persons and the priests themselves! Where are we now? Are these monks and priests who talk in this manner? Are they Christians? or, are they Turks? Are they men? or, are they demons? Are these *the mysteries revealed to his Society by the lamb*, or are they abominations suggested by the dragon to those who are of *his* party?

What would you wish to be esteemed, Fathers? Children of the Gospel or enemies of the Gospel? You must belong to one class or the other—there is no middle condition: " he that is not with Christ is against him:" these two descriptions divide mankind. There are ac-

20*

cording to St. Augustin, two people and two worlds diffused over the earth—the world of the children of God, constituting a body of which Christ is chief and king; and the world at enmity against God, of which the devil is chief and king. For this reason, Jesus Christ is called the king and God of the world; because, in every part of it, he has his subjects and worshippers; and the devil is also denominated in Scripture, the prince of the power of the air, and the God of this world, because he also has every where his supporters and slaves. Jesus Christ has enacted such laws in his church, which is his kingdom, as he has thought proper, according to his eternal wisdom: and the devil has enacted such laws in the world, which is *his* kingdom, as he wishes to be established. Jesus Christ has made it honourable to suffer; the devil *not* to suffer. Jesus Christ has commanded those who receive a blow on *one* cheek to turn the other also; the devil would have them kill the persons who intend to inflict this injury. Jesus Christ pronounces them to be happy who partake of his ignominy; the devil declares such as endure shame to be miserable and accursed. Jesus Christ says, *Woe unto you when all men shall speak well of you;* the devil says, " Woe to those of whom the world does not speak with esteem."

Now, Fathers, to which of these kingdoms do you belong? You have heard the language of the city of peace, called the mystical Jerusalem, and you have heard the language of the city of strife, in Scripture termed *spiritual Sodom;* which of these languages do you understand? Which of them do you speak? Those who belong to Christ are, as Paul expresses it, " of one mind with him;" and those who are the children of the devil, *ex patre diabolo,* who was " a murderer from the beginning," follow the maxims of the devil according to the testimony of Christ. Let us hear the language of your school and inquire of your authors—if one is struck with a blow on the ear, is it right to endure it, or to kill the person who gave it; or, is it lawful to kill a man in order to prevent such an affront? *It is lawful,* say Lessius, Molina, Escobar,

Reginaldus, Filiutius, Baldellus, and other Jesuits, *to kill the person who intends to give you a box on the ear!* Is this the language of Jesus Christ?—Again, is a man without honour who suffers a blow on the ear without killing the man who struck it? "Is it not true," asks Escobar, "that whilst the person who has given you a box on the ear is suffered to live, he who has submitted to it is without honour?" True, Fathers—he is without *that* honour which the devil has transmitted from his own proud spirit into that of his proud descendants. It is that honour which has always been idolized by men possessed of the spirit of the world. It is to preserve this kind of glory, of which the devil is the real dispenser, that mankind sacrifice their lives to the madness of duels, their honour to the disgrace of punishments to which they expose themselves, and their salvation to the danger of damnation, while they are deprived of Christian burial by the ecclesiastical canons. We ought to praise God for bestowing upon the mind of the king a purer light than that of your theology. His edicts, which are so severe upon this subject, do not make duelling criminal; they only punish the crime inseparable from duels. Through the fear of his rigorous justice, he has deterred those who could not be influenced by the justice of God: and his piety has shown him that the honour of Christians consists in observing the commands of God, and the rules of Christianity; not in that phantom of honour which you represent, frivolous as it is, as a legitimate apology for murder. Thus your murdering decisions are execrated by the whole world, and you had better be admonished to change your sentiments, if not from a religious principle, at least from a political motive. Prevent, Fathers, by a voluntary condemnation of these barbarous maxims, the sad effects so likely to result, and for which you must be responsible: and, to inspire you with the greater horror, remember that the first crime of depraved nature was a murder, committed upon the person of the first righteous man; that the greatest crime of mankind was the murder of him who was the head of all the just, and that murder is the only crime which at once destroys the state, the church, nature, and piety.

I have just been reading the reply of your apologist to my thirteenth letter. But if he can give no better answer to this, which solves most of his difficulties, it will merit no reply. I pity him, when I see how he flies off from the subject every moment, and levels his calumnious reproaches both against the living and the dead. But to gain credit to the notes with which you furnished him, you should not have made him disavow, in so public a manner, so notorious a circumstance as that of the box on the ear at Compiegne. It is certain, Fathers, from the acknowledgment of the offended party, that he received a blow on the cheek from the hand of a Jesuit; and all that could be accomplished by your friends, was to render it doubtful, whether it was given with the palm or with the back of the hand; and then, whether a stroke upon the cheek with the back of the hand ought to be called a box of the ear or not?

I cannot tell whose office it may be to determine this puzzling question, but I am of opinion it was at least a *probable* box on the ear. My conscience therefore is at ease.

LETTER XV.

The Jesuists omit Calumny in their Catalogue of Crimes, and make no scruple of using it against their Enemies.

Nov. 25, 1656.

REVEREND FATHERS,

As your impostures are daily increasing, and you make use of them, to scandalize in so cruel a manner, all persons of piety who oppose your errors, I feel myself obliged, on their account and for the service of the church, to expose a part of your mysterious conduct, which I promised to do some time since, that it may be fully known from your own maxims, what reliance may be placed upon your accusations and injurious conduct.

I am well aware, that persons who are not sufficiently acquainted with you, feel it extremely difficult to come to any decision upon this subject, because they are necessitated either to believe those incredible crimes of which you accuse your enemies, or to deem you impostors, which would seem equally incredible. If these things were untrue, say they, would a religious society publish them—thus resisting the dictates of conscience, and giving themselves up, by such atrocious calamities, to damnation? In this manner they reason; so that obvious and striking as are the proofs by which your falsities are exposed, yet, being so diametrically opposed to the opinion they cherish of your sincerity, they are held in suspense between the evidence of the truth which they cannot deny, and the duty of charity which they are apprehensive of violating. As, therefore, the only hinderance to their rejection of your scandal, is their respect for your character, if they should find that you really do not entertain that bad opinion of calumny for which they give you credit, but think it to be no impediment to your salvation, no doubt the force of truth will immediately determine them to disbelieve your impositions. You see, Fathers, the subject of the present letter.

It is my purpose to advance a step further, than merely to show that your writings are replete with calumnious representations. Falsehoods may be stated under an impression that they are truths, but lying is characterized by the *intention* to deceive. I shall show, that you design to deceive and calumniate, and that you purposely impute crimes to your enemies, of which you know they are perfectly innocent, because you believe it may be done without falling from a state of grace. And though you may be as well acquainted as myself with this point of your morality, I shall beg permission to state it, that no further doubt may exist, by showing that I challenge you personally and individually on the subject, without even your being able to deny it with all your assurance, unless at the same time you own that for which I reproach you. For this is a doctrine so common in your schools, that you have not only maintained it in your writings, but even in your public theses, which is an act of the utmost presumption; as, for example, in that of Louvain, in the year 1645, in the following words: " It is only a venial sin to calumniate and ruin the credit of such as speak evil of you, by accusing them of false crimes—*quidni non nisi veniale sit, detrahentis autoritatem magnam tibi noxiam falso crimine elidere ?"* This doctrine is so current amongst you, that whoever dares to attack it, you treat as an ignoramus and a stupid fellow.

Not long ago, this took place in regard to Father Quiroga, a German capuchin, who opposed this doctrine, and was immediately attacked by Father Dicastillus, who speaks of this dispute in these terms—*de Just.* l. 2. tr. 2. disp. 12. n. 404 : " A certain grave friar, barefooted and deep cowled—*cucullatus, gymnopoda*—whose name I shall conceal, had the temerity to decry this opinion amongst some women and ignorant people, as pernicious and scandalous, contrary to good manners, subversive of the peace of states and societies, and opposed not only to all the Catholic doctors, but to all who may become so. But I have maintained against him, and still maintain, that calumny, when made use of against a calumniator, though it be a lie, yet is not a mortal sin, nor contrary to justice or charity; and, as a demonstration of this, I furnished him with a crowd of our Fathers, and whole universities whom I consulted: among others, the reverend Father John Gans, confessor to the Emperor; the reverend Father Daniel Bastele, confessor to the archduke Leopold; Father Henry, who was the tutor of these two princes; all the public and ordinary professors of the university of Vienna (consisting entirely of Jesuits;) all the professors of the university of Gratz (all Jesuists;) all the professors of the university of Prague (of which the Jesuits are masters;) from all of whom, I have in my possession, a written, signed and sealed approbation of my opinion; in addition to which, I have Father Pennalossa, a Jesuit, preacher to the Emperor and the king of Spain; Father Pilliceroli, a Jesuit; and many others, who have all judged this opinion probable, previous to our dispute." You see, Fathers, there are few opinions which you have taken so much pains to establish; and, in fact, there are few which are so serviceable to you. For this reason, you have impressed so much authority upon it, that your casuists have made use of it as an indubitable principle. "It is certain," says Caramuel, n. 1151., "it is a probable opinion, that it is no mortal sin to bring a false accusation for the sake of preserving one's honour: for it is maintained by upwards of twenty grave doctors, Gaspar Hurtado, Dicastillus, &c. Hence, if this doctrine be not probable, there is scarcely any one that is so in the whole system of divinity."

O, what an execrable system is this, and how utterly corrupt in all its main points and principles—that if this doctrine be not probable and safe in conscience, "that a person may be accused falsely in order to preserve one's honour," there is scarcely any one that is! What can be more probable, Fathers, than that those who hold this principle, should sometimes put it in practice? The depraved passions of mankind hurry them on with such impetuosity, that it is inconceivable, when all conscientious scruples are done away, how violently they proceed. For instance, Caramuel writes, in the same place, "This maxim of Father Dicastillus, the Jesuit, respecting calumny, was taught by a German countess to the daughter of the Empress, who, believing that calumnies were but venial sins, spread abroad so many scandals and false reports every day, that the whole court was put into a state of ferment and alarm. It is easy to perceive the use they made of it; so that, to quiet this tumult, it was found necessary to apply to a good Father, a capuchin, named Quiroga, of exemplary conduct (which was the reason Father Dicastillus had such a quarrel with him,) who told them plainly, that this maxim was very pernicious, especially as held by women, and then took such especial care, that the Empress totally abolished the practice of it."

It is by no means surprising that this doctrine should have produced some bad effects: it would have been more so had it been otherwise. Self-love is always ready to persuade us that an attack made upon ourselves is unjust; much more you, Fathers, who are so blinded by vanity, that you would make all the world believe, from your writings, that an injury attempted against your society, is an injury done to the honour of the church; and thus it would be strange, if you were not to put this maxim in practice. We must not say, as those who do not know you do—how is it these good Fathers calumniate their enemies, since it is endangering their own salvation? but we must say, on the contrary—how is it these good Fathers would lose any opportunity of decrying their enemies, when they can do it without risking their own safety? Let us then no longer be astonished at finding the Jesuits calumniators: they are so with a safe conscience, and cannot be otherwise; since, by the credit they have acquired in the world, they may revile others without any apprehension from the justice of men, and by that which they have acquired in cases of conscience, they have established maxims, by which they are empowered to do as they choose, without dreading the justice of God.

Such, Fathers, is the origin of so many base impostures. From this source, your Father Brisacier drew, till he brought upon himself the censure of the archbishop of Paris. It was this which led your Father d'Anjou, openly in the pulpit of the church of St. Benedict at Paris, on the eighth of March, 1655, to decry those persons of quality who received the subscriptions for the poor of Picardy and Champagne, to which they had so liberally contributed themselves; and to declare (which was a horrible falsehood, and enough to have destroyed all charity, had your impostures obtained any kind of credit,) " that he knew for certain that these persons had misapplied this money, to employ it against the church and state; which obliged the curate of the parish, a doctor of the Sorbonne, to preach next day, for the express purpose of confuting these calumnious representations. Your Father Crasset, upon the same principle, published from the pulpit so many impostures in Orleans, which rendered it necessary for the bishop to interdict him as a public impostor, by a mandate of the ninth of September last, in which he declares, " that he prohibits brother John Crasset, priest of the society of Jesus, from preaching in his diocese; and all the people from hearing him, under pain of being guilty of a mortal disobedience; he having been apprised that the said Crasset had delivered a discourse from the pulpit, full of falsehoods and calumnies against the clergy of that city, falsely and maliciously charging them with maintaining such heretical propositions as these—that it is impossible to keep the commandments of God—that internal grace is irresistible—and that Christ did not die for all men, with others of a similar nature, condemned by Innocent X." This, Fathers, is your ordinary imposture, and the first with which you attack those whom you deem it important to decry. And though it be as impossible to prove your charges, as it is for Father Crasset to substantiate his against the clergy of Orleans, your conscience is quite easy, " because you believe that this mode of detraction is so certainly allowable," that you are not afraid to declare it openly in the face of a whole city.

A remarkable instance of this occurred in your disagreement with M. Puys, a clergyman of St. Nisier, at Lyons; and, as this affair furnishes a complete illustration of your spirit, I shall relate the principal circumstances. You know, Fathers, that in 1649, Mr. Puys translated an excellent work, written by another capuchin, into French, "On the duty of Christians to their own parishes, against those who wished to entice them away,"—without using any invectives, and without either pointing at any religious order or individual. Your Fathers, however, took it to themselves, and paying no respect to an aged pastor, a judge in the primacy of France, and much honoured by the whole city, your Father Alby wrote a violent philippic against him, which you yourselves sold in your own church on Assumption-day; in which, amongst other charges, he was accused of " becoming scandalous by his gallantries, of being suspected of impiety, of being a heretic, an excommunicated person, and deserving to be burned alive." To this M. Puys replied; but Father Alby, in a second publication, persisted in his former criminations. Is it not then evident, Fathers, either that you must be calumniators, or that you believed all the charges brought against the good priest; and therefore that it was needful that you should have seen him fully exculpated before you deemed him worthy of your friendship? Attend now to what passed at the reconciliation, in presence of a great multitude of the most distinguished persons of the city, whose names are inserted below, in the order in which they were placed in the paper drawn up on the 25th of September, 1650.* In the presence of this assembly, M. Puys made

* M. de Ville, vicar-general of the cardinal de Lyon; Mr. Scarron, canon and minister of St. Paul's; M. Margat, chanter; Messrs. Bouvaud, Seve, Aubert, and Dervieu, canons of St. Nisier; M. du Gué, president of the treasurers of France; M. Groslier, provost of

no other declaration than the following; "that what he had written was not intended for the Jesuits—that he had spoken in general against those who seduce the faithful from their parishes, without at all meaning to attack their society, for which, on the contrary, he cherished a high regard." This is in itself sufficient with regard to his apostacy, his revilings, and his excommunication, without any recantation or absolution. Father Alby afterwards addressed him in these words: " Sir, my conviction that you attacked the society to which I have the honour to belong, induced me to take up my pen to answer you, and I thought my manner of doing it was *allowable;* but having become better acquainted with your intention, I now declare, that there exists *nothing* which can prevent my esteeming you as a person of a very enlightened understanding, of a profound and *orthodox* faith, of *irreproachable* morals, and in one word, a worthy pastor of your church. This declaration I make with high satisfaction, and beg these gentlemen to remember it."

In truth, Fathers, these gentlemen remember it perfectly well, and were more offended at your reconciliation, than at your quarrel. For who does not admire Father Alby's speech? He does not say that he retracts on account of discovering M. Puys has changed his behaviour and his doctrine, but merely " because he found that it was not his intention to attack your society, so that there is nothing to prevent him from being a good Catholic."— He did not, therefore, believe him to be a heretic at all; nevertheless, after accusing him of it, contrary to his own convictions, he does not acknowledge his error, but dares, on the contrary, to affirm, " that he believes the manner in which he used him was *allowable.*"

My good Fathers, what can you be thinking about, thus publicly to show that you only measure the faith and vir-

---

the merchants; M. de Flechere, president and Lieutenant-general; Messrs. de Boissat, de St. Romain, and de Bartoly, gentlemen; M. Burgeois, king's chief advocate in the treasury-office of France; Messrs. de Cotton, father and son; M. Boniel; who all signed the original declaration with M. Puys and Father Alby.

tue of mankind by their opinions of your society ? How came it to pass, that you were not apprehensive of making people believe, by your own confession, that you were impostors and calumniators ? What ! shall the very same individual, and, without any change in himself, but merely as he honours or opposes *your society*, be " pious or impious, blameless, or deserving excommunication, a worthy pastor of the church, or fit only to be burned ; in one word, a Catholic or a heretic ?" To oppose your society, and to be a heretic, are, then, in your language, the same thing ! A pretty kind of heresy, indeed ! So, then, whenever one sees in your writings, so many good Catholics called heretics, the meaning is, that "you believe them to be inimical to *you*." It is desirable to be initiated into this language ; conformably to which, I am, for my part, a terrible heretic ; and this is the sense in which you dignify me with this appellation. You have no reason for excommunicating me from the church, excepting that you believe my letters are adverse to your interests ; and thus the only method left of becoming a good Catholic, is, either to approve of your extravagant system of morality, which I can never do without renouncing every principle of religion, or to persuade you that I have no other design than that of promoting your real interest ; and, if you admit this, you will be wonderfully recovered from your strange infatuation. But I find myself inevitably involved in heresy ; for the purity of my faith being incapable of rescuing me from this error, I shall never be free from it, without either betraying *my* conscience, or reforming *yours*, till which time I shall always remain a wicked monster and impostor ; for, however correctly I have quoted your authors, you will continue to exclaim, " that he must be an agent of the devil, to charge you with things of which there does not exist the slightest mark or intimation in all your writings ;" and yet there would be nothing in this but what would perfectly accord with your maxims and usual practices : so great and extended is the privilege you enjoy of lying. Allow me to produce a specimen, chosen on purpose, because it will furnish an answer at the same time to your ninth imposture, which only merits a transient notice and refutation.

About ten or twelve years ago, you were reproached with this maxim of Father Bauny, "that it is allowable to seek directly, *primò et per se*, the next opportunity of committing simony for the spiritual or temporal advantage of ourselves or our neighbour," tr. 4. q. 14. Of this, he adduces the following exemplification :—" It is lawful for any one to go into public places of ill-fame, in order to convert prostitutes, though it be not improbable, the individual may fall into sin from various experiments which he has already made, having been seduced by their caresses." What reply did Father Caussin offer to this, in 1644, in his Apology for the Society of Jesuits, p. 128 ?— Look at the passage in Father Bauny, read the page, the marginal references, what precedes and what follows ; study, indeed, the whole work, and you will not discover the least trace of such a sentence ; and it could never enter into the mind of any man, whose conscience was not totally depraved ; nor could any one have imagined it, who was not, in fact, an agent of the devil." Your Father, Pintereau, speaks in the same style, part 1. p. 24 : " A man must be lost indeed to all conscience, to teach such a detestable doctrine ; but, whoever attributes it to Father Bauny, must be worse than a devil. Reader, be assured, there is not the least mark or indication of it in his whole book." Who would not believe, but that people who talk at this rate, had a just ground of complaint, and that Father Bauny had been misrepresented ? Was ever any thing expressed in stronger terms ? How can any person dare to imagine, that a passage can be found in the very place, and in the very words referred to, when it is affirmed, that " there is not the least mark or indication of it in the whole book ?"

Unquestionably, Fathers, this is the true way of gaining credit, till an answer appears ; but it is also the way never to be believed again, as soon as the answer is published. For it is so evident that you told falsehoods at that time, that in your answers, you now confess, without any hesitation, that this said maxim is not only to be found in Father Bauny, in the very place whence it was cited, but what seems most worthy of admiration, what was *detestable* twelve years ago, is now so *innocent*, that in your ninth imposture, p. 10, you absolutely accuse me of " ignorance and malice, for quarrelling with Father Bauny, respecting an opinion which was never rejected in the schools." What an advantage it *is* to have to do with people who talk *pro* and *con!* I have no need of any other auxiliaries, for you confute yourselves! It is only necessary to show two things—that this maxim is a bad one—then, that it is the maxim of Father Bauny ; both of which I shall prove from your own confession. In the year 1644, you allowed it to be *detestable*, and in 1656, you admit it is Father Bauny's. This double acknowledgment is quite sufficient for my justification; but it goes further—it discovers the spirit of your politics. Let me ask what end you propose in your writings ? Is it to state your sentiments with sincerity ? No, certainly ; because your answers are self-contradictory. Is it to establish the true faith ? But this is so little the case, that you authorize a maxim, which, according to your own admission, is *detestable*. But remark, that when you said this maxim was *detestable*, you, at the same time, denied that it was Father Bauny's, and so he was innocent ; and, when, afterwards, you allow it to be his, you maintain it is a good one—so he is innocent still! This Father's innocence, then, being the only thing in common to both your replies, it is obviously your sole aim ; the object being to defend your authors, by saying of the same identical maxim, it *is*, or, it is *not*, in your books ; it is good, or it is bad ; not according to its conformity to *truth*, which is immutable, but to *your interest*, which changes every moment. What can I say after this, which is absolutely demonstrative ? and yet this is your common method of proceeding every day, and, omitting an infinity of other examples, you will, I dare say, deem it enough to produce one more.

You have been censured on various occasions for another proposition of Father Bauny, tr. 4, quest. 22, p. 100: " Absolution ought not to be denied or deferred to those who live in the habit of transgressing the laws of God, of nature, and of the church, though there should be no hopes of amendment—*etsi emendationis futuræ spes nulla appareat.*" I beg to know who has furnished, in your view, the best answer to this ; your Father Pintereau, or your Father Brisacier, who justify Father Bauny in both your peculiar methods of defence : the one condemning this proposition, but denying it to be Father Bauny's ; the other admitting it to be his, but at the same time vindicating it ? Pray, listen—Father Pintereau asks, p. 18, " What is it to break all the bounds of modesty and to outface impudence itself, if it be not to impute to Father Bauny this damnable doctrine, as universally admitted to be his ? Judge then, reader, of the vileness of this calumny, and see with what kind of people the Jesuits have to do ; then say, whether the author of such an atrocious falsehood ought not henceforward to be deemed the interpreter of the father of lies ? Now attend to Father Brisacier, part 6, p. 21. " It is true Father Bauny says what you have related"—(this, by the way, is giving Father Pintereau the lie direct)—" but if you, who condemn this, wait, when a penitent is at your feet, till his guardian angel pawns all his title to heaven for the individual's goodness, or till the eternal God swears by himself that David lied, when he said by the Holy Spirit, that ' All men are liars,' deceitful and frail ; and that this penitent is not a greater liar, more frail, or fickle, or sinful than others—you could never apply the blood of Jesus Christ to any one."

What think you, Fathers, of these extravagant and impious expressions, importing, that to wait till there is some hope of amendment previous to giving absolution, is the same as waiting till the eternal God swears by himself, that a sinner shall fall no more ? What, is there no difference between *hope* and *certainty ?* How reproachful is it to the grace of Jesus Christ to say, there is so little possibility that Christians should abandon their sins against the law of God, against nature, and against the church, as to render it quite hopeless, *unless the Holy Spirit be a liar:* so that, in your view, if absolution be not given to those *whose amendment is to be expected, the blood of Jesus Christ would be useless, and could never be applied to any one.* To what condition, Fathers, has your immoderate desire of maintaining the glory of your authors, reduced you! for you can discover only two methods of justifying them, imposture or impiety; and the most innocent of the two seems to be boldly to disavow the most evident facts, which is the reason you so frequently adopt this plan.

This is not all: you forge writings expressly to render your enemies odious; as, for instance, the "Letter from a Minister to Mr. Arnauld," which you dispersed in every direction throughout Paris, to impress the idea that the book of "Frequent Communion," approved by so many bishops and divines, (which was, in fact, however a little contrary to your opinions,) was written by some secret understanding with the ministers of Charenton. At other times, you attribute to your adversaries writings full of impiety, as the "Circular Letter of the Jansenists," whose impertinent style evinces the grossness of the deception, and shows but too clearly the ridiculous malice of your Father Meinier, who had the audacity to make use of it, p. 28, to support the blackest of his misrepresentations. Sometimes you cite books which never existed, as "The Constitutions of the Holy Sacrament," whence you produce passages which you have chosen to fabricate, and such as would make any man's hair stand on end, who was ignorant of your effrontery in inventing and circulating falsehoods. In truth, there is not a single species of calumny which you have not adopted, and certainly the maxim which excuses it, could never have been in better hands.

These representations, however, are too easily refuted; on which account you avail yourselves of others, of a more subtle nature, in which you take care to avoid particularizing, in order to remove all possibility of being detected and answered; as, when Father Brisacier says, "that his enemies perpetrate horrible crimes, but they will not do to be named." Does it not seem imposible to convict such an indefinite accusation as this? A certain clever fellow, however, has found out this secret; and who do you think it is?—A *capuchin*. You are really, my good Fathers, you are really unfortunate in your capuchins, and I foresee, you will, some time or other, be as unlucky in Benedictins. This capuchin is called Father Valerian, of the house of the Counts de Magnis. You shall see, by this little history, in what manner he answered your calumnies. He had happily succeeded in converting prince Ernest, landgrave of Hesse-Rheinsfelt; but your Fathers, as if sorry for the conversion of a sovereign prince, without their assistance, instantly wrote a book against him (for you uniformly persecute good people every where), and, falsifying one of the capuchin's passages, accused him of *heretical* doctrine; publishing moreover a letter against him, in which they said, "O, how many things could we discover against you (without a syllable of *what* things,) and how would they torment you! For if you do not behave better, we shall be under the necessity of reporting you to the Pope and Cardinals." This is no bad device, and I doubt not. Fathers, but you tell them the same things of me. Now, observe his answer in his book printed at Prague last year, p. 112 et seq. ' What shall I do against those vague and indefinite slanders? How shall I refute what is not explained? There is one method, and I declare loudly and publicly to those who threaten me, that they are the most notorious impostors, the most artful and most impudent liars, if they do not publish these crimes to the whole world. Come forward, then, all ye mine accusers, and proclaim those things upon the house-tops which hitherto you have only whispered, and by this secrecy you have told falsehoods with the greater boldness. Some people regard these disputes as scandalous; and truly it is an infamous scandal to impute to me such a crime as heresy, and thus make me suspected of many other. But the only remedy I propose for this scandal is to maintain my innocence."

Really, Fathers, you seem to be sadly off, for surely never was a man more completely justified. You cannot possibly produce the least shadow of a crime against him, since you have not answered such a challenge. Really you have some troublesome affairs to manage, but you do not seem to become any wiser; for some time afterwards you attacked him again in a similar manner upon another subject; and he makes the same kind of defence, p. 151, in the following words: "These people, who are insupportable to all Christendom, aspire, under pretence of good works, to greatness and domination, by perverting almost all laws, divine, human, positive and natural, to answer their own designs. They engage on their side, either by their doctrine or by fear or hope, all the great of the earth, and then abuse their authority to promote their own detestable intrigues. But their schemes, however criminal they may be, are neither punished nor checked: on the contrary, they are rewarded, and they proceed with the same confidence as if they were serving God. This is known to all the world, and all the world speaks of it in terms of execration; but few are able to oppose this powerful tyranny. I have, notwithstanding, ventured to do so. Already I have succeeded in putting a stop to their insolence, and I shall do it again in the same manner. I affirm then, most unhesitatingly, that they are most impudent liars—*mentiris impudentissimè*. If their accusations against me be true, let them be proved, or let these accusers stand convicted of impudent falsehood After this, it will be seen who is in the right. I beg of every body to mark their proceedings, and to observe how these people, who cannot endure the least affront without resenting it to the utmost of their power, will, in appearance, suffer very patiently those which they have it not in their power to revenge, and cover their real impotence under the veil of pretended virtue. It is for this reason I have used the more vigorous endeavours to provoke their modesty, that the most illiterate may acknowledge, if they should remain silent, their patience will not result from meekness, but from a troubled and guilty conscience."

So says the capuchin, and concludes thus:—" These men, whose history is so well known to the whole world, are notoriously wicked, and so insolent, in consequence of the impunity they enjoy, that I must have renounced Jesus Christ and his church, if I had not, thus publicly too, expressed my detestation of their conduct, both for my own vindication, and to prevent the seduction of the simple-hearted."

My reverend Fathers, you have no way of retreat left: you must be set down as convicted slanderers, and have only to recur to your maxim, that this species of calumny is not criminal. This capuchin has discovered the secret of shutting your mouths; and this is the only method whenever you bring forward accusations unsustained by evidence. The best answer we can give you is that of the capuchin Father—*mentiris impudentissimè*. What other reply can be given, for instance, to Father Brisacier, when he says of his opponents, " They are the gates of hell, the high-priests of the devil, people destitute of faith, hope, and charity, who build up the treasury of antichrist; which," he adds, " I do not say to injure them, but as compelled to it by the force of truth." It would be a curious kind of employment for any person to set about proving, " that he is not the gates of hell, and does not build up the treasury of antichrist!"

What other answer, again, could be given to all the idle nonsense of the same kind to be found in your writings and advertisements about my letters? For instance —" that some appropriate to themselves the produce of restitutions, and thus reduce creditors to beggary—that bags of money have been offered to certain learned monks who have refused them—that benefices have been bestowed in order to sow heresies in opposition to the faith—that some pensioners are among the most dignified ecclesiastics and in sovereign courts; and that I myself am a pensioner of Port-Royal, and wrote romances before I composed my letters."—I write romances!—I who never read one in my life—and do not even know the names of *those written by your apologist!!*—What is to be said to all this, Fathers, but—*mentiris impudentissimè;*—unless you will point out the individuals—their words—time and place. Either be silent, or relate and prove all the circumstances, as I have done in my stories of Father Alby and John d'Alba; otherwise you can hurt nobody but yourselves. Your fables, perhaps, might have obtained some credit before the world knew your principles; but these being now disclosed, when you endeavour to whisper about—" a person of honour, who would not have his name mentioned, told you most terrible things of such and such people,"—you will be instantly reminded of the *mentiris impudentissimè* of the good Father capuchin. You have already imposed upon mankind too long, and abused the credit which has been given to your mis-statements. It is time to restore the reputation of so many slandered individuals. For what innocence can be so universally known as not to suffer some stain from the bold calumnies of a society, which has extended itself through the whole world, and which, under the garb of religion, conceals souls so totally destitute of it, as to perpetrate a crime like slander, not only without opposing, but in direct conformity and subservience to their own avowed doctrines. I shall not, surely, be blamed for destroying the confidence which has been reposed in you, since it is far more just to preserve for so many persons whom you have decried, that reputation for piety, which they ought indeed never to have forfeited, than to leave you a reputation for sincerity which you never deserved to possess. And, as one cannot be done without the other, how important is it to exhibit to the world your real character! I have made a beginning, but it will require some further time and labour to complete the design. It shall, however, be done; nor will all your policy, Fathers, screen you from it : since, all the efforts you make to hinder it, will only serve to prove, even to persons of the smallest discernment, that you are in a state of alarm ; and that your own consciences reproaching you with what I have yet to state, you have used every possible means to prevent the full disclosure.

LETTER XVI.

The horrible Calumnies of the Jesuits against pious Ecclesiastics and holy Monks.

Dec. 4, 1656.

REVEREND FATHERS,

I now propose to proceed to the rest of your calumnies, and shall, in the first place, answer what relates to your *advertisements*. But, as all your other publications are equally full of them, I shall have an ample supply of matter to entertain you as long as I think proper.

As to what relates to the fiction to the prejudice of the bishop of Ypres, which is repeated in all your writings, I will affirm, in a word, that you maliciously abuse some ambiguous expressions in one of his letters, which, being capable of a good sense, ought to be so understood, according to the charitable spirit of the church, and cannot be taken otherwise, but in conformity to the spirit of your Society. Why, when addressing a friend—" Do not trouble yourself so much about your nephew, I will undertake to supply him with whatever money is necessary, from what I have in hand;"—why should you interpret this language as if he meant to take that money without any intention of returning it, and not that he simply designed to advance a sum which was afterwards to be replaced? It was not necessary, however, to be guilty of such an imprudence as to convict yourselves of falsehood by other letters of the bishop of Ypres, which you have published, clearly proving, that what he expended, was, in fact, only money *in advance*, to be afterwards reimbursed. This appears from the letter dated July 30th, 1619, which contains these words: "Do not trouble yourself about the money *in advance;* he shall want for nothing during his continuance here:" and from that of January 6th, 1626, in which he says, "You are too urgent; and whenever the account is required, the little credit I have in this place will, I dare say, be sufficient to find the money, when necessary."

You are as great impostors, then, on this subject, as respecting your ridiculous story about the poor's box of St. Merri: for, pray, what advantage have you derived from the accusation preferred against the clergyman whom you wished to ruin, by one of your beloved friends? Are we to infer, that a man is guilty because he is accused? Surely not. Persons of his exemplary piety, may be always accused, while the world contains such calumniators as you. He is not to be judged of from his accusation, but from his verdict; and, the sentence pronounced on the twenty-third of February, 1656, was a complete justification: and, moreover, the very person who rashly engaged in this iniquitous suit, was disowned by his colleagues, and absolutely obliged to retract his charge. As to your statement, in the same place, respecting a "famous director, who enriched himself in a moment, to the amount of 900,000 livres," it is sufficient to refer you to the clergymen of St. Roch and St. Paul, who can testify to all Paris, his perfect disinterestedness in this affair, and your inexcusable malice.

But these falsities are comparatively trifling—only, in fact, the attempts of your novices, and nothing to the grand performances of your professors. I come, then, to one of the blackest calumnies that ever entered into the human mind; I refer to the insufferable audacity of imputing to holy nuns, and their directors, a disbelief of the mystery of Transubstantiation, and the real presence of Christ in the Eucharist. This is worthy of you, Fathers. This is a crime which God only can punish, and you only could commit. One need be as humble as those humble and aspersed women themselves, to endure this with patience; and as wicked as their wicked calumniators, to believe it. I do not, therefore, undertake to vindicate them, for they are not even suspected. If they had any need of advocates, they would soon find better than I pretend to be. What I have to say, will not be for the purpose of showing their innocence, but displaying your malice. I wish to make you abhor yourselves, and to convince the world that you are capable of any thing.

You will not fail to assert, notwithstanding all this, that I belong to Port-Royal, which is the first thing you have to say against your opponents, as if nobody could be found, but at Port-Royal, with sufficient zeal to defend the purity of the Christian system against your mis-statements. I know the merit of those pious recluses who have retired into solitude, and how much the church is indebted to their edifying and valuable works. I know their piety and wisdom; for though I was never settled amongst them, as you represent, without any sort of idea who I really am, I am acquainted with *some* of their community, and admire the virtue of *all* of them. But God has not included in their number all whom he will employ in opposition to your irregularities: I hope, by his aid, to convince you of this; and if he bestow his grace, to enable me to accomplish my design of employing all the talents he has given me, in his service, I shall speak in such a manner as will, perhaps, excite in you some regret that you have not to encounter a Port-Royal man. And, fathers, to prove my meaning, while those whom you have so much and so calumniously misrepresented, are contenting themselves with offering up to God their ardent intercessions for your forgiveness, I, who am not personally implicated in your calumny, feel myself under the necessity of making you ashamed of it before the whole church, in order to produce that salutary confusion mentioned in Scripture, which is almost the only remedy for such insensibility as yours: " Fill their faces with shame, that they may seek thy name, O Lord—*Imple facies eorum ignominiâ, ut quærant nomen tuum, Domine.*"

It is necessary, however, to silence this insolence, which violates the most sacred places: for who can be safe after such atrocious calumnies? What! to proclaim publicly in Paris there is a book so scandalous, with the name of your Father Meinier prefixed to it, and with this infamous title, " Port Royal and Geneva in concert against the most holy Sacrament of the Altar:" in which you accuse of this apostacy, not only M. de St. Cyran and M. Arnauld, but, also, Mother Agnes, his sister, and all the nuns of that monastery; of whom you say, p. 96; "that their faith is as suspicious with regard to the Eucharist, as that of M. Arnauld," whom, in page 4, you maintain to be an "absolute Calvinist!" I appeal to all the world, if, in the whole church, there be any persons, against whom you could bring so serious a charge with so little propriety: for, if these nuns, and their directors, act in concert with Geneva, against the most holy sacrament of the altar, which is horrible to think of, tell me how they came to take for the principal object of their devotions, the very sacrament which they so abominate? Why add to their rule the institution of the holy sacrament? Why take the habit of the holy sacrament? Why take the name of the nuns of the holy sacrament? Why call their church the church of the holy sacrament? Why solicit and obtain from Rome the confirmation of this institution, and the privilege of repeating every Thursday, the office of the holy sacrament, in which the faith of the church is so fully expressed, if they had conspired with Geneva to abolish that faith? Why should they have obliged themselves by a particular devotion, approved also by the pope, constantly, night and day, to have nuns standing before the sacred host, to atone, by their incessant adorations of this perpetual sacrifice, for the wickedness of that heresy which aims to annihilate it? Tell me, Fathers, if you can, why, of all the mysteries of our religion, they should renounce those which they believe, to choose those which they do not believe? and why should they devote themselves so entirely to that mystery of our faith, if they consider it, as heretics do, as the mystery of iniquity? What answer can you give, Fathers, to these evidences, which consist not of words only, but actions; and not of some occasional actions only, but of a whole course of life, entirely consecrated to the adoration of Jesus Christ, residing upon our altars? What reply can you give to those books which you impute to Port-Royal, and which abound with the most precise terms made use of by the Fathers and councils to express the essence of this mystery? It is at once ridiculous and shocking, to see how you answer this in your libel: "M. Arnauld," you say, "speaks well upon the subject of *transubstantiation;* but, perhaps, he means a *figurative transubstantiation.*" He pretends, indeed, to believe in the *real presence,* but who has informed us, that he understands it of a *true and real figure?* Where are we arrived now, good Fathers, and who is there you could not exhibit to the world as a Calvinist, whenever you chose, if it be allowable to pervert the most canonical and pious expressions, by the malignant subtleties of your new equivocals?—Who ever used any other terms than these, especially in plain discourses upon religion, where controversy is out of the question? And yet the affection and respect they cherish for this sacred mystery, has so pervaded their writings, that I defy you, with all your artifice, to discover the least trace of ambiguity, or the least coincidence with the Genevan creed

Every body knows perfectly well, that the heresy of Geneva essentially consists, as you yourselves state, in believing that Jesus Christ is not contained in this sacrament—that it is impossible he should be in a variety of places at the same moment—that he is really nowhere but in heaven, and there only he ought to be adored, not upon the altar—that the substance of the bread remains—that the body of Christ neither enters into the mouth nor into the stomach—that he is only eaten by faith, and consequently the wicked do not eat him at all—and that the mass is not a sacrifice, but an abomination. Let us see, then, how far the writings of Port-Royal and Geneva agree; and you will find to your confusion, "that the flesh and blood of Jesus Christ are contained in the species of bread and wine," Mr. Arnauld's second letter, p. 259—"that the Holy of holies is present in the sanctuary, and ought to be adored there," *ibid.* p. 243—"that Jesus Christ dwells in sinners, who communicate by the true and real presence of his body in their stomach, though he be not by the presence of his spirit in their heart," *Freq. Com.* part iii. ch. 16—"that the dead and mouldered bodies of the saints derive their chief dignity from that seed of life which remains in them from touching the immortal and life-giving flesh of Jesus Christ," part i. ch. 40—"that it does not arise from any natural power, but from the omnipotence of God, to which nothing is impossible; that the body of Jesus Christ is contained in the host, and in the least particle of every host," *Theolog. Fam.* lec. 15—"that the divine virtue is present to produce the effect which the words of consecration signify," *ibid.*—"that Jesus Christ, who is abased and laid upon the altar, is at the same time elevated in his glory—that he is by himself and by his usual power in a variety of places at the same time, in the midst of the church triumphant, and in the midst of the church militant, and sojourning," *On Suspension*, reason 21—"that the sacramental species remain suspended and subsist in an extraordinary manner, without being sustained by any subject, and that the body of Jesus Christ is also suspended under the species, but does not depend upon them as substances depend upon accidents," *ibid* 23—"that the substance of the bread is changed, the accidents remaining immutable"—In the repose hours of the blessed sacrament, "that Jesus Christ reposes in the Eucharist with the same glory which he has in heaven:" *Letters of Mr. de St. Cyran*, t. i. let. 93—"that his glorious humanity resides in the tabernacles of the church, under the species of bread, which visibly cover it; and knowing our gross conceptions, he thus leads us to the adoration of his divinity, present in all places, by that of his humanity, which is only present in one particular place," *ibid.*—"that we receive the body of Jesus Christ upon the tongue, which he sanctifies by his divine touch," Let. 32—"that he enters into the mouth of the priest," Let. 72—"that though Jesus Christ, through his amazing love and mercy, becomes accessible in the holy sacrament, still he retains his inaccessible nature therein, as an inseparable condition of his divinity; because, though there be only the body, and blood, by virtue of the words—*vi verborum,* as the schools say—yet this does not prevent his whole divinity, as well as his whole humanity, being unitedly present." *Defence of the Chaplet of the Holy Sacrament,* p. 217—"that the Eucharist is both a sacrament and a sacrifice, *Theol. Fam.* lect. 15—"and though this sacrifice be commemorative of that of the cross, there exists this difference, that the mass is offered only for the church, and for believers in her communion; but the sacrifice of the cross was offered, as Scripture states it, for the whole world," *ibid,* p. 153. This, Fathers, is surely sufficient to show, most convincingly, that there never was a piece of more flagrant impudence than yours upon this topic; but I shall still make you pronounce sentence against yourselves. What do you require of any man to clear him from the imputation of secret concert with Geneva? "If M. Arnauld" (to quote your Father Meinier, p. 83) "had said, that in this adorable mystery, there was no substance of bread under the species, but only the flesh and blood of Jesus Christ, I should have allowed, that he had been in direct opposition to Geneva." O shameless impostors, confess it then at once, and make a public reparation for the public injury you have done him. How often has this been repeated in the preceding passages: and, besides, the *Familiar Theology* of M. de St. Cyran, as approved by M. Arnauld, contains the sentiments of both. Read the whole of the fifteenth lecture, particularly the second article, and you will there find the words you demand, even more formally expressed than by yourselves: "Is there any bread in the host, or wine in the cup? No—for the whole substance of the bread and of the wine is taken away to make room for the body and blood of Jesus Christ, which alone remains there, covered with the qualities and species of bread and wine."

Will you now, Fathers, affirm, that Port-Royal teaches nothing but *what Geneva admits,* or that M. Arnauld says nothing in his second letter, but *what might have been said by a minister of Charenton?* See if you can make Mestrezat speak as M. Arnauld does in his letters, p. 237, "that it is an infamous falsehood to accuse him of denying transubstantiation; that he takes for the basis of his writings the truth of the real presence of the Son of God, in opposition to the heresy of the Calvinists; that he deems himself happy to be in a place where the Holy of holies is continually adored as present in the sanctuary." This is much more opposite to the Calvinistic creed than the real presence itself; because, as Cardinal de Richelieu says in his Controversies, p. 536, " the new ministers of France having united with the Lutherans, who believe the real presence of Jesus Christ in the sacrament, have thereby declared, that they do not separate from the church as to this mystery, but in reference to the adoration which the Catholics render to the Eucharist." Obtain the signature of Geneva to all the passages I have cited from the books of Port-Royal, and not only to these, but to entire treatises respecting this mystery, as the book on frequent communion—the Explication of the Ceremonies of the Mass—the Exercise during Mass—the Reasons of the Suspension of the Holy Sacraments—the Translation of the Hymns of the Hours at Port-Royal, &c.—in a word, establish at Charenton this holy institution of constantly adoring Jesus Christ, contained in the Eucharist, as it is at Port-Royal, and you will be doing the greatest service that can possibly be rendered to the church: for then Port-Royal will no longer *act in concert with Geneva,* but Geneva with Port-Royal, and the whole church.

Really, Fathers, you could never have hit upon a worse expedient than to accuse Port-Royal of disbelieving the Eucharist—but I will explain what induced you to adopt this proceeding: I understand, you know, a little of your policy, which on this occasion has been of some service. If M. de St. Cyran and M. Arnauld had only been good enough to inform us what our faith in this mystery ough'.

to have been, and not what ought to be done as preparatory to it, they would have been the best catholics in the world, and no kind of ambiguity would have been found in the terms *real presence* and *transubstantiation.* But as it is necessary to look upon all who oppose your laxity as heretics, and must be so in every particular which they venture to question, how could M. Arnauld be otherwise upon the Eucharist. after having written a book expressly against your profanations of this sacrament? Could he possibly say, with impunity, " that we ought not to give the body and blood of Christ to such as frequently relapse into the same sins, and discover no signs of amendment? and that they ought to be separated some time from the altar, in order to purify themselves by a sincere repentance, that they may afterwards approach it with profit?" Pray, Fathers, do not suffer people to talk at this rate, otherwise I am apprehensive your confessionals will not be very crowded; for your Father Brisacier says, " if you pursue this method, you can apply the blood of Jesus Christ to nobody." You had better follow the practice of your Society, which Father Mascarennhas mentions in a book approved by your doctors, and by the reverend Father General himself, namely, " Persons of every class, and even the priests, may receive the body of Jesus Christ the very day they are polluted with abominable crimes. So far from such communions manifesting any irreverence, on the contrary they are praiseworthy. Confessors ought not to put them off, but should advise those who come from the commission of such iniquities, to communicate immediately : for though the church has forbid it, this prohibition is abolished by the universal practice of the whole world." *Mascar* tr. 4. disp. 5. n. 284.

See, Fathers, see what it is to have Jesuits dispersed over the whole surface of the earth! see the universal practice you have introduced, and constantly uphold! It signifies nothing what abominations you bring to the table of Jesus Christ, provided your churches be full. Be sure and prove that every opponent to this principle is a heretic against the sacrament. It *must* be done, at any rate.

The difficulty is how this can be shown, after so many incontestible evidences of their faith. And now are you not alarmed, lest I should produce the four grand proofs you have adduced of their heresy? You ought to be so; and I think I ought not to spare you the shame of them.

With regard to the first: "M. St. Cyran states, that Father Meinier, to console one of his friends on the death of his mother, tom. i. let. 14, says 'the most acceptable sacrifice that can be offered to God on such occasions, is patience:' then he is a Calvinist!" Very fine, Fathers; very clever, indeed—though I question whether any one can see the reason why. But this we have from himself: "because," adds this great polemic, "he does not believe the sacrifice of the mass, for *that* is the most acceptable of any."

Will any person *now* pretend that the Jesuits are not famous reasoners? They are, in truth, such adepts, that they can make any thing they please heretical—nay, Scripture itself; for, pray, would it not be a heresy to say, as in Ecclesiastes, "Nothing is worse than the love of money—*nihil est iniquius quàm amare pecuniam?*" as if adultery, murder, and idolatry were not greater crimes! In fact, who does not say something of a similar nature every day; as, for instance—the sacrifice of a contrite and broken heart is the most acceptable with God—because, in such propositions, the intention is only to compare together certain internal virtues, and not these with the great sacrifice of the mass, which is quite of a different order, and infinitely superior. Are you not, then, extremely ridiculous? or is it necessary to complete your confusion by introducing a quotation from the same letter, in which M. St. Cyran speaks of the sacrifice of the mass as the *most excellent* of all: "We offer to God every day, and in all places, the sacrifice of the body of his Son, who could not find a *more excellent method* than this of honouring his Father." He adds, "Jesus Christ has required us, when dying, to partake of his sacrificed body, to make the sacrifice of our own more acceptable o. God? and that, by thus uniting himself to us in death, he may strengthen us, through sanctifying by his presence the last sacrifice we make to God of our life and body." But, Fathers, dissemble all this—persevere in stating as you have done, p. 33, that he diverted men from the sacrament at the hour of death, that he disbelieved the sacrifice of the mass; for nothing is too bold for slanderers by profession to assert.

Your second proof furnishes new evidence on this point. To make out M. St. Cyran (to whom you attribute the book of Petrus Aurelius) a Calvinist, you introduce a passage where Aurelius, p. 89, explains the conduct of the church towards priests and bishops whom she wishes to depose or degrade. "The church," he says, " not being able to take away the power of the order, because the character cannot be effaced, she proceeds thus—she blots that character from her memory which it is impossible to exterminate from the souls of those who have received it: she considers them as no longer her priests or bishops; so that, according to the common consent of the church, we may say they are no longer such, though they still remain such as to the character—*ob indelebilitatem characteris.*" You see, Fathers, that this author, approved by three general assemblies of the clergy of France, expressly affirms the character of the priesthood *is* indelible; and yet you make him say precisely the contrary in the very same place, " that the character of the priesthood is *not* indelible." Now this is a most *monstrous calumny*—that is to say, as *you* would term it, a *venial, trifling offence.* This book has affected you deeply, by refuting the heresies of your English brethren respecting episcopal authority. But how prodigious is your extravagance! for having falsely imagined that M. St. Cyran holds this character capable of being effaced, you hurry on to the conclusion that he does not believe in the real presence of Jesus Christ in the Eucharist.

You do not, I suppose, expect me to reply to this absurdity; for if you have not common sense, really I cannot give it you. All who have, however, will be abundantly amused both with you and your third proof, which is founded on the following words in the *Frequent Communion*, part iii. ch. 11 : " God gives us in the Eucharist the *same food* with which he supplies the saints in heaven, without the least difference, excepting it be this, that here he takes away the sight and sensible taste, reserving both for the heavenly world." Surely, my good Fathers, these words so naturally express the sense of the church, that I cannot imagine at this moment how you can pervert them. I can see nothing in them but what the Council of Trent teaches, *Sess.* 13. p. 8, that there is no other difference between Jesus Christ in the Eucharist and Jesus Christ in heaven, but *here* he is veiled, *there* he is not. M. Arnauld does not say there is no other difference in the manner of receiving Jesus Christ ; but, simply, there is no other difference in Jesus Christ who is received. But in contradiction to all reason, you would make him assert in this passage, that Jesus Christ is no more eaten with the mouth here than he is in heaven : *ergo*, he is a heretic !

I really cannot help pitying you, Fathers. Shall I explain again ? How is it you confound this divine food with the manner of receiving it ? The only difference, as I have just stated, between this food on earth and in heaven is, here it is hidden under veils which conceal it from our sensible taste and sight : but there are many differences in the manner of receiving it, both on earth and in heaven ; of which the principal, according to Mr. Arnauld, part iii. ch. 16, is " Here Christ enters into the mouth and stomach both of the righteous and the wicked,"—but it is not so in heaven.

If, Fathers, you continue ignorant of the occasion of this diversity, allow me to inform you that the reason why God appointed the different modes of receiving the same food, is the difference which subsists between the condition of Christians in the present life and that of the blessed in heaven. " The state of Christians," observes cardinal du Perron after the Fathers, " is a medium between the blessed and the condition of the Jews. The blessed possess Jesus Christ really, without a figure and without a veil. The Jews never possessed Christ but under figures and veils, as in the manna and the paschal lamb; and Christians possess Jesus Christ in the Eucharist truly and really, but still under veils." " God, says St. Eucharius, " made himself three tabernacles—the synagogue, which had nothing but shadows, without truth—the church, which has both shadows and truth—heaven, where there are no shadows, but truth alone." We should depart from the state in which we are, that state of faith which St. Paul places in opposition to the law as well as to perfect vision, were we only to possess figures without Jesus Christ, because it is the property of the law to have the shadow of things only and not the substance; and we should err again if we possessed him visibly, because " faith," as the apostle affirms, " is the evidence of things not seen." The Eucharist, therefore, is precisely adapted to our state of faith, because it contains Jesus Christ truly, though veiled. Hence, this state of faith would be destroyed, if Jesus Christ were not really under the species of bread and wine, as heretics pretend: it would also be destroyed, if he were received unveiled as in heaven, because this would be to confound our present condition either with the state of Judaism or that of glory.

This, Fathers, is the mysterious and divine reason of this mystery, which is itself altogether divine; this is the reason why we hold the Calvinists in abhorrence, because they would reduce us to the state of Judaism; and this makes us aspire to the glory of the blessed, where we shall enjoy the full and eternal presence of Jesus Christ. By this you perceive there exists a variety of methods in which he communicates himself to Christians on earth, and to those in heaven; and, amongst others here below, he is received into the mouth—not so in heaven; but they all depend upon the difference which subsists between the state of faith in which we are, and the state of perfect vision in which they are placed. This, Fathers, led M. Arnauld to speak so explicitly in these terms: " There ought to be no other difference between the purity of those who receive Christ in the Eucharist and that of the blessed, but what there is between faith and the full vision of God, on which alone depends the different manner in which he is eat on earth and in heaven." You ought to have reverenced the truths contained in these words, instead of perverting them to detect a heresy which never was there and never can be; namely, "that Jesus Christ is eaten only by faith, not by the mouth," as your Fathers Annat and Meinier maliciously affirm, making it the chief point of their accusation.

Your proofs, then, my good Fathers, seem very defective; which occasions your having recourse to a new artifice, that of falsifying the Council of Trent, in order to show M. Arnauld's disconformity to it; such are your methods of making the world heretical. This is done by Father Meinier in fifty places of his book, and eight or ten times in the single page 54, where he pretends that it is not enough, as a true Catholic, to say, "I believe that Jesus Christ is really present in the sacrament;" but, "I believe, *with the Council,* that he is present there by a true local presence, or locally." He then cites the Council, *Sess.* 13. can. 3. can. 4. can. 6. Who would not suppose, as soon as he saw the phrase *local presence* quoted from three canons of a general council, it was really there? —This might have passed very well previous to the publication of my fifteenth letter; but now, Fathers, people are not to be caught: they look at the Acts of the Council, and find you out to be impostors: for, positively, the words *local presence, locally, locality,* were never there! And I further declare that they are in no other part of that council, nor indeed of any other council, nor in any Father of the church. After this, I should be glad to be informed whether you will pretend to throw a suspicion of being Calvinistic upon all those who have not adopted this phraseology? If so, the Council of Trent is itself suspicious, and all the holy Fathers, without exception. Can you devise no other method of making M. Arnauld heretical, but that of offending so many other people who never did you the slightest injury; as St. Thomas, who is one of the most strenuous advocates of the Eucharist and who, so far from adopting, absolutely rejects this phraseology, p. 3. 9. 76. a. 5. "*Nullo modo corpus Christi est in hoc sacramento localiter.*" Who then are you, Fathers, to impose, by your single authority, new terms, which you pronounce to be better adapted to express the faith of mankind; as if the profession of faith drawn up by the popes according to the decree of the Council, where this term is not to be found, were defective, and left an ambiguity upon the faith of Christians which you only have discovered! What temerity, to prescribe terms to the divines themselves! What falsehood, to impute them to general councils! What ignorance, to know nothing of the objections of the most enlightened saints! Blush—blush for your ignorant impostures, and remark what Scripture says to such characters: "*De mendacio ineruditionis tuæ confundêre.*

Relinquish, then, I beseech you, all further attempts at dictation: you have neither character nor credit for the purpose. If you would introduce your propositions with more modesty, one might pay them some attention, for though the term *local presence* was rejected, as you have seen, by St. Thomas, because the body of Jesus Christ is not in the Eucharist, in the ordinary sense in which other bodies occupy certain spaces; nevertheless, the term has been received by some modern controversialists, understanding by it merely, that the body of Jesus Christ is truly under the external species, which being in a particular place, the body of Christ must be so likewise. In this sense, M. Arnauld will feel no difficulty in admitting it, since M. de Cyran and he have frequently declared that Jesus Christ, in the Eucharist, is really in a particular place, and miraculously in many different places at the same moment. So that all your refinements fall to the ground, and you have not the slightest pretence for an accusation, which ought never to have been brought forward without irrefragable proofs.

But of what avail is it, Fathers, to oppose their innocence to your calumnies? You do not charge them with these errors from any conviction that they maintain them, but from a belief that they are calculated to injure you:

and, according to your theology, that is quite sufficient innocently to calumniate them: and you may, without confession or penitence, say mass, at the very time you represent the priests, who perform it every day, as believing it to be a piece of pure idolatry; which is such a shocking sacrilege, that you yourselves ordered your own Father Sarrigus to be hung in effigy, because he had celebrated mass at the time he maintained an understanding with Geneva.

I am really astonished, Fathers, not indeed at your charging such crimes upon people with so little scruple, but at your imputing such improbable crimes with so little prudence: for though you dispose of the sins of mankind as you please, do you suppose you can also dispose of their faith? If the suspicion of Calvinism must fall either upon them or upon you, I really think you would be in a bad plight. Their statements are as catholic as yours; but their conduct confirms their profession, yours belies it. If you truly believed, as they do, that the bread is changed into the body of Jesus Christ, why not demand, as they do, that the stony and icy hearts of those whom you advise to participate it should be sincerely changed into hearts of flesh and love? If you believe that Jesus Christ is under a state of death in the sacrament, to teach those who partake of it to die to the world, to sin, and to themselves, why do you invite those whose vices and criminal passions are still alive and prevalent? And how can you esteem those to be worthy of eating the bread of heaven, who do not deserve to eat that of earth?

Noble worshippers of this holy mystery, whose zeal is employed in persecuting those who honour it by so many holy communions, and flatter such as dishonour it by so many sacrilegious ones!!—How worthily do these advocates of this pure and adorable sacrifice fill the table of Jesus Christ with abandoned and inveterate sinners, just come from their infamous abominations; and among them placing a priest whose confessor has sent him from his impurities to the altar, to offer there, in the place of Jesus Christ, that holy victim to the God of holiness, and with his polluted hands put it into mouths no less defiled! Does it not well become those who, according to the approved maxims of their own General, practise in this manner *all over the world* to charge the author of Frequent Communion, and the nuns of the Holy Sacrament, with not believing in the holy sacrament?—But this is not sufficient; for, in order to satisfy their passions, it is found necessary to accuse these nuns of having renounced Jesus Christ and their baptism. These are not inventions, Fathers; they are the sad, the awful extravagances by which you have filled up the measure of your calumnies. Such a prodigious forgery was not in proper hands to support it while remaining with your good friend Filleau, to whom, however, you were indebted for it: but your whole Society has openly appropriated it; and your Father Meinier has maintained, as an *indisputable truth* that Port Royal has been engaged, for this five and thirty years, with M. St. Cyran and M. Ypres, as the principal partizans, in forming a secret cabal "to destroy the mystery of the Incarnation, to make the Gospel pass for an apocryphal history, to exterminate the Christian religion, and to elevate deism upon its ruins." And is this all, Fathers? And shall you be satisfied, if all this should be believed of them which your hatred suggests? Will your animosity be satiated, if you could make them abhorred, not only by all who belong to the church, *by a secret coalition with Geneva* of which you accuse them, but also by all believers without the pale of the church, by the *deism* you charge upon them?

But who do you imagine will be convinced upon your mere word, without the shadow of a proof, and amidst all possible contradictions, that priests who preach nothing but the grace of Jesus Christ, the purity of the Gospel, and the obligations resulting from baptism, have really renounced baptism, the Gospel, and Jesus Christ? Who I say, will give credit to such a statement? Do you really believe it yourselves, base as you are? To what an extremity are you reduced? for you must of necessity either prove that they are not believers in Christ, or be deemed the most infamous of calumniators. Prove it then Fathers. Adduce your evidence. Name *the worthy ecclesiastic* who you say, assisted at the assembly of Bourg-Fontain in 1621, and disclosed to your Filleau the project of destroying the Christian religion. Name the six individuals who as you affirm conspired for this purpose. Name the person intended by the letters A. A. who, you assert, p. 15, is not *Anthony Arnauld*, because he has convinced you he was not at that time more than nine years of age, " but another, who," you declare, " is still alive, and too good a friend of Mr. Arnauld to be unknown to him." You know him then, of course ? and, consequently, if you have a spark of religion left, you are under an obligation to bring this impious individual before the king and parliament, that he may be punished according to his demerits. You *must* speak out, Fathers ; you *must* name him, or endure the shame of being regarded as liars who will never more deserve a moment's credit.

This is the method taught us by good Father Valerian, of putting such impostors as you *to the rack*, and driving them to the utmost extremity. Your silence will be a full and perfect evidence of this diabolical calumny. The very blindest of your adherents will be compelled to acknowledge that this silence " is no proof of your virtue, but of your weakness ;" and will be astonished that you could be so wicked as to launch out even against the nuns of Port-Royal, and to say, as you have done, p. 14, that " *the secret chaplet of the holy sacrament*, composed by one of them, was the first fruit of that conspiracy against Jesus Christ ;" and in p. 95, " that they are inspired with all the detestable maxims of that book, which is," according to you, " instruction in *Deism*." Your representations, with regard to that performance, have been already completely refuted in " the defence of the censure by the late archbishop of Paris against your Father Brisacier," to which you have not replied ; yet you continue to abuse still more scandalously than ever those pious females, well known as such to all the world, as impious in the extreme. Cruel and merciless persecutors!—cannot the most retired cloisters be an asylum against your calumnies? Whilst those holy virgins adore Jesus Christ in the holy sacrament, day and night, according to their institution, you cease not, night and day, to proclaim publicly that they do not believe either that he is in the sacrament, or at the right hand of the Father; and while they are praying in secret for you and the whole church, you are as publicly engaged in cutting them off from membership. You revile those who have neither ears to hear, nor tongue to answer. But Jesus Christ, in whom they are hidden till they appear with him in glory, hears you, and answers for them. Even now we hear that holy and tremendous voice which startles nature and consoles the church; and I am apprehensive, Fathers, that such as harden their hearts, and proudly refuse to attend when he speaks as a God, will be forced to listen with horror when he speaks to them as a Judge.

Oh, Fathers, what account will you be able to render of your numerous calumnies, which he will examine, not according to the fantastic notions of your Fathers Dicastillus, Gaius, and Pennalossa, who excuse them, but upon the principles of eternal truth, and the holy ordinances of his church, by which they are so far from being excused, that they are condemned and punished as wilful murderers. For the church has suspended calumniators as well as murderers from communion, till the hour of death, by the first and second council of Arles. The council of Lateran adjudged those who were convicted of this crime, although reformed, to be unworthy of holy orders. The popes threatened such as had slandered bishops, priests, or deacons, with a refusal of the communion until death; and the authors of any defamatory publication, who are unable to bring proof of what they assert, are condemned by pope Adrian *to be whipped*—yes, reverend Fathers—*flagellentur!*—So offensive have the errors of your corrupt Society always been to the church—a society which excuses in others such prodigious crimes as calumny, in order to commit them herself with the greater freedom!

Assuredly, Fathers, you would be able to do much mischief, if God had not so ordered it, that you should yourselves furnish the means of prevention, and render all your impostures inefficient. For it is only necessary to publish that extravagant maxim which exempts them from guilt, to annihilate all your reputation. Calumny is useless, unless its propagators be in great esteem for sincerity. A backbiter could by no means succeed, unless he could induce mankind to believe that he abhorred backbiting, and was utterly incapable of it. And thus, Fathers, your own principle betrays you: for you wished to backbite without being damned, and to be esteemed those "holy and pious calumniators," of whom St. Athanasius speaks. For the purpose, therefore, of saving yourselves from perdition, you have embraced that maxim which will certainly save you, according to your doctors; but yet, this very maxim which guarantees you from the miseries you have reason to apprehend in a future world, takes away from you, in this life, all the advantage you might expect from it: so that while you think of avoiding the vice of slander, you lose the benefit of it, so contrary is wickedness to itself, confounding and destroying itself by its own malignity.

You might slander others with more advantage, by professing to agree with St. Paul, that mere evil speakers—*maledici*—are unworthy of seeing God; for your calumnies would at least be better credited, though, in fact, you must condemn yourselves. But, by saying as you do, that it is no crime to slander your enemies, your misrepresentations will be disbelieved, and your souls exposed to perdition. Certain it is, Fathers, that as your grave authors can never annihilate the justice of God, so you cannot furnish a more decisive proof of your having abandoned the truth, than by having recourse to falsehood. If truth were on your side, she would fight and she would conquer for you; and whatever enemies you might have, she would, according to her promise, "deliver you from them all." You recur to falsehood only to flatter sinners, and to support the calumnies with which you load those pious persons who oppose you. Truth being contrary to your views, you must *put your trust in lies*, as the prophet expresses it—" We have made lies our refuge, and under falsehood have we hid ourselves :" and what is the prophet's reply, " Because you have trusted in calumny and oppression—*sperastis in calumniâ et in tumultu*—therefore this iniquity shall be to you as a breach ready to fall, swelling out in a high wall, whose breaking cometh suddenly at an instant. And he shall break it as the breaking of the potter's vessel that is broken in pieces—he shall not spare : so that there shall not be found in the bursting of it a sherd to take fire from the hearth, or to take water out of the pit ;" " because," as another prophet represents it, " because with lies ye have made the heart of the righteous sad, whom I have not made sad ; and strengthened the hands of the wicked, that he should not return from his wicked way, by promising him life : I will deliver my people out of your hand, and ye shall know that I am the Lord."

It may be hoped, therefore, if you do not change your behaviour and spirit, God will take out of your hands, those whom you have so long deceived, either by leaving them to their misconduct through your wickedness, or by poisoning them with your slanders. He will lead some to perceive that the erroneous rules of your casuists will not screen them from his displeasure, and will impress on others a just fear of their own perdition, if they listen and believe your impostures, while you will destroy yourselves by inventing and circulating them in the world. Be not deceived, God is not mocked. No man can break his commandments with impunity, which enjoin us not to condemn our neighbour till we are assured of his guilt : consequently, whatever profession of piety may be made by those who receive your falsehoods with an unexamining carelessness, and whatever pretence of devotion they have for it, may justly apprehend an exclusion from the kingdom of heaven, for accusing Catholic priests and holy nuns of such enormous sins as heresy and schism, without any other evidence than your gross impositions. " The devil," says the bishop of Geneva, " is upon the tongue of the slanderer, and in the ear of the person who listens to him;" and " slander," observes St. Bernard, *Serm.* 24, *in Cant.* is a poison which extinguishes charity in both: so that one single calumny may prove fatal to an incalculable number of souls, because it destroys not only those who publish it, but those also who do not reject it."

Reverend Fathers, my letters have not usually followed each other in such rapid succession, nor have they been in general so long; the little time I have had is the reason of both. I should not have extended this so much, but that I cannot command leisure to shorten it. What occasioned my haste is, in fact, better known to you than to myself. Your replies succeed miserably, and you have done quite right to alter your method of proceeding; but I doubt whether you have now adopted a proper one, and whether the world will not be ready to say you have been afraid of the Benedictins.

I learn that the person whom the world calls the author of your apologies disavows them, and is vexed that they are attributed to him. He has, indeed, reason enough to be so, and I was wrong to suspect him; for, from whatever quarter it proceeded, I ought certainly to have given him credit for too much sense to believe your impostures, and too much honour to publish them without such belief. Few people are capable of such extravagances as yours—they are so completely your own, so truly characteristic—that I am inexcusable for not perceiving their source. Common report misled me. But I am aware that this apology, too good for you, does not suffice for me, who profess to affirm nothing without substantial evidence, and who have not done so, this instance excepted. I therefore regret it—I renounce it—and I sincerely wish you may profit by my example.

LETTER XVII.

TO THE REV. FATHER ANNAT, JESUIT.

By the unanimous Consent of all the Divines, and particularly of the Jesuits, the Authority of the Popes and of Œcumenical Councils is not infallible in Questions of Fact.

January 23, 1657.

REVEREND FATHER,

Your mode of proceeding induced me to suppose that you were desirous of a cessation of hostilities on both sides, to which I was quite disposed; but you have since produced so many pieces in so short a time, that it seems as if it were not very easy to establish peace when it depends on the silence of Jesuits. I cannot tell whether this rupture will be serviceable to *you;* but for *my part*, I am by no means sorry that it affords me an opportunity of refuting that common-place charge of heresy which abounds in your writings.

It is time, once for all, to put a stop to that audacity with which you treat me as a heretic, and which increases every day. You have ventured to do so in the book you have just published with such insufferable and unceremonious boldness, as would really render me suspected, were I not to reply to this reproach in the manner it deserves. I had passed over this injury with the same contempt with which I treated a multitude of others, indiscriminately thrown together in the writings of your fraternity. My fifteenth letter contained a sufficient answer; but now you assume another tone—you make it the very chief point of your defence, and almost the only one of which you avail yourselves: "for," say you, "to answer all my fifteen letters, it is sufficient to say fifteen times over, that I am a heretic, and, being declared such, deserve no credit." My apostacy, then, is not to be doubted, which, being laid down as a fundamental principle, you proceed boldly with your superstructure. Very good, Fathers; and since you treat me as a heretic, I must in earnest sit down to answer you.

A charge of this nature, my good Fathers you know very well, is so important, that to advance it without proof would be an intolerable piece of rashness. I ask, then, where are your proofs? When was I seen at Charenton? When did I neglect to attend mass, or to perform the duties to which all Christians are bound in their respective parishes? When have I done any thing to unite with heretics or to promote schism in the church? What council have I contradicted? What papal constitution have I violated?—You must answer these questions, Father, or————you know my meaning. But you *do* reply. Well—I beg every body to pay particular attention to your answer. In the first place, you suppose that " the writer of the letters belongs to Port Royal:" then you add, " Port Royal is avowedly heretical;" hence you infer, " the writer of the letters is a declared heretic;" this accusation does not fall upon my poor head, but upon Port Royal; and you only charge me with it because you imagine me to be one of that community. However, I can very easily parry this thrust, by simply saying, I do not belong to them; and, as a proof, referring you to my letters, in which I have stated, " I am alone," and in express terms, " I am not of Port-Royal." Pray, turn to my sixteenth letter, which appeared previously to the publication of your book.

You must devise, then, another method of proving me to be a heretic, or every body will see your inability to do it. Prove, by my writings, that I reject the constitution: they are not so very numerous, you have only sixteen letters to examine, in which I defy you—yes—I defy you and the whole world, to produce a syllable of the kind; but you shall there see quite the reverse. When, for instance, I said in the fourteenth letter " that whoever, according to your maxims, kills any of his brethren in a mortal sin, damns them for whom Christ died," did I not plainly acknowledge that Jesus Christ died for those lost souls? It is therefore false to say, " that he died only for the predestinated," which doctrine is condemned in the fifth proposition. It is certain, therefore, my good Father, that I have not advanced any thing in support of such impious propositions, which I abhor from my very heart: and if Port-Royal hold them, I aver that you can furnish no proof against me, because, thanks be to God, I have no attachment to any society whatever but to the Catholic, Apostolic, and Roman church, in which I wish to live and to die, in communion with the pope, its supreme head, and out of which I am persuaded there is no salvation.

What can you do with a person of this stamp? Where can you attack him? since neither my conversations nor writings furnish the least pretext for your accusations of heresy, and I am secure from your menaces by the obscurity which conceals me. You are struck by an invisible hand, which exposes your extravagances to the whole world, and you endeavour, but in vain, to attack me in the person of those with whom you imagine I am connected. But I am neither afraid of you for myself or any one else, not being attached either to any particular fraternity or individual. All your power is unavailable. I neither hope, nor fear, nor wish any thing in this world: thanks be to God, I neither want any person's property or influence. So, my good Father, I am out of your reach; you cannot take hold of me in any way. You may touch Port-Royal, but not me. You may expel as many as you please from the Sorbonne, but you cannot expel me. You may act with the utmost violence against priests and doctors, but you cannot affect me, who possess neither of these characters. And thus, perhaps, you never before had to deal with a person so completely out of reach, and so qualified to combat your errors, being free, without engagement, without attachment, without connexion, without relation, without business, well acquainted with your maxims, and fully resolved to pursue them as far as I think Providence calls on me to do so, independently of all those human considerations which might tend to retard my progress.

What use is it then, Father, as you can do nothing against me, to publish such calumnies against persons who have no concern in our differences. This proceeding, however, shall not avail you. You shall feel the force of that truth which I produce against you. I maintain that you annihilate Christian morality by separating it from the love of God, from which you dispense mankind; and you, by way of reply, tell me *that Father Mester is dead*, whom I never saw in my whole life! I state that your authors permit " murder in revenge for an apple, when it is disgraceful to lose it"—and you reply, that " a poor's box was broke open at St. Merry." Tell me, I beseech you, what you mean by every day fastening upon me the book of *The Holy Virginity*,* composed by a Father of the oratory, whose face and book are equally unknown to me. I am all astonishment, Father, for you seem to regard all your opponents as one person. Your hatred seizes them all together, forming them into one compact body of reprobates, and thus obliging every individual to answer for all the rest.

There is a prodigious difference between the Jesuits and their opponents. You compose one body united together under one head, and your regulations, as I have shown, prohibit the publication of any thing without the approbation of your superiors, who make themselves responsible for the errors of each member of the society; so that

---

* This book is a translation from St. Augustin, by Father Seguenot, priest of the oratory. There was, in reality, nothing reprehensible in the book itself, but this Father added some strange notes to it, well deserving of censure; and, as it proceeded from the oratory, which society was always attached to the doctrine of St. Augustin, an attempt was made to make the blame of it fall upon the Janseniste.

it cannot be any excuse to say that " they did not observe the errors taught in the said book," because it was their duty to observe them, according to your ordinances and the letters of your generals Agaviva, Vitelleschi, &c. It is perfectly reasonable, therefore, to reproach you as responsible for the extravagant sentiments of your fraternity, whose works are approved by your superiors and divines. But it is quite otherwise with me. I never subscribed to the book of *The Holy Virginity*. I should not be less a Catholic, were all the poor's boxes in Paris broke open; and, in one word, I declare loudly and plainly, that no one is responsible for my letters but myself, and for nothing else do I hold myself accountable.

Here I might finish, without alluding to those other individuals whom you treat as heretics, merely for the purpose of involving me in the accusation; but since I am the occasion of this charge, I feel myself under some obligation to avail myself of the present occasion to deduce three advantages from it. A very considerable one, is to clear up the innocency of so many aspersed characters; another, quite to my present subject, is to expose the artifices of your policy in this accusation; but the most important of all is, that I shall convince the whole world of the falsehood of that scandalous report, which you are circulating in every direction, " that the church is divided by a new heresy." And, as you involve a number of people, by inducing them to believe that the points about which you raise such a dreadful disturbance are essential to faith, I deem it of the utmost consequence to destroy those false impressions, by distinctly explaining in what they consist, to show that there are, in reality, no heretics in the church.

Is it not a fact, that were the question proposed, in what the heresy of those whom you term Jansenists consists, the immediate answer would be in their saying, " that the commandments of God are impossible, that grace cannot be resisted, that no man is a free agent in doing good or evil, that Jesus Christ did not die for all men, but for the elect only; and, lastly, that they maintain the five propositions condemned by the pope?" And pray, do you not assure every body that this is the very reason why you persecute your opponents? Is not this avowed in your writings, in your conversations, in your catechisms, as at St. Louis at Christmas, by asking one of your little girls, "For whom did Jesus Christ come into the world, my child?"—"For all men, father."— "You are not then, my child, one of those modern heretics who say, he came only for the elect?"—The children, of course, give you implicit credit, and so do many others whom you entertain with stories in your sermons similar to those of your Father Crasset at Orleans, who was accordingly suspended. I must here confess, that I was one of your credulous hearers formerly, when you instilled the same ideas respecting these people: so that when you urged them upon these propositions, I carefully noticed their reply, determining to pay no further regard to them if they did not protest their solemn renunciation of such obvious impieties: but they did so, and most openly; for M. de St. Beuve, professor to the king in the Sorbonne, in his writings, censured these five propositions long before the pope and the doctors issued many other publications (among others, that on *victorious grace*,) in which they reject these propositions as heretical and strange. They say, in the preface, "These propositions are heretical and Lutheran, fabricated and forged at pleasure, and nowhere to be found in Jansenius or any of his supporters." This is an exact quotation of their words, and they complain of having such doctrines attributed to them, addressing you in the language of Prospero, the first disciple of their master St. Augustin, to the semi-Pelagians of France, who accused him in the same manner to make him odious—"There are people," says this saint, "who are influenced by so blind a rage to decry us, as to have adopted a method well calculated to ruin their own reputation; for they have purposely invented certain propositions, full of impiety and blasphemy, which they circulate in all directions, to make people believe that we maintain them in the same sense they have chosen to express in their writings; but our innocence and their malignity in charging us with impieties which are solely of their own invention, will be seen by this reply."

When, Father, I heard them speak in this manner before the constitution, when I saw that they afterwards embraced it with all possible respect, that they offered to subscribe it, and that M. Arnauld, in his second letter, had declared all this more strongly than I can represent, I should have considered it a sin to disbelieve their faith ; and, in fact, they who had refused to give absolution to their friends, previous to the publication of M. Arnauld's second letter, have since declared, that after he had so plainly condemned the very errors which were imputed to him, there existed no sufficient reason for either his or his adherents' excommunication from the church. But you did not concur in this, for which reason I began to suspect you were under the misguidance of passion. You threatened to make them sign the constitution, when you thought they would refuse it ; but when you saw they were inclined to it of themselves, you then said nothing more upon the subject. And though you ought after that to be satisfied with their conduct, you must still, to be sure, treat them as heretics, "because," as you allege, "their hearts belied their hands—they were outwardly Catholics and inwardly heretics." This is your language in your answers to certain questions, p. 27 and 47.

How strange a mode of proceeding, Father, does this appear ! Of whom may not the very same thing be said ? And what disturbance might not be excited by such pretences? "If," says Pope Gregory, "we refuse to believe those who confess their faith, conformably to the sentiments of the church, we should render the faith of every Catholic questionable." *Regist. l. 5. ep.* 15. I began, Father, to think, "that it was your design to make them heretics though they were not so," as the same pope says of a dispute of a similar kind in his days, "because," he adds, "to refuse believing those who by their confession witness they are in the true faith, is not opposing, but making heresies—*hoc non est hæresim purgare, sed facere,* Ep. 16." But I knew, in fact, that there were no heretics in the church when I saw they were so well vindicated from all these heresies, that you could not accuse them of any error in faith, and that you were reduced to the necessity of contending with them only upon questions of fact relating to Jansenius, which could never be a heresy; for you would oblige them to acknowledge, " that these propositions were in Jansenius, word for word, all of them, and in express terms," as you stated in your own hand-writing—*singulares, individuæ, totidem verbis apud Jansenium contentæ,* in your Cavilli, p. 39.

From this moment your dispute began to be quite an indifferent matter with me. So long as I believed you were contending about the truth or falsehood of the propositions, I heard you with attention, for it regarded the faith; but when I perceived the object was merely to know whether they were *word for word* in Jansenius or not, as religion was not at all concerned in it, neither was I. Apparently you said what was true, for to state that a sentence is *word for word* in an author is what cannot be mistaken; for which reason I am not astonished that so many persons, both in France and Rome, should have believed, from a statement so little suspicious, that Jansenius had really taught such doctrines. I was therefore not a little surprised to find, that this matter of fact, which you exhibited as so important, was false; and you were then challenged to quote the pages of Jansenius, where you discovered those propositions *word for word,* which you have never been able to do.

I beg to state the whole, because it appears to me it will sufficiently explain the spirit of your Society in this affair, and excite great surprise to see that, notwithstanding all I have said, you do not desist from publishing that they are heretics still; but you have only changed their heresy with the times. For, in proportion as they vindicated themselves from one heresy, you substituted another, to prevent their ever being innocent. Thus, in 1653, their heresy respected the quality of the propositions;

afterwards, the *word for word*—then you placed it in the *heart;* but now, nothing is said of all this, and they must be heretics if they will not sign and seal, that " the sense of the doctrine of Jansenius is found in the sense of these five propositions."

Such is the subject of the present dispute. You are not satisfied that they condemn the five propositions, and every thing in Jansenius conformable to them and contrary to St. Augustin, for all that they do; so that the question is not to know, for example, " if Jesus Christ died only for the elect"—they condemn that as well as yourselves—but whether Jansenius be of that opinion or no; on which account I now declare more firmly than ever, that your dispute concerns me as little as it does the church. For though I am no more a doctor than yourself, I can see, however that faith has nothing to do with the question, since the only point is to know the sense of Jansenius. If they believed that his doctrine were conformable to the proper and literal sense of these propositions, they would condemn it, and refuse to do it, only because they are convinced that it differs exceedingly from that sense; consequently though they should misunderstand it, they would not be heretics, since they understood it only in a Catholic sense.

To explain this by an example, I will take the diversity of opinion between St. Basil and St. Athanasius, respecting the writings of St. Denis, of Alexandria, in which St. Basil thinking they were of the Arian principle, opposing the equality of the Father and the Son, condemned them as heretical; but St. Athanasius, on the contrary, believing them to contain the true sentiment of the church, upheld them as Catholic. Do you suppose, Father, that St. Basil, who held these writing to be Arian, had any right to treat St. Athanasius as a heretic, because he defended them? And what good reason could he have, since it was not Arianism that Athanasius defended, but the true faith which he believed them to contain? If these two saints had been agreed about the true sense of those writings, and had both acknowledged that heresy contained in them, doubtless St. Athanasius could not approve them without being heretical; but, as they differed merely with regard to the meaning, St. Athanasius was a Catholic in maintaining them, though he had even misunderstood them, for it could only be an error of fact, and he merely defended the Catholic faith which he believed to be contained in that doctrine.

I say the same thing of you, Father. If you agree about the meaning of Jansenius, and your adversaries agree with you that he holds, for instance, *that grace cannot be resisted*, those who should refuse to condemn him, would be heretics; but while you dispute about this meaning, and they believe that, according to his doctrine, *grace may be resisted*, you have no reason to treat them as heretics, whatever heresy you attribute to him yourselves, since they condemn the sense which you impute to him, and you dare not condemn that which they impute. If, therefore, you would completely refute them, show that the sense they attribute to Jansenius is heretical, then they will be so themselves. But how could this be effected, since it is certain, from your own admission, that the meaning they gave him was never condemned?

To set this in the most obvious point of view, I will take as a principle, what you receive as such yourselves; "that the doctrine of efficacious grace was not condemned, and the pope did not touch upon it in his constitution." When, indeed, he wished to examine the five propositions, the article of efficacious grace was screened from all censure. This is apparent, from the opinions of the counsellors to whom the pope committed them for examination. I have these in my hands, and so have many persons in Paris; amongst others, the bishop of Montpellier, who brought them from Rome. It is plain their opinions were divided, and the principal persons among them, as the master of the sacred palace, the commissary of the Holy Office, the general of the Augustines, with others, thinking that these propositions might be taken in a sense conformable with efficacious grace, were of opinion that they ought not to be censured; while the others, agreeing that they ought not to be censured if this were their real sense, deemed it right, however, that they should be condemned; because, by their own declaration, it is very far from their proper and natural sense. For this reason, the pope condemned them, and all acquiesced in his judgment.

It is certain then, Father, that efficacious grace was never condemned. It is moreover so powerfully maintained by St. Augustin, St. Thomas, and all his school, by so many popes, by so many councils, and by an universal tradition, that it would be impious to tax it with heresy. But all whom you treat as heretics, aver that they find nothing in Jansenius but this doctrine of efficacious grace; and this was the only point they maintained at Rome. You have yourself admitted the same, *Cavill.* p. 35, where you have declared, " that while speaking in the presence of the pope, they did not mention a single syllable respecting the propositions—*ne verbum quidem*—but employed the whole time upon the subject of efficacious grace." Mistaken, therefore, or not, it is at least certain that the sense they suppose Jansenius to have is not heretical, consequently they are not so. To say the truth in one word, either Jansenius taught only the doctrine of efficacious grace, in which case he cannot be charged with error, or, he taught something else; and in this case he has no supporters. The whole question, then, comes to this, did Jansenius really teach any other doctrine than efficacious grace? If it can be discovered that he did, you will have the glory of understanding him best, but they will not have the misfortune of erring in the faith.

Let us bless God, Father, that there is in reality no heresy in the church, for, in this case, the question refers to a point of fact, out of which it cannot arise. The church decides all articles of faith by divine authority, and excommunicates such as refuse to receive them; but she proceeds differently in matters of fact; and the reason is, that our salvation is attached to the faith which has been revealed to us and preserved in the church by tradition, but it does not depend on any other particular facts which God has not revealed. Thus, we are obliged to believe that the commandments of God are not impossible, but we are not under the same obligation to know what Jansenius has taught upon the subject. God, therefore, conducts his church in determining points of faith by the aid of his Holy Spirit, which cannot err ; but, in matters of fact, he leaves her to act according to the dictates of reason and sense, which are the natural judges upon such occasions. None but God can communicate instruction in matters of faith ; but it is only necessary to read Jansenius, to know whether the disputed propositions be or not in his book. Hence, it is heretical to resist the decisions of faith, because it is to set up our mind in opposition to the Spirit of God. But to disbelieve particular facts is no heresy, though it may be a piece of rashness, because that is merely opposing reason, which may be clear, against an authority which, however considerable, is not infallible.

In this all the divines concur, as appears from the following maxim of cardinal Bellarmin, of your Society. " General councils legally assembled, cannot err in defining doctrines of faith, but they may upon questions of fact." Again—" The pope, as pope and even as the head of a general council, may err in particular controversies respecting facts, which chiefly depend on the information and evidence of the witnesses." Cardinal Baronius says the same—" The decisions of general councils must be entirely submitted to in points of faith ; but, as to what concerns individuals and their writings, censures inflicted upon them have not been observed with so much severity, because no one can be sure of never being deceived." For this reason, the archbishop of Toulouse deduced this rule from the letters of two eminent popes, St. Leo and Pelagius II., " that the proper object of councils is faith, and every thing which is determined there, independently of faith, may be reviewed and re-examined ; but we ought not to enter into any further investigation of what has been determined as a matter of faith, because, as Tertullian says, the rule of faith is alone unalterable and irretractable."

Hence, we have never seen general councils, legally collected, contradict each other in points of faith, " because," as the archbishop of Toulouse says, " it is not lawful to examine afresh what has been already decided as a matter of faith." We have sometimes seen the same councils oppose each other on articles of fact, when the dispute referred to the sense of an author, " because," says the archbishop, quoting from the popes, "every thing which has been decided in councils, excepting faith, may be reviewed and re-examined." Thus, the fourth and fifth councils appear contradictory in the interpretation of the same authors; and the same circumstance happened to two popes, about a proposition of some monks in Scythia: for, after Pope Hormisdas had condemned it, in consequence of understanding it in a bad sense, Pope John II. his successor, upon examining it anew, and understanding it in a good sense, approved and declared it catholic. Will you assert, that one of these popes was heretical? Must it not be confessed, then, that, provided the heretical sense is condemned, which a pope supposed to be in a certain publication, a person is not heretical for not condemning that publication in a sense in which it is certain the Pope never condemned it; otherwise, one of these popes must be in an error?

I felt desirous, my good Father, of familiarizing you with the contradictions which occur between Catholics, upon questions of fact, with regard to the real sense of an author, by showing you one father of the church in opposition to another; one pope against another pope; one council against another council, in order to conduct you to other examples of a similar opposition, though less equalized; for you will see councils and popes on one side, and Jesuits on the other, opposing their decisions upon the sense of an author; notwithstanding which, you refrain from accusing your fraternity of heresy, or even of rashness.

You very well know, Father, that the writings of Origen were condemned by several councils and popes, especially by the fifth general council, as containing heresies; among others, that of "the reconciliation of the devils at the day of judgment." Pray, do you believe it absolutely necessary, in order to be a true Catholic, to confess that Origen really held these errors, and that it is not sufficient to condemn them, without attributing them to him? If so, what will become of your Father Halloix, who has maintained the purity of Origen's faith, as well as many other Catholic writers, who have engaged in the same undertaking, as Pico de Mirandola, and Genebrard, doctor of the Sorbonne? And is it not, also, certain, that this very same fifth general council condemned the writings of Theodoret against St. Cyril, as "impious, contrary to the true faith, and containing the Nestorian heresy?" Father Simond, a Jesuit, has, nevertheless, defended him, declaring in the life of that Father, "that those writings were perfectly free from the Nestorian heresy."

You perceive, then, Father, when the church condemns any writings, she supposes an error in them, which is the object of condemnation, and then it is to be taken for granted, that error is condemned; but it is not necessary to believe, that the writings in question actually contain the error which the church supposes. This, I think, is sufficiently proved; and, I shall finish these examples with that of Pope Honorius, who is so generally known. At the commencement of the seventh century, when the church was troubled with the heresy of the Monothelites, this pope, to settle the difference, issued a decree, which seemed to favour those heretics, which was very offensive to many. It passed, however, during his pontificate, with little clamour; but, fifty years afterwards, when the church assembled in the sixth general council, and Pope Agatho presided by his legates, this decree was brought forward, and, after being read and examined, was condemned, for containing the heresy of the Monothelites; and, as such, burned in full assembly, with the other writings of those heretics. This decision was received with so much respect and unanimity throughout the whole church, that it was afterwards confirmed by two other general councils, and even by Popes Leo II. and Adrian II. who lived two hundred years afterwards, without an individual venturing to disturb that universal and peaceable agreement during seven or eight centuries. But some more modern authors, and, among others, cardinal Bellarmin, have maintained, without any apprehension of being termed heretics, in contradiction to so many popes and councils, that the writings of Honorious are free from the error of which they have been accused ; " because," says he, " general councils being capable of erring in questions of fact, it may be said, with the utmost confidence, that the sixth general council was mistaken in that particular case ; and that, not having clearly understood the meaning of Honorius's letters, wrongly placed that pope among the number of heretics."

Observe, then, Father, that no one can be a heretic for saying, that Pope Honorius was not one, though many popes and councils have pronounced him one, and that too after an examination of the subject. Now, then, I come to our present question, and I will allow you to make your own cause as good as you possibly can. What will you say to render your adversaries heretical ? " That Pope Innocent X. has declared the error of the five propositions is in Jansenius ?" Very well—and what do you infer ? " That it is heretical not to admit that the error of the five propositions is in Jansenius ?" What think you of this, Father ? Does not our question, then, relate to a fact of the same nature with the preceding ? The pope has declared, that the error of the five propositions is in Jansenius, in the same manner as his predecessors had declared, that the error of the Nestorians and Monothelites was in the writings of Theodoret and Honorius. Upon which, your Fathers have published, that they readily condemn these heresies, but that they do not admit these authors ever maintained them ; as your present adversaries say, they readily condemn those five propositions, but do not allow that Jansenius taught them. Really, Father, these cases are amazingly similar ; and, if any difference exist, it is easy to see the advantage on the side of the present question, by a comparison of many particular circumstances, very obvious of themselves, and which I shall not, therefore, detain you to explain. Pray, whence does it arise, that in the very same case your fathers are Catholics, and your adversaries heretics? By what strange exception do you deprive them of a liberty, which you concede to all other Christians? Will you say, "that the Pope has confirmed his constitution by a brief?" To this, I should answer, that two general councils, and two popes, have confirmed the condemnation of the letters of Honorius. What stress do you lay on the words of this brief, by which the Pope declares, "that he has condemned the doctrine of Jansenius in those five propositions?" But what is this to the *constitution*, and what follows from it? but that, as the sixth council condemned the doctrine of Honorius, believing it to be the same with that of the Monothelites; in the same manner, the pope says he condemned the doctrine of Jansenius in the five propositions, because he supposed it to agree with those five propositions. And how could he believe otherwise? Your Society avowed nothing else; and you, Father, yourself said, they were there *word for word,* and were at Rome at the very time of the censure:—you see I meet you every where! Could the pope distrust the sincerity or capacity of so many grave religious men? How could he resist the conviction, that the doctrine of Jansenius was the same with that of the five propositions, assured that they were *word for word* in that author? It is obvious, therefore, if it be found that Jansenius never held these doctrines. It need not be said, as your Fathers have intimated in their examples, that the pope mistook this point of fact, which is always mischievous to publish, but only that you misled the pope, which will bring no scandal upon *you,* because you are so well known already.

Thus it appears, this affair is far enough from constituting a heresy: but being determined to make one at any rate, you have endeavoured to divert the question from the point of fact to that of faith, in the following manner. "The pope," say you, " declares, he has condemned the doctrine of Jansenius in the five propositions the doctrine of Jansenius, therefore, respecting them, is to be deemed heretical, whatever it may be." A strange article of faith, truly, that a doctrine is to be considered as heretical, be it what it may. What! if, according to Jansenius, *we may resist internal grace,* and if, too, it be false *that Jesus Christ died for the elect only,* must that be condemned also because it is *his* doctrine? Shall it be true in the *constitution* of the pope, that we are *free to do good or evil,* and yet false in Jansenius? By what fatality is it, that, in his book, truth becomes heresy? Must it not be admitted, that he is only heretical in case of conformity to those errors which are condemned, since the *constitution* of the pope is the rule to which Jansenius must be applied, to form a judgment of what he is by his conformity to it. In this way the question, *whether his doctrine be heretical,* may be resolved by another, *whether it be conformable to the natural meaning of these propositions;* it being impossible to make it heretical if this conformity be discoverable, or to make it catholic if the reverse. For as, according to the pope, and the bishops, *these propositions are condemned in their proper and natural sense,* they cannot be condemned in the sense of Jansenius, unless the sense of Jansenius be the same with the proper and natural sense of these propositions, which is a point of fact.

Here, then, the question still rests; and it is impossible to make it a matter of right, consequently not of heresy. It may, indeed, become a pretext for persecution, if any expectation could exist of persons being found to enter sufficiently into your interests to sanction such injustice, and comply with your wishes by signing to the statement, *that they condemn these propositions in the sense of Jansenius,* without giving any explanation of that sense. Few people, however, are disposed to sign a *blank* confession of faith, to be filled up afterwards as you might think proper, because you would be left at liberty to put whatever interpretation you pleased upon Jansenius. Explain it, then, previously, or we shall have a second edition of the *next power—abstrahendo ab omni sensu.* But this, you are well aware, will never succeed. Mankind abhor ambiguity, especially in matters of faith, where it is perfectly just that people should at least understand what they condemn. And how can it be, that those doctors who are convinced that Jansenius has no other sense but that of efficacious grace, should consent to declare, that they condemn his doctrine without any explanation of it; since, according to their present and confirmed belief, they must condemn efficacious grace, which would be criminal? Would it not be a strange tyranny to reduce them to this unhappy necessity, either to render themselves guilty in the sight of God, by signing this condemnation against their conscience, or to be treated as heretics, by refusing to do so?

But all this is very mysterious. Your proceedings are all political. I must, therefore, give a reason why you have not explained the meaning of Jansenius. I write merely for the purpose of exposing your designs, and, by this means, rendering them useless. I ought, then, to state, to such as are uninformed of it, that your principal interest in this dispute being to promote the *sufficient grace* of your Molina, you cannot accomplish this without destroying the *efficacious grace* opposed to it. But, as you see that the latter is, at this day, authorized at Rome, and by all the most learned men in the church, being unable to combat it in itself, you have been thinking of an attack which should not be perceived, by giving it the name of the doctrine of Jansenius : and thus you have invented a mode of procuring the condemnation of Jansenius, without examination; and, to succeed the better, you affirm that his doctrine is not that of efficacious grace, to make it believed, that one may be condemned independently of the other. Of this, you have constantly endeavoured to persuade those who are unacquainted with this author. You, Father, have done precisely the same in your *Cavill.* p. 23, by this subtle representation—" the pope has condemned the doctrine of Jansenius, but the pope has not condemned the doctrine of efficacious grace ; consequently, the doctrine of efficacious grace is different from that of Jansenius." If this argument were conclusive, it might be shown in the same manner, that Honorius, and all his adherents are heretics: "The sixth council has condemned the doctrine of Honorius, but the council has not condemned the doctrine of the church; therefore, the doctrine of Honorius is different from that of the church; consequently, all who defend him, are heretics." It is plain, no conclusion can be deduced from this statement, since the pope has only condemned the doctrine of the five propositions, which he was led to believe was that of Jansenius.

But this is of no consequence, for you do not intend long to pursue such a mode of reasoning: still it will last long enough, weak as it is, to answer your purpose. It is merely intended to induce such as would not condemn efficacious grace, to condemn Jansenius without scruple. When this is done, the argument will soon be forgot, but the signatures will remain as an eternal testimony to the condemnation of Jansenius. You will take occasion directly to attack efficacious grace by a superior mode of reasoning, which you will adopt in good time. "The doctrine of Jansenius," you will say, "has been condemned by the universal subscriptions of the whole church; but this doctrine is manifestly that of efficacious grace:" and this you will easily prove; "whence the doctrine of efficacious grace is condemned, even by the admission of its own advocates."

We see, then, the reason of your proposing to sign this condemnation of a doctrine, without explaining it, and also the advantage you profess to gain by this proceeding. But if your adversaries refuse to do the same, you lay another snare for them, on account of such refusal: for, having dexterously blended the question of faith with that of fact, without allowing any separation, or any signing of one without the other, as they cannot sign both, you will publish it every where, that they have refused both together: and thus, though, in fact, they merely decline acknowledging that Jansenius held the propositions they condemn, which, after all, could constitute no heresy, you will boldly assert, they have refused to condemn the propositions in themselves, and that they are on that account heretical.

Behold the advantage you would gain by their refusal, which certainly is not inferior to what you could draw from their consent! So that, if their signatures be required, they will equally fall into your snares, whether they do or do not sign, and you will reap the benefit in either case: yes, such is your exquisite management, that whatever turns up, you will always be the gainers.

How completely I know you, Father! and how grieved I am to see that God has so forsaken you, as to permit your success in such a wretched affair! Your prosperity demands compassion, and can never be envied by any, but such as are ignorant of real happiness. It is really charitable to thwart a success procured by such means, because it is founded on falsehoods, of which you would have us believe one of the two following:—either that the church has condemned efficacious grace, or that its advocates maintained the five condemned errors.

Let all the world, therefore, understand, that efficacious grace is not condemned, by your own acknowledgment, and that no man maintains those errors: and let all be aware, that they who refuse to sign what you require, only refuse it with regard to the matter of fact; and being willing to sign that of faith, their refusal cannot stamp them as heretics: because, though these propositions be indeed deemed heretical, there is no necessity to believe them to be the propositions of Jansenius. His adherents are in no error: that suffices. They may possibly interpret Jansenius too favourably, but perhaps you do not interpret him enough so. Passing this, I am sure that, according to your maxims, you think it no crime to publish that he is a heretic, contrary to your own knowledge; while, according to theirs, they could not innocently affirm he was a Catholic, unless they were fully convinced of it. They are, consequently, more sincere than you, Father; they have examined Jansenius as much as you have: they are no less intelligent than you ; they are, therefore, no less worthy of credit. But let this point of fact be as it may, they are undoubted Catholics ; for it surely is not necessary, in order to establish this claim, to say that another is not so, or to fix a charge of error upon them. It is quite sufficient to clear one's self.

LETTER XVIII.

TO THE REVEREND FATHER ANNAT, JESUIT.

Evidence still more incontestable adduced even from Father Annat's Reply, that no Heresy exists in the Church. Every body condemns the Doctrine which the Jesuits impute to Jansenius; and thus all Christians agree on the Subject of the Five Propositions. Difference respecting the questions of Right and Fact pointed out. With regard to the latter, one ought to rely more upon our own Senses than upon any human Authority.

March 14, 1657.

REVEREND FATHER,

Long, long have you used every effort to discover some error in your adversaries; but, I am persuaded, you will at last confess that nothing can be so difficult as to make out those persons to be heretics who are really not so, and who are solicitous of nothing so much as to avoid it.

I have pointed out, in the preceding letter, how many heresies you have imputed to them in succession, being unable to support a single charge for any length of time; so that nothing remained but to accuse them for refusing to condemn the sense of Jansenius, which you were anxious should be done, without giving any explanation. To be reduced to this measure is, indeed, a proof how much you are at a loss for subjects of accusation: for who ever heard of a heresy incapable of being explained? The reply, therefore, was easy—by only representing to you, that, if Jansenius be not in any error, it is unjust to condemn him; and if he be, it becomes you to declare it, that at least the reason of his condemnation might be understood. This, however, you were by no means disposed to do; but have attempted to corroborate your charge by appealing to decrees, which made nothing in your favour, because they afford no explanation of the sense of Jansenius said to be condemned in these five propositions. This was not the way to bring your disputes to a termination. Could any agreement be concluded respecting the true sense of Jansenius, and were the only point of difference whether this sense ought to be deemed heretical or not, then the opinions which should pronounce this sense to be heretical would bring the question at once to issue. But, as the grand subject of dispute respects the real sense of Jansenius, one party alleging that they can see nothing in it but the sense of St. Augustin and St. Thomas; the other, that they discover an heretical sense, which, however, they do not explain; it is clear, that a constitution which does not say one syllable about this difference, and only condemns in general the sense of Jansenius, without explaining it, determines nothing of the point in dispute.

On this account, you have been repeatedly told, that the subject of your difference relating only to this fact, it will never be brought to a close but by declaring what you understand to be the sense of Jansenius. But as you have always refused to do so in the most obstinate manner, I was obliged to urge you in my last letter; in which I intimated, that it was not without some secret purpose that you undertook to procure the condemnation of this sense without explaining it, and that design was some time or other to make this indeterminate kind of condemnation fall upon the doctrine of efficacious grace, by showing it to be no other than that of Jansenius, which would be no difficult undertaking. This has rendered it necessary to reply; for if you had still remained obstinately determined not to explain this sense, the simplest person must have perceived that you really intended to demolish the doctrine of efficacious grace, which would have been to your utter confusion, on account of the profound respect which the church entertains for this holy doctrine.

You have now been under the necessity of declaring yourself, in your reply to my letter, in which I had represented to you, that " if Jansenius, in these five propositions, had any other meaning than that of efficacious grace, he would find no supporters; but that if he really had no other meaning, he was chargeable with no errors." It is impossible for you to deny this statement; but you make a distinction of this kind, p. 21 : " it is not sufficient, in vindication of Jansenius, to allege that he holds nothing but efficacious grace, because that may be received in two senses—the one heretical, with Calvin, consisting in saying that the will, influenced by this grace, possesses no power of resistance; the other orthodox, with the Thomists and the Sorbonne, which is founded on the principles established by councils; namely, that efficacious grace governs the will, of itself, in such a manner as to admit of resistance.

All this is admitted : but you conclude by saying, " Jansenius would have been a good Catholic if he had defended efficacious grace as the Thomists maintain it; but he is heretical, because he is opposed to the Thomists, and agrees with Calvin, who denies the power of resisting this grace." At present, I shall not examine this question, whether Jansenius really coincides with Calvin : it is enough that you assert it, and now inform us, that by the sentiment of Jansenius you understood nothing else than the doctrine of Calvin. Was this, my good Father, all you intended to say? Was it nothing but the error of Calvin that you wished to condemn under the name of the opinion of Jansenius? Why not, then, distinctly avow this at first? You would, by such a piece of candour, have spared yourself an immense deal of trouble. All the world would have agreed with you in condemning this error, without any bulls or briefs. Well, how necessary was this eclaircissement, and what difficulties it removes! We really did not know what error it was that the popes and bishops were aiming at under the name of the sense of Jansenius. The whole church was in the greatest agitation, and nobody would explain it. But you have now done it, my good Father; you, who are considered by your own party as their head and the prime mover in all their councils, and who know the secret of all this proceeding, have stated that the sense of Jansenius is no other than the sense of Calvin condemned by the council. Behold, then, the resolution of our doubts! We are now assured that the error which they intended to condemn by the phrase, *the sense of Jansenius*, is no other than *the sense of Calvin;* and thus we continue in subjection to their decrees, by uniting with them to condemn that sense of Calvin which they were so desirous of condemning. We are no longer surprised to find that the popes, and some of the bishops, have manifested so much zeal against the sense of Jansenius. How could they have done otherwise, as they cherished the utmost confidence in those who publicly declare that this sense is the same with that of Calvin?

I must insist, therefore, Father, that you have nothing further to censure in your adversaries, for they, most assuredly, detest the very sentiment which you detest. I only feel surprised at your ignorance of it, and of their general opinions on this subject, which are so repeatedly avowed in their writings. I am persuaded that, if you were better informed, you would deeply regret not having been so far disposed to a spirit of peace, as to acquaint yourself with a doctrine so pure and so truly Christian, and which passion has impelled you to oppose without understanding it. You would otherwise have seen that they not only maintain, that these feeble graces, called exciting or inefficacious, from their not achieving the good they suggest, are effectually resisted; but that they are also as strenuous in asserting, in contradiction to Calvin, the power of the human will to resist efficacious and victorious grace, as in affirming, contrary to Molina, the power of that grace over the will, being equally jealous of both these truths. Too well do they know, by experience, that man in his own nature has always the power of sinning and of resisting grace, and that, since his fall he carries about with him a dreadful fund of evil propensities, which inconceivably increases this power ; but, nevertheless, when it pleases God, in infinite mercy, to touch his heart, he makes him do whatever he chooses, and in whatever manner, without this infallible operation of God in any measure destroying the natural liberty of man ; and which is accomplished by the secret and admirable methods by which the Divine Being produces this change, so excellently described by St. Augustin, and which remove all the apparent contradictions which the enemies of efficacious grace imagine to exist between the sovereign power of grace over free-will, and the power of free-will to resist grace. According to that eminent saint, to whom the popes and the church have referred as a guide in this matter, God changes the human heart by a heavenly sweetness of disposition imparted to it, which, overcoming the sensuality of the flesh, causes man, on the one hand, to perceive his mortality and nothingness, and, on the other, to discover the greatness and eternity of God, and produces a distaste for the pleasures of sin, which separate him from incorruptible blessedness. Finding his supreme enjoyment in the God who attracts him, he inclines infallibly, and of himself, to this good, by a bias entirely free, voluntary, and affectionate, so that to be separated from it would be a grief and a punishment. Not that he becomes incapable of departing from it, or of departing effectually if he chose : but could he be so disposed, when the will never propels him to do any thing but what is most pleasing to him ; and nothing pleases him so much, then, as that single good, which comprehends in itself all others ? " *Quod enim amplius nos delectat, secundùm id operemur necesse est,*" as St. Augustin observes.

In this manner, God disposes of man's free-will, without imposing necessity on him ; and that free-will which can always resist grace, but is not always desirous of doing so, leads as freely as it does infallibly when he draws him by the sweet influence of his efficacious inspirations.

Father, these are the divine principles of St. Augustine and St. Thomas, who concur in affirming, that " we are able to resist grace," in opposition to the opinion of Calvin; but, nevertheless, as Pope Clement VIII. says in his epistle to the congregation, *de auxiliis*, " God forms in us the suggestions of our will, and effectually disposes of our heart, by the dominion which his supreme majesty possesses over the will of man, as well as over all the rest of his creatures under heaven, according to St. Augustin."

By these principles, besides, we can act for ourselves, and thus possess a merit truly our own, contrary to the error of Calvin: nevertheless. God being the first principle of our actions, and " working in us what is well-pleasing in his sight," as St. Paul expresses it, " our good works are the gifts of God," according to the language of the Council of Trent.

Hence the impiety of Luther, which is condemned by the same council, is destroyed—" that we do not in any way co-operate in our own salvation more than inanimate things;" and by the same means, the impiety of the Molinist school is destroyed, which refuses to admit that it is the energy of that grace which causes us to co-operate with it in the work of our salvation; by which the principle of faith established by St. Paul is overturned—" it is God that worketh in us both to will and to do, of his good pleasure." In a word, it is by this means all those passages of Scripture which appear most contradictory are made to agree; as, " Turn ye to the Lord—Turn us unto thee, O Lord—Break off thine iniquities—God will subdue our iniquities—Do works meet for repentance—Lord, thou hast wrought all our works in us—Make you a new heart and a new spirit—I will give unto you a new heart and a right spirit."

There is but one mode of reconciling these seeming contradictions, which, at one time, attribute our good works to God, at another, to ourselves; which is to admit, with St.

Augustin, that "our works are our own, because it is our free-will which produces them ; and they are also of God, because it is his grace which causes our free-will to produce them ;" and, as he observes in another place, "God makes us do whatever he pleases, by making us willing to do that to which we should otherwise be unwilling—*a Deo factum est ut vellent quod nolle potuissent.*

Thus, Father, your adversaries are perfectly agreed with the new Thomists themselves, since the Thomists maintain, as well as they, both the power of resisting grace and the infallibility of the effect of grace, which they profess to hold so strongly, according to that capital maxim of theirs, which Alvarez, one of the most distinguished among them, so frequently repeats in his book, and expresses, disp. 72. n. 4. in the following words : " When efficacious grace impels free-will, it infallibly consents, because the effect of grace is to cause, that though it has power not to consent, it does however in fact consent ;" the reason of which he adds, from his master, St. Thomas, " that the will of God cannot fail of being accomplished : so that, when he wills that a man should consent to grace he infallibly does consent, and necessarily, not from an absolute necessity, but a necessity of infallibility ;" by which grace does not impair " the power of resistance, if the inclination to do so exist," because it only makes one not will to resist, the Father Petau admits in these words, tom. 1. p. 602 : " The grace of Jesus Christ causes one infallibly to persevere in piety, though not from necessity ; for we have the power not to consent if we will, as the council says ; but this same grace impels us not to will it."

Here then, Father, we have the uniform doctrine of St. Augustine, St. Prosper, the Fathers who followed them, the councils, St. Thomas, and all the Thomists in general. It is also that of your adversaries, though you have not supposed so ; and it is the same with that which you have yourselves approved in these words, " The doctrine of efficacious grace, which admits the power of resistance, is orthodox, supported by the councils, and maintained by the Thomists and the Sorbonne." Now, Father, speak the truth : if you had really known that your adversaries held this doctrine, probably the interest of your Society would have prevented your giving it this public approbation : but, in consequence of supposing they were opposed to it, the same cause, the interest of your Society, induced you to authorize the sentiments which you believed to be the reverse of theirs; and by this mistake, while anxious to destroy, you have really, and most completely established their principles. So that, by a kind of miracle, the advocates of efficacious grace are vindicated by the disciples of Molina : such are the admirable methods of Divine Providence in making all things concur to promote the glory of his truth!

All the world may now learn, by your own declaration, that this truth respecting efficacious grace, essential to every pious action, so dear to the church, and the price of her Saviour's blood, is so truly Catholic, that there is not an individual of this community, not even of the Jesuits themselves, who does not acknowledge it to be orthodox. It will be seen at the same time, by your own confession, that those whom you have so violently accused ought not to be in the slightest degree suspected of error; for when you charged them with concealing sentiments they were unwilling to avow, it was as difficult to defend themselves as it was easy to produce an accusation of this nature : but having now avowed, that the error for which you are obliged to oppose them is no other than that of Calvin, which you suppose they maintain, no person can fail of perceiving they are in reality free from every error, since they are quite opposed to the only one which you impute to them, and protest, both in their discourses, in their writings, and, in short, in every thing they can possibly produce in evidence of their opinions —that they condemn this heresy from the very bottom of their hearts, and in the same manner with the Thomists, whom you allow, without hesitation, to be Catholics, and who have never been suspected of being otherwise.

What have you now to allege against them, my worthy Father? That though they do not concur in the sense of Calvin, they are, nevertheless, heretical, because they are unwilling to admit that the sentiment of Jansenius is the same with that of Calvin? Will you absolutely venture to affirm, that this is a matter of heresy? Is it not a mere question of fact, which really cannot be in any way moulded into a heresy? It would certainly be so, to say that man has no power to resist efficacious grace; but can it be such to question whether Jansenius maintains this doctrine? Is it a revealed truth? Is it an article of faith which must be believed upon pain of damnation? Is it not, after all, notwithstanding all you say, a point of fact, on account of which, it would be ridiculous to pretend there were heretics in the church?

No longer then, I beseech you, my good Father, apply this name to them; but devise some other, which may be more adapted to the nature of your difference. Say they are ignorant and stupid, and do not understand Jansenius—such reproaches would accord with your dispute; but, to call them heretics, has really no relation to the question. And, as this is the only reproach from which I propose to defend them, I need not take much trouble to show, that they do understand Jansenius well. All I have to say, is, that it appears to me, in judging of him by your own rules, it is difficult to make him any thing else than a Catholic; for your mode of examination is indicated by the following statement:—

"To know," say you, "whether Jansenius is innocent, it is necessary to ascertain whether he defends efficacious grace after the manner of Calvin, who denies the power of resisting it—in that case, he would be a heretic; or, in the manner of the Thomists, who admit of such a power—then he would be a good Catholic." Consider, then, Father, if he maintains this power of resistance, when he asserts throughout whole treatises, and, among others, in vol. 3. b. 8. c. 20. "that the power of resisting grace always exists, according to the Council; *that the free-will can always act, or not act, will or not will, consent or not* consent, do good or do evil; and that man has always, during life, these two kinds of liberty, which you call the liberty of contrariety and contradiction." Notice further, if he be not opposed to the error of Calvin, such as you represent it, when he shows, in chap. 21. "that the church has condemned this heretic, who maintains that efficacious grace does not act on the freedom of the will in the latter, so long believed in the church, so that it is afterwards in the power of the free-will to consent, or not consent; instead of concurring with St. Augustin, and the Council, that one has always the power of not consenting, if we choose; and that, according to Prosper, God bestows, even on his elect, the will of persevering, in such a manner, as not to take away the power of willing the contrary." Finally, judge if he do not agree with the Thomists, when he declares, c. 4. "that every thing which the Thomists have written to reconcile the efficacy of grace, with the power of resisting it, is so conformable to his opinion, that it is only necessary to read their books to ascertain his sentiments—*quod ipsi dixerunt, dictum puta.*"

Such is his mode of speaking on all these topics; and, on this account, I suppose that he believes in the power of resisting grace, that his views are opposite to Calvin and coincident with the Thomists, because he expressly says so, and therefore, according to your rules, he must be a Catholic. If you have any way of ascertaining the sense of an author besides his own expressions, and, if without quoting any of his words, you will aver in contradiction to them, that he derides the power of resisting, and is on the side of Calvin and against the Thomists, nevertheless, you need be under no apprehension of my accusing you of heresy; I shall only say, it seems to me that you do not well understand Jansenius, but we shall not, on this account, be less the children of the same church.

How is it, my good Father, that you conduct yourself in this dispute in so violent a manner, and treat as your cruellest enemies, and the most dangerous of heretics, those whom you cannot accuse of any error, or indeed of any thing excepting their not understanding Jansenius as you do? For what is the subject of dispute, but the meaning of this author? You wish then to condemn him, but they demand what you mean? You say that you understand the error of Calvin: to which they reply that they condemn it; and therefore, if you do not contend about words but things, you surely ought to be satisfied. If they refuse to say they condemn the sense of Jansenius, it is simply because they believe it to be that of St. Thomas: so that this word is very ambiguous it seems: in your mouth it signifies the sense of Calvin—in theirs, of St. Thomas; and hence, as the different ideas which you have of the same term, occasions all these divisions, if I were arbitrator of your controversy, I should interdict the word *Jansenius* on both sides. By which means, as you would be compelled to express nothing but what you understand by it, it would be seen that you require nothing but the condemnation of the sentiment of Calvin, in which they concur; and that they wish for nothing but the defence of the sense of St. Augustin and St. Thomas, in which you are both agreed.

For myself, then, I declare, Father, I shall always regard them as good Catholics, whether they condemn Jansenius, if they should find him erroneous, or do not condemn him if they find nothing but what you affirm to be Catholic; and I shall address them as St. Jerome did John, bishop of Jerusalem, who was accused of holding eight propositions of Origen. "Either," said this saint, " condemn Origen, if you admit that he has maintained these errors, or at once deny that he held them—*aut nega hoc dixisse eum qui arguitur, aut si locutus est talia, eum damna qui dixerit.*"

In this manner they act who aim at the errors of men only, not their persons: while you, attacking their persons instead of their errors, think it useless to resist error, unless the persons to whom it is imputed, be also condemned.

My good Father, what a violent mode of proceeding is this, and how ill adapted to become successful! I have said elsewhere, and now repeat it, violence and truth can never affect each other. Never were your accusations more outrageous, and never was the innocence of your adversaries more notorious: never was efficacious grace more artfully attacked, never was it more firmly established. You use your utmost efforts to induce people to believe, that your controversies respect points of faith, and never was it more completely apparent, that the whole dispute turns upon a question of fact. You leave no method unattempted to circulate the impression, that this point of fact is true, and never were people more inclined to doubt it. The reason is obvious—you avail yourself of none of the natural modes of obtaining credit to a point of fact, which are to convince the senses, and to show, in the book itself, the words it is said to contain. But you go in search of devices so remote from this simplicity of proceeding, that the greatest ignoramus must be necessarily struck with it. Why not pursue the same method to which I have uniformly adhered in my letters, in detecting so many of the bad doctrines of your authors, that of giving a correct reference to the places where each quotation is to be found? The curates of Paris did the same, and it will never fail to convince mankind. What would you have said, or what would have been thought, when you were reproached, for instance, with this proposition of Father Launy, " that a monk may kill the individual who threatens to publish calumnies against him, or his society," if he can defend himself by no other means, if your accusers had not quoted the places where these words are written? And if, however urgently you requested their authority, they had always obstinately persisted in refusing to inform you, and, instead of it, had gone to Rome to procure a bull to enjoin all the world to admit it? Would it not have been considered certain, that they had surprised the pope into such a measure, and only had recourse to it, because they failed in all those natural modes of proof, with which the truth of a fact supplies those who possess it? Hence, they have only stated, that Father Launy teaches this doctrine in vol. 5. disp. 36, n. 118. p. 544, of the Douay edition; so that those who wish to see this passage, have found it, and nobody is in any doubt upon the subject. This is a very easy and ready method of deciding questions of fact, when one is in the right.— How is it, therefore, my good Father, that you have not adopted it? You say, in your *Cavilli*, "that the five propositions are in Jansenius, *word for word,* in the express terms—*iisdem verbis.*" But you have directly assumed, *they are not!* What remained, therefore, but a reference or quotation from the very page, if you had really seen them, otherwise to have confessed your mistake? Neither of these, however, has been done : on the contrary, perfectly conscious that all these passages from Jansenius, which you sometimes allege, in order to dazzle the eyes of mankind, are not " the individual and particular propositions condemned," which you engaged to produce from the book, you present us with certain constitutions which declare they are extracted thence, but *without pointing out the place!*

I am aware of the reverence which Christians owe to the Holy See, and your adversaries sufficiently evince their resolution never to depart from it; but you are not to imagine it was any deficiency of respect which led them to represent to the pope, with all the submission due from children to a Father, and from members to their head, that he might have been surprised in reference to this fact; that he had not investigated it since his being elevated to the pontificate : and that his predecessor, Innocent X., had merely examined whether these propositions were heretical, but not whether they were attributable to Jansenius. This induced a commissary of the Holy Office, one of the principle examiners, to say, that " they could not be censured as the idea of any author— *non sunt qualificabiles in sensu proferentis*—because they had been presented for examination without any reference to any person as the author—*in abstracto, et ut præscindunt ab omni proferente*"—as appears from their opinions recently published; that upwards of sixty doctors, and a great number of other intelligent and pious persons, have carefully read this book, without being able to discover these propositions in it; but they found the very reverse, that those who succeeded in giving the pope this impression, might well be supposed to abuse his confidence, interested as they are to decry that author, who has convicted Molina of more than fifty errors. And what renders this the more credible, is their holding the following maxim as one of the most established in their system—" that it is not criminal to calumniate those persons by whom they deem themselves unjustly attacked." As their testimony is so suspicious, and that of others so considerable, there is some reason to supplicate his Holiness with all possible humility, to have this fact examined in the presence of the doctors of each party, in order to come to a solemn and regular decision. " Let able judges be assembled." said St. Basil, on a similar occasion, ep. 75, " and every one be free to examine my writings—let them see if there be any errors in the faith —let them read the objections and the answers to them that they may pass a judgment from knowing the cause, and with proper formality, and not deal in defamatory representations without examination."

Pray then, Father, do not aim to make those who should act in this manner looked upon as deficient in submission to the Holy See. The popes are far from treating Christians so tyrannically as some who act in their name. " The church," observes St. Gregory, *in Job, lib.* 8. *c.* 1. " which was formed in the school of humility, does not command in an authoritative manner, but persuades by reason, whatever she teaches her children, whom she supposes addicted to any error—*recta quæ errantibus dicit, non quasi ex auctoritate præcipit, sed ex ratione persuadet :*" and so far from deeming it a dishonour, to retract a decision into which they have been surprised, they, on the contrary, glory in it, as St. Bernard testifies, ep. 180 : " The Apostolical See possesses this excellence, that it does not pique itself upon a point of honour, but is willing to revoke a judgment into which it has been led by surprise, and it is right that no one should profit by such an injustice, especially before the Holy See."

These are the proper sentiments to inculcate upon the minds of popes, since all divines are agreed, that they are liable to surprise; and their supremacy is so far from being an effectual safeguard, that it really exposes them the more to such deceptions, on account of the variety of concerns that devolves upon them. This is what the same St. Gregory intimated to certain persons, who were astonished that another pope should have permitted himself to be misled. "Why," says he, *l. 1. c. 4. Dial.* "why are you so struck with wonder at our being deceived—we, who are but men? Have you never read of David, who had the spirit of prophecy, confiding in the impositions of Ziba, and giving an unjust judgment against the son of Jonathan? Who, then, will consider it strange, that we should sometimes be surprised by misrepresentations—we, who are not prophets? The multiplicity of our affairs overwhelms us, and our mind, being distracted by so many different concerns, pays the less attention to each one in particular, and is, therefore, the more easily deceived in any of them." I do believe, my good father, the popes know much better than you, whether they are liable to be surprised or not. They tell us, themselves, that the popes and the greatest monarchs are more exposed to deception than persons who are occupied with less important engagements; and I really think we ought to believe them. There is no difficulty in imagining in what manner they may be surprised. St. Bernard has given a description of it in a letter to Innocent II. "It is nothing either so remarkable, or so novel, that the mind of man should be capable of deceiving and being deceived. Some monks are come to you with the spirit of falsehood and illusion. They talked against a bishop whom they detest, but whose life has been exemplary. These people bite like dogs, and would make what is good pass for evil; while you, holy father, are displeased with your son; but why have you given his adversaries an occasion of triumph? Believe not in every spirit, but prove them whether they are of God. I trust, when you come to know the truth, whatever has been founded on false information, will be dismissed; and I entreat the Spirit of truth, to give you grace to separate the light from darkness, and to reject the evil, that you may favour the good." Thus you see, Father, that the elevated station which the popes occupy, does not exempt them from surprise: but, in fact, it renders the mistakes into which they are hurried, more dangerous and important. This is what St. Bernard represents to pope Eugenius, *de Consid. lib. 2. c. ult.* "There is another fault so general, that I have never yet found an individual amongst the great who escaped it. It is, holy Father, a too great credulity from which so many disorders proceed. To this, may be traced violent persecutions against the innocent, unjust prejudices against those who are absent, and terrible passions in affairs of no consequence—*pro nihilo.* This, holy Father, is an universal evil, and, if you are exempt from it, I must say you are the only one that possesses this advantage over your brethren."

I fancy, my good Father, you are now beginning to be convinced that the popes are liable to surprise; but to show this still better, I only beg to remind you of some examples, which you have yourself related in your book of popes and emperors, who have been completely surprised by some of the heretics. You state, that Apollinarius surprised pope Damasus as Celestius did Zozimus. You say, also, that a person named Athanasius, deceived the emperor Heraclius, and occasioned his persecuting the Catholics; and that Sergius obtained from Honorius that decree which was burnt at the sixth council, *through his being,* as you say, *the parasite of that pope.*

It is evident then, by your own statement, that those who attend upon kings and popes, sometimes artfully engage them to persecute the true faith, while they imagine they are exterminating heretics. Hence the popes, who are exceedingly fearful of such surprises, have adopted a letter of Alexander III. as an ecclesiastical enactment, inserted in the canon law, to allow a suspension in the execution of their bulls and decrees, when it is supposed they have been deceived. "If," observes this pope to the archbishop of Ravenna, "we should sometimes send to your fraternity decrees which oppose your own views, do not be uneasy; for either you must execute them with obedient reverence, or send us the reason why you do not think you should, because we shall not be dissatisfied that you do not execute a decree which may have been drawn from us by artifice and surprise." Such is the conduct of the popes, who are solicitous of clearing up the differences of Christians, and not of gratifying the passions of those who would fill Christendom with confusion. They do not claim an authority like that of St. Peter and St. Paul, after Christ, but their conduct evinces a spirit of peace and truth. Hence, they generally insert this clause in their letters, which is understood to be in all—"*si ita est—si preces veritate nitantur*—if the thing be as we understood it; if the facts alleged be true." It is apparent from this statement, that since the popes give no authority to their bulls, only in proportion as they are founded on established facts, the bulls alone cannot prove the truth of facts; on the contrary, according to the canonists themselves, it is the truth of the facts which gives weight and effect to the bulls.

But how shall we ascertain the truth of the facts? *By our eyes*, my good Father, which are the lawful judges, as reason is of natural and intelligible things, and faith of those which are supernatural and revealed. For, since you compel me to it, I must tell you, that, conformably to the sentiments of two of the greatest doctors of the church, St. Augustin and St. Thomas, these three principles of knowledge, the senses, reason, and faith, have each their distinct objects, and their certainty within their own sphere. And, as God has seen fit to make use of the senses as the medium of faith—*fides ex auditu*—so far is faith from destroying the certainty of the senses, that it would be destructive to faith to call in question the fidelity of the senses. St. Thomas, therefore, expressly says, that God has appointed sensible accidents to subsist in the Eucharist, that the senses, which judge only from these accidents, might not be deceived—*ut sensus à deceptione reddantur immunes.*"

We may hence infer, that whatever proposition is presented for our examination, it is necessary, in the first place, to ascertain the nature of it, to know to which of these three principles we must have recourse. If the question refer to any thing supernatural, we must neither judge of it by the senses nor by reason, but by Scripture and the decisions of the church: if it be an unrevealed proposition, and within the sphere of our natural sense, that must be the judge; but if it relate to a point of fact, we must believe our senses, to whose cognisance it naturally belongs.

This rule is so general, that, according to St. Augustin and St. Thomas, when Scripture itself presents a passage, of which the first literal meaning is contrary to that which the senses and reason know with certainty, we must not endeavour to disavow them, to subject them to the authority of this apparent meaning of Scripture, but must interpret Scripture, by searching out another signification, which agrees with the truth obvious to our senses; because, the word of God being infallible in the facts themselves, and the report of the senses and reason acting within their appropriate spheres being also certain, these two truths must agree; and, as Scripture may be variously interpreted, and the testimony of the senses but in one way, we ought, in such cases, to receive that as the true interpretation of Scripture, which is conformable to the faithful evidence of the senses. "Two things," remarks St. Thomas, p. 1. q. 68. a. 1. " must be observed, according to St. Augustin, the one, that Scripture always has a true meaning, the other, that it may be received in more senses than one, when we find one which reason convinces us is unquestionably false; it must not then be obstinately affirmed,' this is the natural meaning,' but another coincident with sense and reason must be sought."

This he explains by an example from the book of Genesis, where it is written, " God made two great lights;

the greater light to rule the day, and the lesser light to rule the night; he made the stars also;" by which the Scripture seems to state that the moon is greater than all the stars; but since it is certain, from incontestable demonstrations, that this is not the case, we ought not, says this Father, pertinaciously to adhere to the literal sense, but seek for another more conformable to fact, as by observing, "that the word only indicates the greatness of the moon's light, with respect to us, and not the greatness of that body in itself."

Were we to do otherwise, we should not render the Scripture venerable, but expose it to the contempt of infidels; "because," as St. Augustin remarks, "should it be said that we believe in things contained in Scripture, which they know to be false, they would ridicule our credulity in other things more concealed from human discernment, such as the resurrection of the dead, and eternal life:" "and thus," adds St. Thomas, "our religion would be rendered contemptible, and their conversion to it utterly prevented."

This would, moreover, operate as an entire prevention to the change of heretics, and render the pope's authority despicable, if we refuse to consider them as Catholics who will not believe certain words to be in a book where they cannot find them, upon the assurance of a pope, taken by surprise, that they were there. For nothing but the examination of a book can ascertain whether it contains certain words or not. Matters of fact can only be proved by the senses. If what you maintain be true, show it; if not, pray desist from soliciting any one to believe it, for this is perfectly useless. All the powers of the world cannot, by their utmost authority, persuade a person of a point of fact, any more than they can alter it; for nothing can make that which is, not to be.

It was all in vain, for example, that certain monks of Ratisbon, obtained from Pope Leo IX. a solemn decree, by which it was declared, that the body of St. Denys, first bishop of Paris, and commonly held to be the areopagite, had been carried away from France, and conveyed to the church of their monastery. That decree does not prevent the body of the saint in question from having always been, and still remaining, in the celebrated abbey which bears his name; and you would find it difficult enough to procure this bull a reception, though the pope avers he had examined the matter "with all possible diligence, *diligentissimè*, and, with the council of many bishops and prelates:" so that he strictly enjoins all Frenchmen, "*districtè præcipientes*, to acknowledge and confess that they no longer have these sacred relics." Notwithstanding which, the French, who knew this was not the fact, from the evidence of their own eyes, (for, having opened the shrine, they found in it all the relics entire, as the historians of that time declare,) believed then, and always have continued to do so the contrary to what this holy pope enjoined them to believe; convinced, that even saints and prophets are liable to surprise and deception.

In vain did you obtain a decree from Rome against Galileo, which condemned his opinion respecting the motion of the earth. This will never prove that it stands still; and, if it have been ascertained, from careful observations, that it turns, all mankind together, cannot prevent its turning, nor prevent their being carried round with it. Do not imagine, that the letters of Pope Zachary for the excommunication of St Virgil, for asserting we had antipodes, have annihilated that new world, though he declared this opinion to be a dangerous error; or, that the king of Spain has derived no considerable benefit from believing Christopher Columbus, who came from those regions, instead of the pope, who had never been there; or that the church has not received great advantage, for this discovery has sent the knowledge of the gospel to great multitudes of people perishing in unbelief.

Hence, my good Father, you see the nature of matters of fact, and by what principles we ought to regulate our judgment; and, from this statement, it is easy to conclude, with regard to our subject, that if these five propositions do not belong to Jansenius, it is impossible they should be extracted from his book; and, the only means of coming to a conclusion, and convincing the world, is to examine his work in a regular conference, which you were requested to do long, long ago. Till this is done, you have no right to stigmatize your adversaries as obstinate; for they are certainly blameless as to this point of fact, as they are free from error on points of faith—*Catholics* in reference to *right,* *reasonable* with regard to *fact,* and *innocent* in *both cases.*

Who can help feeling surprised, Father, to see on the one side a justification so complete, and on the other accusations so violent? Who would suppose that the question between you related to a fact of no importance, which you wished to be believed without evidence? And who would dare to think so much clamour was excited in the church for nothing, absolutely nothing—*pro nihilo,* as St. Bernard says? But this is a part of your grand policy, to make people imagine every thing is at stake, in an affair really about nothing; and to give it out to the great people who attend to your representations, that your disputes refer to Calvin's most pernicious errors, and the most important principles of faith, for the purpose of inducing them to exert their zeal and authority against your adversaries, as if the safety of the Catholics depended upon it! Whereas, if they come to know that the question relates merely to this insignificant point of fact, they would not proceed another step; but, on the contrary, regret extremely having made so many efforts to gratify your private passions, in an affair of no consequence to the church.

Lastly, to take it in the worst point of view, if it should prove true that Jansenius held these propositions, what would it matter if some persons doubted it, provided they detest them, as they do publicly? Is it not sufficient they are universally and without exception condemned, even in the very sense in which you have explained that you were desirous of their condemnation? Would the censure be more complete if it were really admitted that

Jansenius maintained them? What is the use of exacting this acknowledgment, unless it be to decry a doctor and a bishop, who died in the communion of the church? I cannot see that, in this case, the good would be so considerable as to repay the trouble. What advantage would it be to the state, the pope, the bishops, the doctors, or the church at large? It does not in any way affect them; and it is, in fact, merely your Society, Father, that would receive any pleasure from defaming an author who has done you a trifling injury. But every agent is set in motion, because you declare every thing is at stake; and this is the secret cause of all these mighty movements, which, so soon as the true state of the case was known, would instantly cease to operate. As, therefore, the peace of the church depends upon this exposition of the business, it was extremely important to attempt it, that, all your disguises being detected, the whole world might see, that your accusations are groundless, your adversaries without error, and the church without heresy.

The object I had in view is thus apparent: and it seems to be so important to the general interests of religion, that I can scarcely comprehend how those whom you have so provoked to speak can remain silent. Though your injurious conduct should not affect them, its influence upon the church itself ought, I think, to induce them to complain: besides, I cannot think ecclesiastics ought to abandon their reputation to calumny, expecially in matters of faith. They allow you, however, to say whatever you please; so that, independently of the occasion which you have happened to give me, perhaps there might have been no opposition to the scandals you were disseminating on every hand. I am, therefore, astonished at their patience, especially as it cannot be attributed to timidity or weakness: for I well know they neither want arguments for their vindication, nor zeal for the truth. Still they maintain such a religious silence, that I fear it is carried to an excess. For my part, Father, I doubt whether I can imitate them in this particular. Leave the church in peace, and I will readily and heartily consent to let *you* alone : but while you are aiming to stir up trouble, depend upon it there will be found children of peace who will think themselves obliged to use the utmost exertion to preserve its tranquillity.

THE END.

ImTheStory.com

Personalized Classic Books in many genre's

Unique gift for kids, partners, friends, colleagues

Customize:

- Character Names
- Upload your own front/back cover images (optional)
- Inscribe a personal message/dedication on the inside page (optional)

Customize many titles Including
- Alice in Wonderland
- Romeo and Juliet
- The Wizard of Oz
- A Christmas Carol
- Dracula
- Dr. Jekyll & Mr. Hyde
- And more...

CPSIA information can be obtained at www.ICGtesting.com
Printed in the USA
LVOW01s1623270813

349860LV00019B/1368/P